Role Change

ROLE CHANGE

A Resocialization Perspective

MELVYN L. FEIN

PRAEGER

New York
Westport, Connecticut
London

Library of Congress Cataloging-in-Publication Data

Fein, Melvyn L.
   Role change : a resocialization perspective / Melvyn L. Fein.
      p.   cm.
   Includes bibliographical references.
   ISBN 0-275-93358-X (alk. paper)
   1. Social role.   2. Role conflict.   3. Clinical sociology.
   I. Title.
   HM131.F385   1990
   302'.15—dc20   89-23038

Library of Congress Catalog Card Number: 89-23038
ISBN: 0-275-93358-X

First published in 1990

Praeger Publishers, One Madison Avenue, New York, NY 10010
A division of Greenwood Press, Inc.

Printed in the United States of America

The paper used in this book complies with the
Permanent Paper Standard issued by the National
Information Standards Organization (Z39.48-1984).

10 9 8 7 6 5 4 3 2 1

Contents

Preface

This volume was conceived in conjunction with a workshop developed for the Sociological Practice Association. Ray Kirschak, then the SPA's training coordinator, wanted a program that would help clinical sociologists learn the basics of individual counseling. What evolved from the planning and writing of this work was much more: it became a general theory of role-change processes. By taking sociological concepts and applying them to ordinary problems in living, it developed into an explanation of why people become trapped in dysfunctional roles and how they can escape from them. As such, it is not merely applicable to sociological practice, but is equally valid for psychology, social work, and even psychiatry.

Historically, sociology's involvement with clinical concerns has been a checkered one. Most helping professionals are unaware of its relevance to their own efforts because it has not often been explicitly applied to them. While the concept of clinical sociology has been around for some time, it and its practitioners have largely been on the sidelines in the great "psychotherapeutic" revolution of the twentieth century.

The phrase "clinical sociology" seems to have been born in a 1931 *American Journal of Sociology* article by Louis Wirth. In it he advocated the application of a "cultural" approach to the then burgeoning field of child guidance. He wished to see sociologists attached to clinics so that they could use their special expertise in understanding how children get into trouble. Unfortunately for him and his fellow sociologists, the guidance clinics coming into existence at that time soon fell within the purview of psychiatry. Since this discipline was not especially re-

ceptive to the incursions of a rival profession, Wirth's initiative came
to naught.

In subsequent years, clinical psychologists were to establish a presence in mental health facilities, although they too faced concerted medical opposition. Sociologists, however, continued to be excluded. While
other groups sought and obtained licensure to validate their clinical
aspirations, sociologists concentrated on academic and policy-oriented
issues. Their influence on clinical practice became indirect. Thus it was
through figures such as the psychiatrists Harry Stack Sullivan and Karen
Horney that sociologically informed views came to have an impact. The
importance of "relationships" and "family interactions" became well
established, but most professionals had no idea of their provenance.

The closest to direct sociological representation in the helping professions came via social work. Many pioneering social workers obtained
their training as sociologists and hence had a social orientation (Deegan
1986). Still, in recent decades this field developed into an independent
discipline primarily influenced by medicine and psychology (Zander et
al. 1957). Sociologists, however, continued to do research about clinical
concerns rather than participate in the task of aiding individuals.

It was not until the 1970s that a new breed of sociologist began exploring the possibility of reasserting their discipline's applicability to
practice (Glass and Fritz 1982). These pioneers believed that sociology
had developed a body of knowledge which, although appropriate to
addressing personal problems, was not being used to do so. As a first
step to changing this situation, they sought to alert their sociological
colleagues to missed opportunities. John Glass, in particular, was instrumental in founding the Clinical Sociology Association (later to be
renamed the Sociological Practice Association).

In 1979, a year after its founding, I became aware of the CSA's existence. At the time, I was pursuing a Ph.D. in sociology precisely because I believed a social perspective was vital to comprehending personal problems. After years of having worked as a human services
counselor, I felt the need to more fully understand the dynamics of
social structure and human relationships (matters that turned out to be
the essence of sociology). It seemed to me that these, more than an
individual's psychological quirks, were responsible for most client
problems. The coming of the CSA reinforced this viewpoint and gave
me the comfort of knowing that others shared my perceptions.

My theoretical views about the role of social relationships in the
etiology of human distress began with a reading of Sullivan. He opened
my eyes to the fact that people are not isolated creatures, but exist, of
necessity, in a rich tapestry of human interactions. Through him and,
later, George Herbert Mead, I learned to appreciate that even the con-
tents of the individual human mind are in large measure a social prod-

uct. The contribution of John Bowlby to my thinking must also be mentioned, for he made it plain that a disruption of social attachments can have grave, even lethal, consequences. It became evident that personal happiness has interpersonal roots, and that for people to be satisfied with their lives, they must solve their social as well as personal problems.

The more I have thought about these matters, and the more I have worked with clients, the more convinced I have become that most personal unhappiness is instigated by social role problems. If this is true, the inevitable corollary is that for unhappiness to be abated, dysfunctional roles must be changed. This is the resocialization perspective. It holds that painful roles are created in socialization processes; to be overcome, they must be relinquished and new ones constructed in their place.

Resocialization is not, and should not be, a mystery. Role change is a normal human phenomenon. It may be painful and confused, but for those not caught in its grip, it is relatively easy to understand. In what follows, special attention will be paid to the process by which social coercion generates unsatisfying roles, and how, once established, normal role-conservation mechanisms keep them from changing easily. A central thesis is that role-loss mechanisms similar to those found in the mourning of loved ones must be set in motion, if change is to occur. Since these of necessity involve anguish and fear, resocialization is not tranquil. Still, when successful, it can be among the most rewarding of all human endeavors.

My work with the resocialization paradigm has not proceeded in isolation. The help I have received has been real and extensive. The first debt I must acknowledge is to Joanne M. Jacobs of the Rochester Institute of Technology. She was my partner in the workshop we developed for the SPA, and despite her busy schedule, has several times read and assessed my manuscript. Her many insights and continuing support have been invaluable. Elizabeth Clark, former president of the SPA, was instrumental in keeping the project alive, and David Kallen, editor of the *Clinical Sociology Review*, forced me, through his gentle mandates, to clarify my thoughts. Martin Lean, who once taught me philosophy, and Elaine Ruskin, who introduced me to the realities of psychotherapy, may be credited with many of the ideas which have emerged here. I must also thank my former secretary, Sandy Cottingham, for her inspiration and prayers. Last, I gratefully acknowledge the numerous and (unfortunately) anonymous clients, who are the real source of most of what I have learned.

1

Role Problems

ANGELA

"Why do they always keep doing this to me?"

Angela, a woman in her mid-twenties, was distraught. She was explaining to a counselor that her mother had turned her down once more. Her brother, in whose house Angela was living, had threatened to evict her and now her mother would neither intercede nor help out financially. Since the welfare department had already rejected her pleas for more aid, Angela was beside herself. All she could imagine was that very soon she and her infant son would be out on the street.

As Angela unfolded her story, it became a recitation of all the times people had rejected her. There were, of course, her mother, brother, and the welfare department, but also her boyfriend, former employers, her other siblings, the kids she used to go to school with, and those who even today professed to be her friends. No one seemed to be on her side; no one was there when she needed them. They always seemed to say "No" when she asked for something; and the more critically she needed it, the more certain she was of a negative reply. It seemed to her that people were always telling her to "get out of here" and to "disappear."

"Why do they always do these things to me?" she complained. "What's wrong with me?" Were these repeated rejections her own fault, she wondered. As far back as Angela could remember, people seemed to be trying to get rid of her. It was almost as if this were her role in life, and it probably was.

Angela had been born out of wedlock. To her mother, a woman who desperately sought respectability, she was an embarrassment. For her father, who was not ready for marital entanglements, she was an excuse to leave. Their solution was to ship Angela to her grandparents, and she remained with them even when her mother married another man and began having children by him.

In her early years, Angela was the outcast. She was her family's "rejected child." It was as if she did not belong, and never would. When, as her teen years approached, her mother did allow her to return home, it was as a second-class citizen. Angela was certain she was not receiving the same love, attention, or material benefits as her siblings. Rather, it seemed she was always the one in the wrong, always the one punished. This rejection dogged her everywhere she went. Now as an adult, it was still with her and she didn't know why. All she could think was that it must be her fault. There must be something about her that made people recoil in horror. Although she plaintively asked her counselor why she was always being scorned, her question was somewhat disingenuous. There already existed an answer in which she had confidence. The reason for her plight, she was sure, was that she was unlovable. People were shunning her because there was something about her which invited revulsion.

It did not occur to Angela that her problem might not be due to some quality she possessed, but rather to her on-going relationships. She did not even suspect she was trapped in a "role problem." That the circumstances of her birth had cast her in a particular role within her family did not enter her thoughts. She believed that if she were treated in a certain way, that's probably the way it was supposed to be. If everywhere she went, people rejected her, maybe it was because she carried a personalized curse in her "genes." Angela may have hated being the rejected daughter, but it was a role she knew well, and she played it to the hilt. It may not have met her needs, but it seemed to be her. She clearly perceived herself as a rejected daughter, and established relationships that enacted this basic pattern. Though she might protest against her situation, it was as if she possessed a radar for unearthing role partners who helped her relive it, over and over again.

THE UBIQUITY OF ROLE PROBLEMS

Angela's dilemma is by no means unique. Role problems are a ubiquitous phenomenon. They are a major cause of personal unhappiness, and the reason that many people feel trapped in unsatisfying lifestyles. Social roles are the primary mechanism through which human beings interact with one another. If they are not geared toward meeting personal needs, they are bound to create dissatisfaction. Normal roles are then transformed into role problems, and frustrations are institutionalized.

People do not often realize how much of their behavior is, in fact, role behavior. In consequence, they are not usually aware that many of their most intimate and intractable predicaments are really role problems. Yet social roles are at the core of our individual identities. They determine how we perceive ourselves and are perceived by others. Each of us, for instance, is a man or a woman. These are more than biological categories; they are highly complex patterns of living (Garfinkel 1967). In addition, we are all a particular type of man or woman, such as a super-woman, a macho-man, or a stud. We may further be designated the "good one" in our family, or the scapegoat, the smart one, the artist, the clown, or the rebel. Some of these roles may serve us well, but others seriously undermine our happiness. The most important personal roles are generated within intimate relationships, and may include such restrictive patterns as caretaker, dreamer, spoiled brat, wounded bird, troublemaker, family hero, lost child, or family mascot (Scarf 1987; Wegscheider-Cruse 1980).

Bad roles make it difficult for people to fulfill their needs for safety, love, or respect. But without these requirements being met, it is almost impossible for us to be happy. Still, when they are not achieved, we usually don't know why. Though we may be actively miserable, or quietly desperate, we mistake the cause of our distress. We tend to blame ourselves, without realizing that we are being victimized by an interpersonal problem rather than a personal defect.

Taking Role Problems Seriously

Helping professionals have long been aware of role problems. They have been highlighted by Grinker (1961) and Szasz (1961), and recently have figured prominently in family therapies (Gurman and Kniskern 1981) and the treatment of depression (Klerman et al. 1984). Nevertheless, they have rarely been treated as a separate entity worthy of direct exploration. More commonly, they are relegated to a systems approach or to adjunctive status within a personality or medical approach. Little effort is made to understand exactly how roles are formed, how they go wrong, or how they can be corrected.

If, as we have been asserting, role problems are a major source of human misery, this is an egregious oversight. If role failures are a major cause of individual pain, then they deserve to be taken seriously. The fact that they have not is probably an artifact of the institutional structure of the helping professions. Traditional helping services have been in the hands of medicine and psychology. These have typically understood their subject in terms of either physical or personality dis-

orders. Only within the last decade or so have they come to appreciate
that role relationships are a formative factor in the difficulties they attempt to solve. Nevertheless, medical schools and graduate programs
in psychology do not make roles or role relationships a significant focus of their programs. It is therefore inevitable that they are not at the
center of attention for academic psychologists or psychiatrists.

It would seem that the only way this situation can be rectified is by
institutionalizing a profession that does focus on relationships and social roles. Historically, this niche has been filled by sociology. It is this
field that inaugurated the study of role relationships, childhood socialization, and the organization of family structures. Unfortunately, it is
also historically true that it did not apply these insights to helping individuals solve personal problems.

The time has come for this to change. Sociology must be admitted to
the pantheon of disciplines that address individual human difficulties.
Sociologists must be encouraged to focus attention on role problems
and to investigate their development and alteration. Moreover, clinical
sociologists need to have the same professional authority as psychiatrists and psychologists to employ their unique insights in helping individual clients. Only then will the psycho-social approach, which most
practitioners already advocate, become a reality. Only then will role
problems be accorded their proper status.

A Role Perspective

Social roles are complex patterns of human behavior. They can be
identified by what people do and how they interact; they can also be
highlighted by examining what people are trying to do or trying to
convince others to do. Roles are patterns of interpersonal action that
are guided by both internal and external directions. They are shaped
by a person's plans, thoughts, and feelings, and by the demands made
by others. Exactly how this occurs will be described in succeeding
chapters.

Social roles are a joint construction of people and their role partners.
If they cooperate, they may succeed in developing role patterns that
are mutually satisfying. If not, one or both will be frustrated. The arrangements they evolve will be burdens rather than sources of pleasure. Moreover, these roles must be maintained. They are not constructed once and for all, then frozen irrevocably in place. Rather, they
must be modified and adjusted to meet ever-changing circumstances.
If, however, the interpersonal negotiations that shape these alterations
are coercive, the results may not suit their purposes. The modified roles
will be out of synch with underlying needs.

Roles and Needs. Since roles are a primary mechanism for meeting personal needs, they must be such that they do fulfill them. They must especially satisfy a person's requirements for safety, love, and respect (Maslow 1954). The reason roles are so essential to achieving needs is that they are the preeminent human arrangement for allowing people to do things together. In short, they organize human interactions. The role of husband largely prescribes what a man will do with his wife qua wife. If these patterned interactions do not include loving behaviors, it is unlikely that either of their needs for love will be satisfied, at least within their relationship. Similarly, if a parent does not respect his child, the child's need for respect is not likely to be met.

Yet the relationship between a social role and needs satisfaction is not one-to-one. It is not as if particular behaviors, when indulged in, immediately and reliably bring safety, love, or respect. Needs fulfillment follows in uncertain ways from combinations of role behaviors. Therefore it becomes very difficult to predict whether a particular role will have a desired effect. To a great extent, discovering which behaviors lead to what results is a matter of trial and error. This means that satisfying roles must be capable of adjustment. To the degree that people are frozen into patterns they find difficult to alter, they are often trapped in dysfunctional behaviors.

Types of Role Problems. There are several ways in which social roles can cause problems:

1. The initial construction of a role may have gone wrong. Instead of a viable one developing, an unfinished and unsatisfying muddle can result. Such a role may be thought of as having been aborted. It is like a marriage that has never been happy and eventuates in a squalid divorce.
2. A role may work when it is initially constructed, but become dysfunctional in a new social context. In such a case, it will no longer meet a person's needs and hence may be said to have failed. It is like a marriage that has been happy, but which is prematurely severed by death.
3. A dysfunctional role may be dysfunctionally maintained. Apart from the lack of satisfaction that derives from a role being aborted or having failed, the process of changing it into something better may be very painful and hence itself a problem. When this pain is so intense that it prevents a remedy, the difficulty is compounded.

Aborted Roles. When roles are initially socialized, especially in childhood, a person's role partners (e.g., parents) may force unsatisfactory bargains upon him. They may demand, for instance, that he be a good boy, then disqualify him from conforming with their wishes by judging everything he does as bad. In so doing they put him in a "double bind" which precludes successful role resolution (Berger 1978). Much to his chagrin, the child is left with the fragmented role of "bad boy," which is acceptable neither to himself nor his parents.

When this child becomes an adult, he may carry the albatross of being a bad boy with him, all the while wishing to be a good one. The role he enacts is incomplete and distorted. For him, it represents unfinished business that pushes for a more successful resolution. Sometimes an aborted role will not be impossibly bad, but only naggingly so. The role may allow some satisfactions, but not the ones the person wants. For example, a child's parents may demand that he become an athlete, when he is more interested in music. Such a role is not impossible in the same sense as the good boy role, but it will not be fully pleasing. Despite the child's overt submission, he will try covertly to sabotage it. Given such resistance, this kind of role never works very well, and hence it too is aborted. In adulthood, the person trapped in it finds himself uneasy. He may experience a sense of guilt that he finds difficult to fathom. It will not occur to him that his own lingering resistance is making it impossible for him to be gratified.

Failed Roles. Sometimes a role that is useful in childhood makes it impossible to satisfy needs in adulthood. For example, in order to please her parents, a child may assume the role of caretaker. Her task in the family will be to protect her parents. One of her jobs may be to stay close to mother to help allay her anxieties. Or she may be required to be the family spokeswoman and guard father from external threats. In return for these services, she will be rewarded with love and protection. Indeed, being a caretaker may be her only way of fitting into her family, and while a child she may succeed tolerably well.

When the child becomes a woman, the situation will be different. In order to succeed in life, she will need roles which can be maintained outside the bosom of her family. If she has been raised as a caretaker, she will probably believe that the only niche others will allow her to fill is that of caring for them. She will conclude that the sole avenue for gaining love and protection lies in sacrificing herself for their good. In consequence, she receives far fewer personal satisfactions than she would if she were looking after her own needs too. Since she has eschewed self-determination and entrusted herself to the tender mercy of others, unless they take special precautions in her behalf, she will be trapped in a failed role.

Failed roles cannot be entirely separated from aborted ones. Most failed roles are never entirely successful. Thus to some extent a caretaker role is usually aborted before it fails. Childhood caretakers may have some of their personal needs met, but at considerable personal expense. If, for instance, caretaking means remaining by the side of an anxious mother, it clearly interferes with the satisfactions to be gained from playing in the street with one's friends. A more clear-cut case of a failed role would be that of "family genius." Such a child may be exalted by his parents, but if he doesn't have the intellectual tools to maintain his genius status in a wider world, he will eventually encounter a very traumatic disillusionment.

Dysfunctional Role Maintenance. Role change can be an extraordinarily painful process. The more central a role is to a person's identity, the more intolerable it is to modify. This means that many people do not attempt to alter or replace failed or aborted roles because the pain of change is worse than the pain of living with the role.

The most significant factor in the dysfunctional maintenance of bad roles is intense emotion. It is the discomfort induced by very potent feelings that dissuades most people from attempting role change. They are distressed at having to face the fear, anger, and sadness inherent in resocialization. Neither do they relish the guilt, shame, or unrequited love that also figure prominently in such efforts. Nevertheless, before basic roles can be relinquished, emotions must be faced and disarmed.

It must also be pointed out that the mechanisms that discourage people from changing unsatisfying roles are merely a variation of the mechanisms that hold functional roles in place. The same fear, anger, and sadness that make it difficult to relinquish a failed role also make it difficult to inadvertently slough off a satisfying one. The difference between functional and dysfunctional role maintenance sometimes lies merely in what is being preserved.

Role maintenance is a vital part of any social structure. There is a normal inertia built into role behavior without which no society could function. Individual behavior would be too unpredictable for large numbers of people to coordinate their activities. There thus needs to be something that inhibits arbitrary changes in patterns of behavior. This is the function of role-maintenance mechanisms. Ordinarily they are very useful, but when roles are dysfunctional they become a trap. It is then that the difficulty inherent in changing any role forces people to remain caretakers or scapegoats. It is precisely because change is painful that someone attempting to alter her roles finds herself forced into repeating the same dreary patterns. This is why it is often necessary to have a helper who can increase the odds of making resocialization work.

Demoralization. When people seek professional help for personal problems, they often do not realize they are trapped in dysfunctional roles. Instead, they feel "demoralized" (Frank 1973) and are acutely aware that their own efforts to improve their situation have been unavailing. They feel helpless, depressed, angry, anxious, or confused. All of these emotions are signs of aborted roles, failed roles, or dysfunctional role maintenance.

The Locus of Fault

Clients such as Angela usually want to know who is at fault for their suffering. Like Angela, most suspect, and have been told by friends and relatives, that their plight is of their own doing. The guilt this imposes becomes an additional burden, one that is totally unnecessary. In contrast, a role-problem perspective assigns the cause not to the person himself, but to the interpersonal relationships in which his dysfunctional roles were formed, and/or to the normal mechanisms that perpetuate roles. A person trapped in a failed or aborted role may be participating in the maintenance of his own discomfort, but he was not its original cause. Neither does he prolong it because there is something wrong with him. On the contrary, his role behaviors started as a defensive reaction to the coercive maneuvers of others, and the reason he maintains them is that basic roles are always difficult to change.

Most clients who seek help are told that they have a medical disorder or a personality problem. In either case, the fault for their distress is placed squarely on their own shoulders. The medical model implies that it is the client who has a disease and asserts there is something physically wrong with him (Miller 1978). The personality model places the burden on some personal defect of his and insinuates that he is incompetent. Either way, a finger of blame is pointed at the person in pain and an implicit demand is made that he shape up.

Medicalizing Distress. When people are feeling, thinking, or doing things they really don't want to feel, think, or do, when these don't appear to make sense, and when, furthermore, they find it difficult to change them, they and others are liable think them crazy. Breaking important social rules, especially rules about emotional expression, logical thinking, and acceptable behavior, and doing this without apparent reason or an ability to stop, is precisely what is meant by being crazy. No wonder then that when people become depressed for no apparent reason, enraged with no visible cause, confused without knowing about what, or frightened when there seems to be nothing to fear, they are suspected of being ill. At least this hypothesis has the virtue of making sense of the seemingly senseless.

In reality, these feelings, thoughts, and behaviors are more comprehensible if they are recognized for what they are: evidence that a person is trapped in dysfunctional roles. There is no need to take recourse in the various psychiatric diagnoses of the DSM-III (APA 1980). Most anxiety, affective, dissociative, psychosexual, impulse, adjustment, and personality disorders are better understood as aspects of role problems than as diseases. The intense feelings and confusions they engender result from failed and aborted roles and from miscarried attempts at role change, not from a physical or functional illness.

There are, to be sure, real mental illnesses. Schizophrenia and cyclothemia are two such. Both are precipitated in large measure by inherited biological vulnerabilities (Wynne et al. 1978; Beckham and Leber 1985). When a person's dysfunctional behavior is a result of a genetic defect, an infection, a nutritional deficit, or an injury, it is proper and fitting to speak of disease. When, in contrast, the primary evidence of disorder is the person's behavior itself, and especially when there is reason to believe that this behavior has been socially induced, talk of illness is misplaced and inappropriate.

One of the glaring ironies of current therapeutic practice is that Gerald Klerman, an M.D. who has successfully introduced a role perspective to the treatment of depression, simultaneously stresses the medical model of depression. Following the DSM-III, he insists that depression is a mental disorder because it "represents significantly *abnormal behavior or function*" (Rounsaville et al. 1985). Among the causative agencies he cites are "interpersonal role disputes," "role transitions," and "interpersonal deficits." But however much these factors may lead to abnormal behavior or function, they are not physiological problems. To stretch the notion of disease to cover them takes it well past the breaking point. If all significantly abnormal behavior counts as disorder, then no dysfunctional behavior is excluded, and criminal activity, error, and foolishness become disease. Doctors are then cast as the arbiters of morality, competence, and social acceptability, a role for which they are ill-prepared. One is surely entitled to wonder how an expertise in biochemistry or physiology validates their moral judgments.

Psychologizing Distress. Although most psychologists readily admit that their field deals with psycho-social problems, their training biases them to psychologize behavior. For obvious reasons, they are sensitized to what happens within people and so are inclined to give interpersonal dynamics short shrift (Dorpat 1985). In particular, they are likely to see personal problems as an outcome of personality dilemmas. Psychologists readily interpret unhappiness as a derivative of personal traits, disordered thoughts, or inappropriate instincts.

Personality traits have traditionally been thought of as discrete qualities that inhere in the individual. If a woman is honest or brave, it must be because she has an inclination to honesty or bravery, much as a glass vase has a disposition to shatter. In recent decades, an awareness has been growing that traits are context specific (Mischel 1968). It has become evident that how a person reacts depends as much on her interpersonal environment as on who she is. Ostensible personal qualities such as honesty depend a great deal upon the situation a person finds herself in. Thus an honest woman will not be honest in all social contexts. When she is playing poker, for instance, she may consider bluffing a virtue rather than a vice. A social role perspective, unlike a trait orientation, asks not only what a person does, but when she does it, and with whom. It is concerned with the complex patterns of her necessarily interactive behavior. Such a framework places an honest woman within the setting of her relationships, and sees the nature of her honesty varying with these.

Some parts of a person's personality are, it must be admitted, very stable. They can profitably be thought of as qualities of his. In particular, traits that can be identified as part of his temperament do seem to belong to him. People are apparently born with some behavioral characteristics that persist for long periods of time (Chess and Thomas 1986). For instance, some are shy, some active, and some aggressive. But the essence of temperament is that it resists change. Unlike dysfunctional roles which can be altered or replaced, temperament must be adjusted to fit its environment. This means that people in distress will find it is their role structures which are amenable to alteration, and not their more stable personality traits.

Thoughts too are often identified by psychologists as the locus of personal problems. Cognitively oriented psychologists have suggested that "errors in logic" (Beck et al. 1979) or "irrational ideas" (Ellis and Grieger 1977) are the root of much unhappiness. Specifically, it is their contention that disordered ideas have a primary causative function in conditions such as depression. No doubt strange ideas do get people in trouble, but there is reason to suspect that they are not the central factor in precipitating personal pain (Beckham and Leber 1985). People with problems don't get that way because their ability to think is impaired; even schizophrenics have a command of logic (Wynne et al. 1978). Rather, ideas become disturbed because they are generated in role relationships that have gone awry. Distorted ideas are a defensive reaction, not a causative agent. Suggesting otherwise is to stigmatize troubled people unfairly.

A Psycho-Social Viewpoint. One of the chief virtues of a role-problem perspective is that it is inherently psycho-social. Social roles of necessity consist of inter- and intra-personal components. They are not solipsistic compositions or stereotyped social impositions, but rather a combination of both. Roles are the negotiated result of individual persons interacting within their social environments. The concept of "role" is thus Janus-faced. It simultaneously looks within and without, and that is its special virtue. Because it is psycho-social, the concept is capable of doing justice to the complexity of human experience. Moreover, it points the way toward more effective problem-solving techniques. Clearly, if roles are generated both inter- and intra-personally, they must of necessity be corrected within relationships.

Levels of Intervention

Personal problems and, more specifically, role problems can be tackled on several levels. People can be helped to cope despite the continued existence of their distress, they can be taught skills that open up new vistas of problem solving, or they can be assisted in altering and replacing their dysfunctional roles. The first of these approaches can be labeled "social support," the second, "socialization," and the third, "resocialization." These three services differ in the degree of change they attempt. The deeper they go, that is, the more they lie in the direction of resocialization, the more effort and pain they entail. The choice of which approach is appropriate to a particular client will depend upon a variety of factors. A client's personal strength, the seriousness of his problem, and the competence of his helper will all have to be considered. Ultimately, the single most decisive factor will be what a person wants to achieve and is motivated to implement.

Supportive Interventions. Support services can be either moral or material. Frequently, when people have problems in living, all they need is someone to be on their side. A clinician who listens with compassion may be sufficient to make a difference. Her moral support may help a client discover his strengths and solve his problems himself. Sometimes this does not happen, but the client acquires the courage to endure nevertheless. This latter goal is one of the chief aims of programs such as Alcoholic Anonymous, which hopes to sustain sobriety "one day at a time" (Bratter and Forrest 1985). A clinician may also be asked to furnish more tangible avenues of help. In some instances she may have to engage in environmental interventions such as finding a client an apartment, arranging for financial support, or providing advocacy services. The point of doing these things is to lighten the burden on a person and give him the room to solve his own problems.

Socialization. Socialization is the process through which roles are initially acquired. For a client who does not have pre-existing roles that must be replaced, it may be the intervention of choice. A person who is dissatisfied with his lot in life may only need to learn new ways of living in order to feel better. If so, an adequate intervention may merely help him develop additional roles that can be used in conjunction with the ones he already possesses. A clinician's task is then to help him achieve these. Socialization usually involves quasi-educational forms of help. Clients may be taught assertiveness, parenting skills, or specific vocational competences. They can even be taught methods of relaxation. These individual techniques can then be melded into more comprehensive ways of interacting with others.

Resocialization. Resocialization is a more far-reaching and radical process than either support or socialization. It is the process through which dysfunctional roles are either altered or replaced. It assumes the pre-existence of roles that must be relinquished before new and more sat-isfying ones can be adopted. Old roles that are incompatible with the new must be dropped (at least in part) before the new ones can be acquired. It is the necessity of relinquishing outmoded roles that often makes resocialization a painful and protracted affair. Given the nature of role maintenance, people are, despite themselves, reluctant to give up even dreadfully painful personal roles. Their fear and rage get the better of them, and they find themselves clinging desperately to pre-cisely what they should release.

Professional Help. Resocialization does not always have to occur under professional auspices. Old roles can be altered or replaced with the help of friends and relatives. Indeed, there is an innate push toward role change (Freud called it the repetition compulsion) which induces resocialization in everyone's life. Nevertheless, the more extensive the role problem, the more necessary is professional intervention. It must be remembered that role difficulties originate in disturbed interper-sonal relations, and hence a person who attempts positive personal change will probably be interacting with the very people who precipi-tated her problem. In short, her normal role partners will be inclined to impede rather than foster change. A professional, however, should have no ax to grind. He is pledged to have sufficient detachment and expertise to correctly perceive what his client needs and to effectively facilitate its achievement.

Professional resocialization is usually identified as psychotherapy or counseling. Unfortunately, both of these designations are misleading in that neither implies role change. "Counseling" connotes only the giving of advice (McKecknie 1971), while "psychotherapy" literally means "curing the mind." Since role change deals with more than the psyche, and not at all with illness, this latter is not the right term either. "Re-socialization" comes much closer to the mark in describing what ac-tually needs to be accomplished when people are trapped in dysfunc-tional roles. It is undoubtedly an ugly word, and an uncommon one, but it fits the facts. Therefore it is the word we will use to specify professionally supervised role change.

2

The Genesis of Dysfunctional Roles

DEFINING ROLES

Before it is possible to facilitate role change, it is necessary to understand what roles are and how they go wrong. One must know what needs to be changed, and how and why it came to require change. Let us start with the definition of social roles. In chapter 1, these were described as "complex patterns of interpersonal behavior." This formulation takes the viewpoint of an external observer. It presumes an objective enumeration of the things people do and how these are integrated with what others do. According to this perspective, the actual behaviors of people are their roles.

If human beings were disinterested creatures who did not inhabit their roles, this definition might be sufficient. In fact, social scientists have found it necessary to define them in other ways as well. One of these, a view that has been identified with structural/functionalist theories of society, sees roles as imposed upon individuals from the outside (Linton 1936; Parsons 1951, 1970). It defines roles in terms of the "expectations" people have of one another (Biddle 1979; Joas 1985). These expectations are really demands that role partners make of each other and through which they confer rights and duties. A person's roles thus are what her role partners say they are.

In contrast, roles may also be defined from the point of view of the role performer. According to this view, a person's own norms and values, that is, her own way of understanding what she is doing, define her role. It is her intentions and understandings which make the role what it is. This perspective has been identified primarily with symbolic/interactionist views of society (Mead 1934; Turner 1985).

In fact, roles are a combination of internal and external factors. The objective behaviors that constitute a person's roles are controlled both by what her partners demand and by what she intends. Her ideas and theirs interact to shape her conduct. Together they define her role. The concept of social role is thus inherently both inter- and intra-personal. Leaving out either aspect diminishes the whole. Turner (1962) has underscored this fact by speaking of role-making. He emphasizes the interpersonal construction that goes into creating role performances. In his words, "the idea of role-making shifts emphasis from the simple process of enacting a prescribed role to devising a performance on the basis of an imputed other role."

Ideal Types. The role behaviors defined by the joint efforts of a person and his role partners are often assigned a name. Earlier Angela was described as a rejected daughter. Another person might be labeled a caretaker, artist, or scapegoat. These words place boundaries on roles and call our attention to them. Yet they can also take on the aura of the role itself. A label can be reified and confused with the complex and variable patterns of behavior it represents. In such a case, the performance associated with it can seem simpler and more stereotyped than it really is. In fact, what role labels delimit are "ideal types" (Weber 1947; Gerth and Mills 1946). They represent the central tendencies of very tangled, convoluted patterns of behavior. In order to comprehend the complexities of the world, we need simplifications. This is how the human mind works (Wittgenstein 1953). Since the "ideal" has sharp borders, it allows for efficient mental manipulations.

Role Variations. It must not be overlooked that the unsophisticated patterns brought to mind by role labels conceal a multitude of variations. Any given role can be performed in many different ways. There is an infinite variety of rejected daughter, caretaker, or family genius subroles (see Tables 2.1 and 2.2). For the specific instance of a role, it is always necessary to inquire how it is played, with whom it is played, and when it is played. Only then can it be clear what is happening.

When a person is a caretaker, if one is to understand his actual role, it is necessary to know whether it is being performed with men or women, with adults or children, with the powerful or weak. One must also know if care is provided in terms of money, emotional support, or physical protection. Similarly, a rejected daughter may be rejected by her family, friends, or employers; she may be given the cold shoulder, actively persecuted, or selectively excluded. Each of these permutations will make a profound difference in her role experience. Ignoring them distorts the reality of the situation. For a clinician, this is an especially treacherous pitfall, since ignoring a client's particular role translates into a failure to help with his true problem.

Negotiated Products. The role-making that Turner spotlights needs to

Table 2.1
Types of Roles

Caretaker	Alcoholic	The Quiet One
Friend	Clown	Born Leader
Scapegoat	The Student	Tough Guy
The Genius	The Generous One	Macho Man
The Fat One	Gloomy Gus	Bum
The Observer	Black Sheep	Saint
Rebel	The Eldest	No. 1 Son
Family Hero	Martyr	The Criminal
Coward	Super woman	The Rival
Fool	The Baby	Life of the Party
Great Beauty	Hermit	The Pursuer
Earth Mother	Artist	The Pursued
Athlete	The Good One	The Selfish One
Mascot	The Lover	Weak One

be taken quite seriously. Roles are constructed phenomena that are hammered out in interpersonal negotiations. They are forever being altered and adjusted as people interact with one another. Social life is pervaded with demands and counter-demands. There are perpetual conflicts about who will do what with whom; and when and how they will do it. This results in bargains that eventually become stabilized, and are then built upon by subsequent bargains.

The negotiated aspect of roles is a familiar fact of everyday life. It is seen in the disputes parents and children have about who will take out

Table 2.2
Role Variations (Caretaker)

- WHO:
  - Parents
  - Children
  - Men
  - Women
  - The Weak
  - The Strong

- HOW:
  - Financially
  - Emotionally
  - Physical Protection
  - Food
  - Information
  - Sexually

the garbage, in the disagreements of spouses about whether the wife will go to work, and in office politics that decide who will be promoted and who won't. Role negotiations are at least a two-way affair. In a negotiation, both parties are "sending and receiving" (Turner 1985). Each has an input into the final product, and neither automatically imposes his will upon the other. Despite the power disparities that exist between people, even the weakest is capable of obstructing the strongest.

Negotiations may be thought of as a mechanism for dispute resolution. They are a medium in which multiple parties can participate to allocate social tasks with relative safety. If war is diplomacy carried on by other means (Clausewitz 1908), then role negotiations are a civilized version of the Hobbesian war of all against all (Hobbes 1956). When functioning properly, they provide controlled structures for achieving mutually acceptable decisions. The "constructed" aspect of role negotiations refers to the fact that the results are a new creation. The bargains generated are not pre-arranged fiats handed down from above or swallowed whole. Negotiated deals depend upon the moment-to-moment decisions of the participants (Garfinkel 1967). In contrast to a view commonly held in psychology, roles are not simply "learned" (Dollard and Miller 1950; Skinner 1953); they are far more than combinations of "reinforced" behavior. Role negotiations incorporate the demands, foresight, and spontaneity of their participants. Hence their product is more than a computer program that is accepted by docile automatons.

Personal Roles. The roles produced through negotiations take many forms. Some can be characterized as personal while others are distinctly impersonal. It is personal roles that typically cause people most pain. They are commonly the ones people need help in changing. Usually, they are deeply significant to individuals because they are identified as parts of the self. When such roles go wrong, people feel as if they have personally gone wrong. Behavior patterns such as caretaker and family genius help define the self. They carry a great deal of emotional freight and are not easily jettisoned.

Personal roles are a product of the face-to-face interactions within primary relationships. They are roles generated within families and intimate relationships, and form the glue of our most valued interpersonal connections. They are decidedly not artificial appendages that can be dropped at the whim of the moment. When a personal role is lost, a yawning gap is created in a person's life. He may no longer know who he is or where he fits. Without satisfying personal roles, people feel incomplete and adrift. No wonder that they desperately resist their loss. Impersonal roles, on the other hand, do not have the same effect. They too can be very important, but they are more often seen as something a person does, rather than who he is. Impersonal roles, that is, roles such as banker, customer, or pedestrian, are characteristic of secondary relationships. They are less likely to be a fundamental part of a person's identity, although some people may be very heavily invested in their occupational stations. Most of the time, impersonal roles are easier to replace than the personal. After all, it is easier to change a job than who one is.

Basic Roles. Just as some roles are more personal than others, some are more basic than others. A basic role is one that forms a platform upon which others are built. Usually, these roles have been constructed in childhood. Like personal roles, they are central to a person's identity; since they provide the foundation for numerous other roles, they are vital to one's sense of well-being. Without them, a person would feel as if his whole world were collapsing.

Roles are forever being altered to fit new circumstances. When a person encounters a new life situation, it is natural for him to try out the old familiar roles first to see if, with a few adjustments, they can be made to work. Roles thus begin to form ramified chains of evolving behavior patterns. Like blueprints of evolutionary descent, they branch out in different directions, sometimes finding brilliantly productive outlets, sometimes leading to dead ends. For instance, a woman who has learned to be a caretaker in childhood may develop many variations of the role as she matures. As a child, her caretaking may have been restricted to remaining at mother's side to ensure her of safety. With increasing age, she may transfer this function to new relationships, for example, to boyfriends, a spouse, children, clients, and so on. She may also develop variations on how she cares for them. Thus she may develop the character of the great mother who is totally protective of her offspring, or become a social worker who works to save a myriad of clients. These new roles, while morphologically connected to that of caretaker, will have added new facets to the basic structure.

Evolving roles, which have grown from a more basic rootstock, form a repertoire of behaviors that can be drawn upon as needed. This repertoire is an ever-expanding structure that includes numerous interlocking variations of simpler childhood models. It is like an inverted pyramid resting on a foundation of basic childhood roles. Striking at this base thus becomes a threat to the whole structure. Should a basic role be extirpated, its loss threatens the integrity of all roles derived from it. Since these are themselves interlocked, changing the base portends the destruction of the whole edifice. It is therefore no wonder that people in the grip of dysfunctional roles balk at the prospect of altering their basic roles. They correctly sense that a lot is at stake, and they are afraid that too much may be lost. Basic roles are too vital to be casually adjusted.

Trans-situational Roles. The basic and personal roles that are at the focus of most resocialization are usually trans-situational (Stryker 1968, 1980). They represent patterns of behavior that remain consistent in different social contexts. Roles are more than patterns of behavior; they are patterns that are associated with particular social positions (often called "statuses"). To give a concrete example, the behaviors that go to make up the role of banker are appropriate to the situations in which a person functions as a banker. It is in the context of a bank that it is most appropriate for him to play the part. It is in this setting that customers and colleagues will define him as a banker and where his concerns about money and interest rates are most appreciated.

Trans-situational roles, in contrast, are not so context-bound. They are roles a person carries around with him that can be used in diverse situations. Many of them come close to what psychologists call traits. Roles like "the smart one" or "the family beauty" come to mind. They may be thought of as qualities of the person, but are actually patterns of behavior. While they may be based on personal qualities, they are much more. To be "the smart one," one does not need to be the smartest in the family; one needs only to be treated as if one were. The "smart one" is expected to show off. She is designated to solve crucial problems and to carry the family's banner. It is not so much her intelligence that defines her status, but the fact that both she and others judge her to be exceptionally bright and grant her the rights and duties pertaining thereto.

People bearing trait-like trans-situational roles import them into all sorts of situations. The "smart one" tries to be smart on the job and at home. The "great beauty" acts the part almost everywhere. We have all met the inveterate intellectual show-off and the constantly preening peacock. Their roles are portable and may be implemented at a moment's notice. We may disagree that a particular person is very smart or attractive, but this will not impede his performance one bit. Given the potential ubiquity of trans-situational roles, they, like the personal and basic roles with which they may be co-extensive, tend to be central to a person's identity, and hence difficult to alter.

Role Scripts

Lurking behind all roles are role scripts. These are the structures that guide people during the performance of their behavior patterns. They give role players a general idea of what is expected of them and with whom they are supposed to interact. These scripts are not explicit sets of instructions, but hints on how to improvise a part. They do not specify most details, but provide parameters for action. A specific role performance is always open to revision at the moment of its enactment. Different times and different circumstances call forth different versions.

Whenever roles are negotiated, the partners to the negotiation collaborate in developing scripts which can then be used to guide their subsequent interpersonal relationships. These scripts, which tend to be very persistent, have both internal and external components. That is, part of a role script resides within the person and part is imposed upon him by his social environment. It is the interaction of these components that determines the final performance.

Historically, internal scripts have been divided into cognitive, affective, and conative constituents (Allport 1985). Recently, under the impact of behavioral psychology, these have been reconceptualized as cognitive, emotional, and behavioral factors (Wolberg 1967). However, this new arrangement seems to be a matter of mixing apples and oranges. Cognitions and emotions are clearly internal to a person, and are capable of guiding behaviors. Behavior, in contrast, is that which is guided. It is external and objective, and belongs to a different category. A more appropriate candidate for the third element of internal scripts is volition. It refers to a person's decisions and intentions, and harks back to the old-fashioned concept of conation (inner striving). As distinguished from behavior, volition is internal and does guide action.

External scripts mirror the internal, but come primarily from the social environment. These script elements consist mostly of the demands that role partners make of a role performer. Just as the components of an inner script guide behavior, so do these exterior parameters. Exactly what is demanded of a person is itself shaped by the cognitions, emotions, volitions, and social environment of his role partners. And these, in turn, are influenced by the internal scripts of the role partner's role partners. Like light bouncing between an infinity of mirrors, external scripts are affected by society-wide considerations. Not just persons, but whole cultures are implicated in individual role performances (Kluckhohn and Murray 1948; Shibutani 1961; Westen 1985).

It is remarkable, considering the omnipresence of social scripts, how often they are neglected. Psychologists are accustomed to taking account of intra-psychic factors, but too frequently find social facts invisible. Yet social pressures are a focal cause of role failure. Indeed, it is the coercive imposition of external scripts that is the single greatest precipitant of role dysfunction. A resocialization agent can not afford to leave them out of his calculations.

Cognitions. The world in which we live is of human fabrication. It is the result of interpretations that we impose upon reality. The meaning of things does not have an existence independent of that which people give it. Moreover, these meanings are fashioned of symbols (Mead 1934). It is ultimately through language and thought that human beings make sense of the world. With these, we impress patterns on an otherwise "blooming, buzzing confusion." That someone is a father, or something a piece of food, is our judgment. Once made and communicated, these judgments act as "maps of the world." They help us predict and determine subsequent actions. How a person understands his environment influences how he uses it. Hence, interpreting something as a table increases the probability that one will eat on it. Similarly, a person who conceives of himself as being very agile may be inclined to become an athlete. Even if he is mistaken in his judgment, his interpretation may still guide his actions. As W. I. Thomas (1928) reminded us, even false beliefs have real consequences. It is the man who imagines he can fly who may decide to jump off a building.

Emotions. Feelings also give us information about the world. They tell us what is dangerous and what is pleasant, they inform us about our frustrations, and they chastise us for our transgressions. It is emotions that alert us when our needs are not being met and guide us as we attempt to satisfy them. No less than cognitions, they reveal the architecture of the world and provide details about our inner state. Indeed, they coordinate our outside and inside worlds.

In addition to transmitting messages, emotions also motivate us to act. They mediate the transition from information to accomplishment. Thus, in the face of danger, it is fear that impels us toward fight or flight. It provides us with the energy for action, and often directs the form that activity will take. Primitive anger, for example, can encourage an assault on an obstacle, or impel us to bite and kick an object of frustration. It is these properties that make emotions the central motivating factor of internal role scripts.

Volition. Volitions might better be called "action schemas," or more simply, "plans." In order to implement role behavior, it is not enough to have a cognitive map of the world, or to be impelled to action by emotions; it is also necessary to have some plan about what to do. It is essential to have what might be compared with an itinerary. Human actions, including role behaviors, are guided by ends and means. These inform us about what we are after and what strategies are suitable for attaining them. Sometimes volitions are confused with cognitions. They are lumped together under a rubric such as "irrational ideas" (Ellis and Grieger 1977). Yet plans are not understandings. They may utilize cognitive maps as tools, but they add another dimension. Theirs is the difference between values and facts, or between rules and descriptions. The former pair direct actions, while the latter paint a picture of the world. Labeling both as "ideas" blurs this distinction. It gives the impression that merely knowing how the world is constructed automatically generates decisions about how to act.

Since there is, in fact, always more than one way to do something, choices must be made. Recognizing these as volitional, and hence subject to individual motivation, dispels the notion that decisions are objective. Though some alternatives may be wiser than others, their rightness cannot be read directly off the facts. Fallible human judgment always intervenes in the planning process.

Social Demands. In the theater, an actor must not only know his own lines, but those of his fellow actors as well. Without a feel for their parts, he cannot recognize the cues to his. Their lines tell him when to begin. Moreover, how they say their lines dictates his pacing and emotional tone. In effect, the lines of the rest of the cast are a part of his. It turns out that in real life the roles of others are an even more integral part of one's own. Not only is there a similarly-cued turn-taking, but given the improvisational nature of real-life roles, the very words of one actor are generated in response to those of others. Roles always come in pairs. This is the point of speaking about role partners (Merton 1949). The behaviors of one role are always integrated with those of others. After all, roles are patterns of interpersonal behavior. One way or another, they must mesh, and in a very real way the role of another becomes part of one's own.

The persons with whom we collaborate on our roles are similar to ourselves. They too have cognitions, emotions, volitions, and role partners who guide their actions. For this reason competent role performances depend on understanding scripts. It is necessary to know what another is doing in order to make the adjustments that help both roles succeed. It is even more important to understand the scripts of role partners when negotiating new roles. Good deals, that is, deals that meet needs, rarely flow from mutual ignorance. Knowing the scripts of another makes it possible to react with insight rather than blindness.

ROLE FAILURE

Since social roles are negotiated products, negotiations that are smooth and cooperative have a good prospect of generating scripts that meet the needs of both parties. When, however, negotiations are conflictual, there is an ever-present danger that dysfunctional roles will emerge. Instead of demand and counter-demand melding into a mutually satisfying bargain, aborted or potentially failed roles ensue. The bargain achieved, or more properly, imposed, will at some point be unacceptable to at least one of the parties. Bad negotiations force one or both to lose. Instead of generating role behaviors that facilitate satisfying relationships, someone is coerced into accepting undesired ways of living. Coercion, or its equivalent, makes it impossible for at least one of the negotiators to influence the developing deal according to his felt needs. Thus a valid deal never emerges and the role is aborted, or an apparently satisfying deal is accepted only to fail under different circumstances.

Losing a role negotiation is an especially traumatic form of loss. When someone dies, the loss is irrevocable, but when someone loses a negotiation, the loss is interminable. A death is final, while a bad negotiation is nagging. It never ends. There is always the feeling that one more proposal or one more counter-demand will rectify the so far unacceptable bargain. No matter how bad the negotiation, it seems amenable to correction. This makes it difficult to accept losing as definitive. Instead of the disadvantaged party letting go, the loss remains incomplete; and because it persists, it festers.

Bad role negotiations make for losses that linger because the losing party cannot let go of what went wrong or move on to new and more appropriate roles. He is in thrall to script elements that make it difficult to adopt alternate scripts. The cognitions, emotions, volitions, and social relationships that were constituted during his original role negotiations remain in place, despite the fact that they ignore his needs. In particular, the ways in which he has come to perceive himself, the fears generated within him, the plans of action he has decided to implement, and the role partners with whom he has been programmed to interact all conspire to keep him bound to role behaviors he hates. When the elements of a role script point in the wrong direction, or are too intense, change is impeded. A person then has difficulty breaking loose from his past.

A person can also be trapped by his own lack of skill as a role negotiator. If he is inclined to bargaining strategies that make unsatisfying consequences the norm, he is likely to perpetuate bad bargains every time he tries to alter them. Much to his chagrin, he will extricate himself from one bad situation only to replicate it somewhere else. Such a person will usually be said to have a personality disorder. His unproductive bargaining strategies will be assumed to reveal a character flaw, and his problems will be blamed on him.

All in all, dysfunctional roles come into existence when role negotiations fail. Their etiology is a social one. Excessive conflict results in bad roles which are then hard to change. The pain of role dysfunction derives from roles that do not meet needs, from fighting to prevent their emergence, and from attempts to change them. Bad roles thus constitute a loss, and fighting to preserve them is itself a losing endeavor.

The symptoms of role problems emerge from these factors. To put the matter more explicitly, the discomfort that impels people to seek professional help is a product of: (1) a felt lack of needs satisfaction; (2) uncomfortable script elements that are hard to alter; or (3) counterproductive negotiating styles. None of these is indicative of a fatal flaw

in the individual, and actually bespeak a lost social battle and its se-
quelae. They result from coercive role negotiations and the normal, if
unsuccessful, reactions to such coercion. Thus it is not the person who
needs to be "fixed," but coercion and its consequences that must be
reversed.

Moreover, bad role negotiations are not an aberration that occurs
only because of unfortunate happenstance. Coercion and its equivalents are themselves a result of normal social structures. Conflict is an
essential part of role construction. That some of this conflict is excessive or misguided is a predictable consequence of the nature of conflict.
Because society of necessity includes a shortage of resources and is
unavoidably hierarchical, some coercion is predestined. And because
social stability requires role conservation, changing social roles, even
bad ones, is an inevitably painful affair.

Coercion and Its Equivalents. Coercion is the application of an excessive
force to get a person to do what she might not otherwise do. When a
person is coerced, she is put in a no-win situation. Whatever she does,
it will not be enough to counter the pressures exerted upon her. The
other party simply has more power, and insists on using it. Coercion,
therefore, implies loss. When it, or its equivalents, are present, their
target is defeated.

Coercion can take many forms. It includes tangible abuse, emotional
manipulation, or just plain neglect (Egeland and Stroufe 1981). These
can encompass: (1) physical coercion; (2) emotional coercion; (3) cognitive or volitional coercion; and (4) emotional or physical abandonment. In each of these instances, the victim sustains an injury that is
difficult to resist unless she has protection. A source of power that can
contest the coercive act will be required. At the very least, she will
benefit from the sanctuary that a safe situation or environment can
provide. Safety and protection are at the heart of any resocialization
endeavor (Weis 1982). Without them, the effects of coercion cannot be
reversed.

1. Physical coercion. Physical coercion includes the literal manipulation of another person's body and/or the imposition of physical pain.
The child who resists a parent's wishes may find himself caught by the
scruff of the neck and physically placed where the parent wants him
to be. Or he may be stretched over his parent's knee and spanked into
submission. In this latter case, the assumption will be that if the pain
is severe enough, he will become compliant. When physical manipulation or punishment are sufficiently egregious they may be deemed
abusive (Garbarino et al. 1986). Ordinarily, physical coercion is reserved for childhood. When it continues into adolescence or beyond, it
is especially likely to be excessive. Normally, the imposition of physical
manipulation is replaced by the use of verbal threats. An adult, or older

child, is told what will be done to him if he fails to comply, and it is hoped that an internal representation of this will produce the desired result. Usually, it is enough to wave a gun in a person's face; it is rarely necessary to fire it. The efficacy of verbal threats is substantially dependent upon the pre-existence of physical manipulation and punishment during childhood. The fact that threats have been associated with actual physical coercion is what makes them effective motivators. It is also why when people talk of physical coercion, they are usually thinking of threats grounded in physical coercion.

2. *Emotional coercion.* It is not only physical harm and/or manipulation that can induce a person to do what he does not desire. Intense emotions can have the same effect. Fear, in particular, can force him to abstain from what he would like to do, or to perform what he abhors. It acts as an internal prison that decisively constrains actions. Indeed, it is fear which mediates the efficacy of physical coercion. The verbal threats that derive from physical coercion work by frightening a person into doing what is demanded. He is made to fear the imposition of physical pain or injury, and then his fear induces him to act as the other desires.

Since fear is such an effective coercive agent, if it can be stimulated by mechanisms other than physical pain, they too become coercive. Thus, intense anger is especially productive of fear. The violent bluster of an unfair role partner can so frighten a person that he does not dare transgress the other's directives. It is as if he had been threatened with a weapon. Anger can also be used to arouse fear indirectly. It can, for instance, induce self-anger (guilt) which bludgeons a person into submission. Indeed, morality may be considered an institutionalized form of anger. More than one person has been made to feel so guilty that he never attempts what is vehemently denounced. The intense self-anger generated makes it impossible for him to win, and is every bit as coercive as a paddle applied to his derriere.

Even ostensibly benign emotions such as shame and love can be used to enforce coercion. Shame works very much in the manner of guilt. When it is induced by ridicule, a person can be embarrassed into immobility. Intense shame is so painful that most of us will do anything to avoid it. The mere threat of it is enough to convince us to do what is demanded. We would rather engage in role behavior we detest than risk being made fun of in public

Perhaps surprisingly, love too can be coercive. It is an emotion that makes us want to do another's bidding almost despite ourselves. When we are in love, we aim to please the object of our affection. It is this very strong desire that imbues love with its potential for abuse. If a loved person threatens to withdraw his love or demands an exorbitant price for his favors, a person in love can be tricked by his own commitments into doing things that are against his interests. To gain love, he may be enticed into accepting very painful role assignments.

Finally, emotions can be indirectly coercive. Even when they are not intended to force someone in a particular direction, they can have this effect. Since emotions can be contagious, one person may inadvertently arouse a coercive emotion in another. Intense anxiety and sadness especially have this result. If one person is anxious, his fear can arouse fear in another. The second person may then be too afraid to do what he might otherwise have desired. This is what happens when an anxious mother dissuades her child from tree climbing by covertly communicating her distress. Because the child "catches" her anxiety, what had previously been attractive becomes terrifying, and this terror forces him to desist from his play. Sadness can have a similar outcome by transmitting the immobility that accompanies depression. Thus a depressed parent can produce a depressed child who, for reasons not originating in himself, may be disinclined to do what will meet his needs. It is not stretching language too far to say that this child is forced by his role partner to renounce vital interests.

3. *Cognitive and volitional coercion.* What a person thinks and what he decides also exercise constraint upon his actions. If, therefore, a role partner forces a person to think or decide in a particular way, he can be quite as coercive as if he had physically manipulated his body. Just as in the case of the emotions, where it is possible to manipulate the cognitive and volitional aspects of a person's internal scripts, it is possible to control him.

There are many ways in which someone's cognitions and volitions can be coercively influenced. If his beliefs are distorted or confused, then his understanding of the world and his options within it can be directed by others. Distorted ideas and plans can be generated by such simple exigencies as secrecy and deception. If the truth is withheld from a person or if he is subjected to outright lies, he will not have the information needed to make an enlightened choice. In short, he will be fooled into deciding against his own interests.

An even more insidious functional equivalent of coercion is cognitive and volitional confusion. Bateson's famous "double bind" (Berger 1978) is a wonderfully effective means of accomplishing this. By issuing inconsistent directives or making contradictory judgments, a person can be thoroughly disoriented by her role partners. If someone is told she is both smart and dumb, or simultaneously to come close and go far away, she will not know what to think. The younger and more uncertain she is, the more vulnerable she will be to such a maneuver. The other's confused communications can make it difficult for her to know whether she is male or female, strong or weak, a winner or a loser. In the end, she is forced into immobility. The effect of a double bind can also be accomplished by multiple role partners who impose incompatible demands and judgments. Once again a person is placed in a no-win situation. She will not know what is wanted or what is true. Whatever she does or whatever she believes, someone will consider wrong, and therefore she will lose.

4. *Abandonment and neglect.* Neglect and abandonment can also be coercive. They too force a person to lose what he desperately wants. When one person seriously neglects or abandons another, he is being insensitive to the other's wishes. His implacable avoidance of his partner's demands makes him an utterly unresponsive role partner. He in effect becomes an immovable force that prevents his partner from realizing his goals. Ego loses because he isn't allowed to win. Passive avoidance forces him to remain unsatisfied.

Insensitivity to another's needs can take many guises. Sometimes it can even masquerade as extreme concern. Overprotectiveness and permissiveness may seem to be opposites, but they accomplish the same end. Protection that does not take into account the desires of its object is oppressive. It does not protect; rather, it exposes its beneficiary to new dangers by forcing him to resist unnecessary demands. Similarly, permissiveness promises freedom, but delivers isolation. It allows its object to face a complex and dangerous world alone and unaided. Instead of providing the right to choose, it really permits the freedom to be frightened. At bottom, neglect and abandonment deny love. Whether or not they are inflicted in the name of protection, they leave their victim alone and unloved. Since love is one of the most important of human needs, its denial is an act of violence. The person without love loses, and he loses big. Life without love is an earthly reflection of hell. Its absence is so painful that the mere threat of its withdrawal becomes coercive.

The Response to Coercion

Coercion leaves its victims with no choice. The person who has been the object of excessive force does not get what he wants. Whether he has been physically manipulated, had his emotions used against him, or been kept in a state of ignorance, he is denied an opportunity to determine his own fate. His voice is silenced and another's will foisted upon him. Not surprisingly, coercion is rarely welcome. Since an individual is usually best situated to appreciate his own needs, decisions imposed from the outside frequently do not meet them. The consequence is unhappiness, resistance, and rejection.

Unfortunately, coercion is a common fact of life. Dysfunctional roles are a routine outgrowth of early socialization, and early mistakes are often perpetuated by the barbarities of adulthood. Parents usually feel it is their responsibility to mold their children's behavior. But when their offspring disagree with them, it may be viewed as an act of impertinence and treated accordingly. Demands, threats, and punishments are then justified as a necessary attempt to prevent "spoiling." Too often, attempts at providing guidance escalate into physical or emotional brutality. In the name of doing what is best for the child, terrible injustices are perpetrated.

In adulthood, the victim of early coercion usually finds himself victimized by unfair role partners once again. His dysfunctional roles incline him to seek out partners who are unfair in the same ways as previous ones. What is more, the vulnerabilities instilled by childhood coercion make it difficult to resist the new. Despite his abhorrence of the life he is living, he is ill-equipped to fight for what he really wants. Hence coercion tends to perpetuate itself.

Resistance. The predictable reaction to coercion is resistance. People do not like being pushed around. Whether or not effective resistance can be organized, human beings instinctively rebel against force. The reflexive reaction to a shove is to shove back. When someone is asked to do something, he may consider the request and then provide a positive or negative response. A choice is possible, since there is no imposed decision that must be resisted. When, however, he is told that he must do something, the initial reaction will almost always be *No!* Even children dislike being restrained. An infant who is force-fed will vigorously work to expel the nipple from his mouth. In fact, one of the major milestones in achieving a separate personhood is learning to say "No." During the "terrible twos," this word becomes the emblem of successful individuation. Initially, rejecting another's demands is a way of establishing the latitude for a choice. Without being able to deny another's overtures, there can be no viable sense of self.

Acceptance. When a very forcible demand is made of a person, he has several possibilities. One of these is to try to withdraw from the situation so that he can ponder his options. It is virtually unthinkable to accede to a forcible demand the moment it is promulgated, but the passage of time makes this possible. If, upon reflection, a person can decide a demand is in fact in his interest, he may decide to accept it. This will make it his own, and henceforth he will act as if the original impetus came from himself. When a potentially coercive demand is accepted, it ceases to be coercive. Rather, it becomes part of the person's own equipment.

Time is a great healer. Despite a person's instinctive resistance to external demands, given time, compliance may emerge. He will have an opportunity to cool off and reverse his initial reaction. Thinking things through can make his own advantage visible. Even if it doesn't, even if complying with the other's demand remains against his interests, a decision to comply may still occur. It may be judged wiser to allow the other to win rather than to continue a bruising battle. Thus, given time and a modicum of utility, even moderately coercive demands can be accepted.

Rejection. When a role partner allows neither time nor utility to do his work, acceptance becomes virtually impossible. Coercive demands that must be endorsed at once offer little inducement for acceptance. They do not permit an opportunity to reverse resistance; neither do they bestow a benefit for doing so. In consequence, they virtually dictate adamant rejection. They convert tentative resistance into ironclad refusal.

If the victim of coercion is a child, he may be put in a bind. His rejection of a parental demand can call forth additional coercion. Most parents do not like to lose to their own children and so when confronted with rejection, redouble their efforts; they use more physical force, more emotional violence, and more cognitive distortion. It is as if they are determined to break their child's spirit. But the young person on the receiving end of such exertions will want to continue resisting. The more he is coerced, the more he will want to make his refusal stick.

Nevertheless, he will understand that coercion can escalate to the point of serious injury. Intuitively he will realize that further overt resistance can be dangerous. No matter how distasteful he may find it, he will have to reconsider his strategy and demonstrate some form of compliance. If the child has the option, he may elect to pursue covert resistance. His goal will be to sustain his rejection, but on the surface he will seem to comply. Ostensibly he will say "yes," but on the inside will continue to fight back. When his parent is around, he will pretend to conform, while surreptitiously seek ways of eluding sanctions or surveillance. As much as possible he will try to have things his way. When he must accede, when there is truly no choice, he will do so without enthusiasm or genuine commitment.

Self-Subjugation. If the child is lucky, pretense will be sufficient. If not, if his parents demand absolute submission, he may have to take additional steps. The parent who requires compliance in heart and mind, as well as behavior, presents a dilemma. His demands make covert resistance as much of an offense as overt resistance. A child of such a parent knows that he must control his feelings and thoughts as well as his actions; he knows that a rebellious interior will invite as much punishment as a recalcitrant exterior.

The child whose internal role scripts are subject to close parental surveillance has to exercise a form of self-subjugation. He will have to internalize parental coercion and begin coercing himself. Indeed, the more impulse to resist he feels, the more he will have to suppress it.

The major mechanism of internal suppression is guilt. It essentially re-peats an external demand internally. Thus, if an angry demand which first comes from a parent cannot be successfully resisted, a child may angrily begin to demand the same thing of himself. Though he hates what is being demanded, he does so anyway. He becomes his own enforcer. Rather than risk the dangers of parental coercion, he tries to force himself into compliance.

Since a child will be immediately aware of his impulse to resist, he may become a more dreadful oppressor than his parent ever was. He will be embroiled in a never-ending battle for self-control. His guilt turns into an incessant self-prosecutor; anger, punishment, and self-reproach become the theme of his internal life. Because he rightly fears that a tendency to resist remains within him, he is terrified that some day it may break its bonds. He will fear that if it does, he will be de-stroyed. In consequence, he multiplies his efforts at self-control and self-subjection becomes habitual.

Defense. A child (or adult) who finds herself bathed in a coercive environment needs protection. Whether excessive force comes from without or within, it represents a real danger. Both physical and emo-tional pressures hurt. They can even precipitate death. The victim of such threats will therefore seek to avoid injury. Though she has be-come the author of some of her own pain, she still tries to defend herself.

There are many devices a person can use for self-defense. Essen-tially, she can try to find ways to convince others not to attack, or she can exclude the pain and its causes from her awareness. Self-suppres-sion is a vital part of the former strategy. The idea is to give the at-tacker no cause for aggression. A similar effect can be achieved by appearing weak and helpless. Displays of submissiveness are a well-established technique for deflecting the wrath of a stronger foe. One tries to avoid more losses by openly demonstrating one's vulnerability. Like the weaker timber wolf who protects himself by exposing his ab-domen to the alpha animal, a human child or adult can make a display of her helplessness to divert an aggressor. The above technique ac-tually does reduce the chance of being injured and so it is a good defense, although of course it is a defense predicated upon losing. It doesn't bring victory; it only cuts losses. But that is enough for many people.

Cognitive and emotional defenses have even less of a chance of bringing victory. They are based not upon ending a threat, but on not perceiving it. Among these defenses are such time-honored strategies as denial, repression, and diversion.

When executing denial, a person refuses to see what is in plain sight. Although injury seems imminent, he simply does not acknowledge it.

Denial works by interrupting cognitive or emotional channels (Dorpat 1985). The brain simply does not interpret the stimuli ordinarily signifying danger as dangerous. Hitler is not seen as a threat, a parent's suicide is not acknowledged as a suicide, or a painful loss of love is not experienced as pain, but as numbness.

Repression is a little different from denial in that what is not acknowledged was once correctly apprehended. If a person's father committed suicide, it may have been understood as such when it occurred, but in time all thought of it can be expunged from consciousness. Repression handles coercive demands by eventually pretending they never existed. Thus the coerced child who grows to adulthood may one day believe that his parents were the kindest people in the world. Instead of trying to suppress his resistance to their demands, he convinces himself that they never issued oppressive mandates and hence he never needed to resist. Repression can also be used to control hazardous impulses. Thus a desire to resist may be excluded from consciousness. A person may come to feel that he has no impulse to rebel. It is not that he now accepts parental demands, but that his desire to resist is not ordinarily experienced.

Another way of excluding what is dangerous from consciousness is to fill the mind with something else. A person can think, feel, or do something different from, and preferably incompatible with, that which is intolerable. Defense mechanisms such as "rationalization" (A. Freud 1966) can be used to divert attention. Rationalization substitutes a spurious understanding of a person's situation for the real thing. Instead of looking at what he is doing, he accepts a non-threatening interpretation of it. Emotions too can be used as a diversion. Perhaps a child finds his anger at his parents very dangerous. Instead of feeling angry, he can feel something else: maybe frightened, disgusted, or sad. All of these potential substitutes will be uncomfortable, but not as objectionable as the excluded emotion. Finally, diversion, and hence defense, can be accomplished by acting in ways that are different from what a person really wants. Rather than punch his boss in the mouth, he can decide to go jogging. Running will rechannel his energies and make it less likely that he will do something untoward. By diverting his actions, he protects himself and others from potentially nasty consequences.

The Repetition Compulsion. No matter how much self-subjugation or defense a person employs, rejected demands remain rejected. Acceptance does not result from failing to display resistance. Guilt, denial, or diversion are necessary precisely because the impulse to resist continues to exist. Coercive demands that are not genuinely accepted endure as a constant irritant. They are a perpetual reminder that one is not getting what one wants. Role negotiations that include these unresolved coercive demands lead to aborted roles. A disguised conflict between the role partners persists. The demands and the resistance to them may no longer take place in public, but continue to be played out within the victim. The contest between him and his erstwhile role partners will be a kind of incomplete losing. The battle may be going against the person, but he will not yet have given up.

Aborted roles represent unfinished business. A person trapped in them is living out a behavior pattern to which he is not reconciled. Like Angela, he may have been forced into a role such as that of rejected child, and like her, desperately want things to be different. His impulse to fight for something better endures, and he will constantly find himself in relationships involving rejection in which he is trying to change the rejection into acceptance.

Freud called this tendency to refight past battles the "repetition compulsion." He noted that his patients often entertained an apparently irrational desire to recapitulate past relationships. They seemed compelled to relive the segments of their lives that caused them distress. This was not, however, because they enjoyed the pain or liked living in the past. Rather, it was because they wanted to win. During the unequal contests of their childhood, the odds were against them. Their parents (or other role partners) had the power to enforce unequal bargains. Now as adults, an impulse to resist remained, but the tools to oppose these demands were much stronger. Thus it was in the hope of renegotiating their losses that they reactivated aborted roles.

Society and Coercion

Coercive role negotiations and their deleterious consequences are not an aberration; they are not an accident of particular relationships. Coercion is an inevitable consequence of human society. Conflict is one of the mechanisms through which social structures are created and maintained. Society is built upon force and counter-force. As a practical matter this means that some excessive force is unavoidable. It also means some people are bound to be hurt.

Freud, in *Civilization and Its Discontents* (1961), speculated that it is the conflict between people's instincts and the demands of civilization that causes neurosis. In fact, it is not civilization, but the nature of social organization that is the culprit. The very means necessary to organize society also puts pressure on individuals. These pressures, in the form of coercion, disrupt role formation and lead to failed and aborted roles. Loss and pain may not themselves be useful to society or individuals, but they are an unavoidable byproduct of the construction of society.

Social Creatures. We human beings are social creatures. Philosophers may speculate about a "state of nature" in which each man wars against all others (Hobbes 1956), but in actuality people have always belonged to societies. Human beings are simply not like unconnected atoms capable of existing in splendid isolation. Even hermits are the product of social affiliation. They too begin as babies who are nurtured and molded in human interaction. Without relationships, they could not survive; neither would they have anything to react against. Yet despite the inevitability of social connections, people are remarkably ambivalent about society. Myths about feral children speak of the profound human need for individual freedom. People know that while social relations afford protection, they also induce pain. The dream of being an isolated individual is a reaction to this social injury. It offers solace, if only in fantasy. Still, the reality is that people and societies inevitably go together. Indeed, *who* an individual is, is a consequence of social interaction. Individual identity and the individual self emerge only in interaction with others.

The Side-effects of Force. Social negotiations are based upon the exercise of power. As has been emphasized, the negotiations from which roles emerge involve demands and counter-demands. These demands are not polite requests; they are attempts to impose an outcome. There is, of necessity, an energy behind them that requires response. The use of this force can have the intended, or unintended, effect of inflicting pain.

According to William Goode (1972), "Whatever else social systems are, they are also force systems. Force constitutes one of the major foundations of all social structures." He goes on to explain that the amount of injury inflicted by force is not due to its presence or absence, but to how it is organized. The difference between civilized and barbarous societies is that in civilization force is more reliably organized and hence tends to be less brutal. It is the stable existence of a constabulary with real power that makes it unnecessary to publicly draw and quarter offenders as proof of governmental power.

Force becomes coercive when it is not accepted or socially integrated. It then spills over into injury. Insecure governments and insecure parents are the ones who are motivated to be brutal. The person who is unsure of his power is the one who uses it to excess. When force is employed judiciously, injury is not necessarily a consequence. In fact, however, society always contains people who are relatively powerless and inclined toward abuse. One has only to look at the excesses of the social climber or the violence of the slum for confirmation (Rainwater 1970; Sennett and Cobb 1972).

The Division of Labor. Social structure includes both a division of labor and a social hierarchy. Force is used to decide who will do what within this organization. The nature of social jobs and who will get them is at stake, but the allocation of these positions is not automatic. It must be negotiated between people each of whom is vitally concerned about the outcome. Human social organization is not transmitted genetically (Lewontin et al. 1984). People are not like social insects, which are born with biological blueprints that tell them how to seek pollen or build a hive. On the contrary, we human beings must acquire a knowledge of who we are and how to perform our assigned tasks after we are born. More particularly, we must construct these positions and tasks among ourselves.

The division of labor in society (Durkheim 1933) enables us to integrate our activities. The roles developed with it allocate social chores and permit complementary undertakings. It is these roles that assign tasks and allow us to predict one another's behaviors. Without them, no one would know what to expect of anyone else. People would work at cross-purposes in utter chaos. But despite its necessity, a division of labor is an invitation to conflict. Any such partition is inherently inequitable because not everyone can have the roles he desires. There is room for only so many TV stars or so many senators. When roles are divided up, someone is bound to be dissatisfied. Even within families there is likely to be a dispute about who will take out the garbage or do the dishes (Nye 1976). More importantly, not everyone can be the favorite child, the family genius, or the family beauty. When there exists an apportionment that allows for only a limited number of specific positions, some losing is inevitable. So is the temptation to avoid defeat by employing duress.

Whenever there are scarce resources for which people compete, someone is likely to be overly zealous. He will resent the direction negotiations are taking, and will apply himself to reversing the decision. The more a person feels deprived, the more he is inclined to believe that the role allocation is unfair. He will feel that his needs are being thwarted and hence that he has a right to pursue his goals with extra vigor. If this vigor is transformed into coercion, then establishing a division of labor will eventuate in excessive force and its side-effects, namely failed and aborted roles.

Social Hierarchy. Another aspect of social structure, namely hierarchy, also has the effect of causing role problems. Societies are stratified (Bendix and Lipset 1966). They have ranking systems that place some people higher than others. Those with greater rank obtain more power, prestige, and economic resources than their less privileged peers. The inequality of this arrangement is redolent with the possibility of strife and injurious conflict.

Stratification is often justly despised, but it is universal. All large-scale societies have class systems and all large-scale organizations have hierarchical offices. Apparently, sizable groups of people require some form of "imperative coordination." While the function of this arrangement is not fully understood, its purpose may be to organize complex activities and/or to ration scarce resources. In any event, it is a reality, and for some, an unfair reality. People have been enslaved, wars fought, and inquisitions imposed all for the purpose of securing hierarchical advantage. The desire to be on top is apparently very strong. To achieve it, people have committed all manner of crimes, including murder.

It should be noted of course that the unfair conflicts generated by a competition for status is hardest on those with the least power. People at the bottom of the social pecking order, that is, the poor, the young, and the outcast, are on the receiving end of a disproportionate share of coercive manipulations. Since they are also the least able to protect themselves from such visitations, they suffer the most.

Role Conservation. The imposition of coercion results not only from the mechanisms used to build social structures, but from the devices that hold social roles in place. For a society to function smoothly, it must be predictable. In addition to having a role structure, that structure must be stable. Roles that change quickly are difficult to forecast, and hence there must be instruments that provide role conservation. There must be what Parsons (1951, 1970) has described as "pattern maintenance."

The mechanisms that keep social roles from changing too quickly seem to be built into our nature. They are internal to each of us and help make us social. These mechanisms are none other than our role scripts. Both internal and external scripts give role behavior a persistence and consistency that would not otherwise exist. The cognitions, emotions, and volitions of a person, and the demands of his role partners, guide his behaviors into well-worn channels. They do not permit dizzying shifts of conduct that would make him seem to be someone other than who he is.

Cognitions, emotions, volitions, and role partner demands, once set in motion by role negotiations, have a staying power of their own. After a person has settled on a cognitive interpretation of her world, developed a particular emotional reaction to it, committed herself to a specifiable coping strategy, or entered unique relationships with role partners who have unique role commitments of their own, a natural conservatism takes over. The things she believes, feels, plans, or which her role partners demand tend to remain the same unless specifically changed. Even when change is intended, altering a script element can be very difficult. Inner change feels like self-betrayal, no matter if the result is self-enhancement. It represents a loss of self and social position that feels intolerable, and is tenaciously resisted. A person's role scripts can exercise an inner tyranny worse than any dictator. Indeed, it is often the most unsatisfying role elements that are the most despotic. For instance, the existence of miserably painful fear may be the very reason a person has difficulty adopting a less frightening lifestyle.

The role conservatism that sometimes results in a person maintaining her own pain may seem perverse, but it provides an individual with benefits too. Not only does it preserve the society upon which she depends, it also protects her from the ordinary pitfalls of life. Consider how a child learns to avoid fire. If he accidentally puts his hand in a flame, he feels extreme pain. This pain then becomes part of his script. It remains as an emotional warning against putting his hand in a flame again. Because this warning is an intense emotional reaction, it provides both strong motivational power and a strong resistance to erosion. This means that a child has only to put his hand in the fire once to learn to avoid it for a lifetime. The pain and fear of the flame will literally restrain him from repeating the experiment. His script elements, namely his pain and fear, will retain their power for years. Their conservatism, that is, their tendency to guide the same sort of response time and time again, will undoubtedly save him from many nasty burns.

Without the mechanism of role conservatism, people would routinely blunder into dangerous situations. No one is capable of creating his world from scratch every time he makes a move. He must have reliable guides to action which are already in place; these are provided by his role scripts. Without their existence, he would be as vulnerable as a newborn babe. Yet role conservatism has its dark side. It can, and does, impede potentially corrective change. The lessons that are incorporated in role scripts are sometimes over-learned. Imagine someone who has learned to avoid fire by incorporating an emotional reaction to its pain. Suppose now he encounters a new form of fire which, instead of burning, heals. His emotions will certainly persuade him that this cannot be true. His eyes may say that this new flame is safe, but his fears will shout that it is not. No doubt it will take considerable effort to convince him to touch this new phenomenon.

This little scenario may sound far-fetched, but it is actually a good replica of what happens when a person's role environment changes. Consider the child who is raised in a coercive human environment. He will surely learn that human beings are dangerous. They will be his flame and he will avoid too close contact with them. Now suppose as an adult he meets a new type of person. Will he believe his senses, or will he consider them dangerous too? Almost surely it will be the latter. Our adult will find it difficult to revise his childhood judgment. His fears, which have protected him many times in the past, will not lightly be relinquished. Casually changing his mind would be both dangerous and foolish. Even though new people may have the potential to provide him with the warmth and protection he always craved, he will be understandably cautious. If he changes his role scripts, he will do so very slowly and very carefully. This means that he may well be deprived of many satisfying relationships. Like the moth who has evolved a camouflage to protect itself in a grimy city but is vulnerable to attack in the pristine countryside, the child who has grown up in a harsh environment may find his once vital defenses have become a burden that prevents happiness in more benign settings.

The fears that prevent a child from changing are part of his internal role scripts, but it must be remembered that external scripts can also impede change. The demands of role partners past and present have a conservatism too. First, role partners themselves have conservative scripts. They too are people with cognitions, emotions, volitions, and demanding role partners that stabilize their behavior patterns. This means that their demands are likely to be constant. Second, people usually choose role partners of the sort to which they are accustomed. A person's own role scripts will attract him to relationships with people inclined to make demands similar to those of earlier role partners. The person will therefore find himself in a social environment that demands that he remain constant.

The conservative bent of role partner demands is dramatically evident in psychotherapy. A person trying to change often discovers, much to his chagrin, that the very friends and relatives who encouraged him to seek help are now upset. Where once they demanded change, now they resist every alteration he makes. Their motto seems to be: "Change now! As long as you remain the same." Like the spouse of an alcoholic who first demands sobriety, then places a bottle into his hands, they go back on their word. Role partners, whatever their spoken message, usually value stability. The other's change may mean that they too will have to change, and this is unwelcome news. In consequence, role partners often demand that a person remain the same, even at the expense of his well-being.

Normal Problems. Role problems are normal. They are not a sign of illness, perversion, immorality, or congenital weakness. People have them because they are social creatures. Such predicaments are an expectable side-effect of the way in which roles are created and maintained. This may not mesh with social ideals, but it is reality. Role dilemmas may not be supposed to happen, but they do with regularity. To be sure, these problems are not uniformly distributed. Some people have more difficulties, and some have more serious ones. Partly this happens because we are not all the same, and partly because social structures are not uniform. Coercion itself is not evenly dispersed. Some have more of a burden than others, and some handle it more adeptly. But this uneven distribution is no reason for labeling those with greater hardships abnormal.

3

The Role Change Process

LOSS AND LOSING

Role change is inherently difficult. Roles do not change easily, especially bad ones. A person cannot pull them on or off like an old shirt. If a bad role is also a basic one, change can involve radical reconstruction. At the very least, the replacement of a dysfunctional role requires that it be partially relinquished. As long as it remains an active part of someone's repertoire, it has the potential to disrupt any new roles which are incompatible with it. It can then emerge at the most inopportune moments to wreak havoc upon his life.

Relinquishing basic social roles is very painful and time-consuming. Since letting go of even a bad role represents a serious loss, its termination feels very like death and is never accepted lightly. Roles are a mechanism through which people relate with one another, and when they are surrendered, so are relationships. The loss of such valued partnerships is not easy. Ordinarily when someone dies, or divorces, the loss is fiercely resisted and inaugurates a mourning process. People grieve the deceased, and they do the same when an important social role misfires.

Failed or aborted roles automatically entail loss. Indeed, loss and losing are equivalent phenomena (Szasz 1961). A role negotiation that is aborted or eventuates in a bad role is a miscarried negotiation. It is one that results in a lost role, that is, in a loss. The role, which one hoped would meet one's needs, does not. An attachment that was forming is wrenched asunder and a prospective role relationship dies aborning. Instead of the satisfying partnership one hoped for, only ashes and misery survive. It truly is as if someone had died.

The Grieving Process

Because failed and aborted roles are truly lost, the role-change process can be directly compared with mourning. In both cases there is a relationship which dies and must be relinquished before new and more vital relationships can emerge. Elizabeth Kubler-Ross (1969) has provided a model of how this grief operates. Her paradigm is derived from her work with the dying, but is applicable to expired roles too. Kubler-Ross posits a grieving process that occurs in predictable stages whether one is contemplating one's own death or coping with the death of a loved one. In her model, loss triggers (1) denial, then (2) anger, (3) bargaining, (4) depression, and finally (5) acceptance. This order is described as stable, but not invariable.

Denial. When a person is first confronted with a loss, there is usually shock. His initial tendency is to disbelieve what has happened or is about to happen. It is as if ignoring the fact can stop it from materializing. His reaction may be: "No, John has not died. He will be coming back shortly," or "This divorce isn't happening. Mary will change her mind." In the case of role loss, a person may persuade himself that his relationship remains intact. Despite being in an unhappy marriage, he may deny that he has any marital problems. He may tell himself, and everyone else, that his is a wonderful union. If trapped in a role as bad as Angela's, he may not be able to deny the pain of his situation, but will fool himself about its source. Instead of recognizing that he is in a failed relationship, he will conclude that he has had bad luck or perhaps is being punished for his misdeeds.

Anger. If the reality of a loss cannot be excluded by denial, anger is likely to follow. A person experiencing ruin protests against what has happened. He unconsciously hopes that his anger will induce fate to rescind its decision. Perhaps he will direct this anger at himself, the lost person, or fate in general. Thus, if his father has died, he may conclude that this was dad's own fault, and that if he had only decided to live, things would be very different. This internal presumption may convince him that if he becomes sufficiently angry, the deceased will be persuaded to return. Losses are frustrating. They are not what a person wants. And anger, of course, is a normal reaction to frustration. It is a mechanism that is used to motivate others to change their minds. During role loss, anger is a natural part of interpersonal negotiations. It is used to forestall frustration by pressuring role partners into making better deals. This was why Angela was angry with her mother. Not only did she want money to meet her present needs, but she hoped her mother would compensate her for past rejections. Her anger was designed to force her mother into meeting her demands, and hence reversing her loss.

Bargaining. While anger can sometimes rescind a bad deal, other forms of bargaining can accomplish the same result. Rather than forcing a turnabout, rewards can be used to cajole a partner into cooperating. If uncle Harry won't come back when we get angry at him, perhaps if we promise to be good, he will change his mind. Of course, in the face of death, this bargaining is futile, but it may make better sense when role loss is involved. For instance, a wife who threatens divorce may indeed be persuaded to return by promises of reform. Nevertheless, serious role failure usually resists bargaining. Angela often promised to do what her mother wished, yet her hope of gaining love was constantly thwarted. Mother had reasons of her own to pursue a different course despite any blandishments Angela might offer. Moreover, whatever acceptance she delivered in the present would not compensate for love that was withheld in the past.

Depression. When deal-making fails, depression sets in. The time comes when a person recognizes that fighting back has not worked, and that loss is inevitable. He must finally accept that what is gone will not return. Uncle Harry is indeed dead. This recognition brings sadness, often profound sadness. The more important a person's loss, the deeper will be his agony. Yet contained within the pain of sorrow are the seeds of renewal. Sadness allows a person to let go of what has been lost. During depression, he can withdraw into a quiet inner self and gradually start breaking the bonds that attached him to the lost person or relationship. The more important these have been, the more points of attachment will need to be severed. All of them will have to be thought through and disconnected in turn. And the more that must be relinquished, the longer and more painful will be the effort.

During the stage of depression, the process of letting go will be the same whether a person or a role has been lost. The primary difference is that the occasion for sorrow is less visible in role loss. If it is uncle Harry who has died, people will know what the tears are for. But if in the middle of her day Angela starts crying, most people will be bewildered. They will see the tears but not what provoked them. The sadness produced by role loss may also be more intractable than that caused by death. The latter is more definitive. When it occurs, all is over and done with; there is no going back. Role loss, on the other hand, lingers. It is similar to a divorce that takes a long time to be decided upon, and which always seems capable of being undone. Thus Angela's "rejected daughter" role regularly offered the hope of reversal; she could always imagine that one day her mother would start loving her. This made it more difficult for her to let go, and so her sadness persisted. It would take her years before she was capable of breaking all ties with her mother.

Acceptance. Eventually, depression does its job. As connections with

Figure 3.1
The Loss Curve

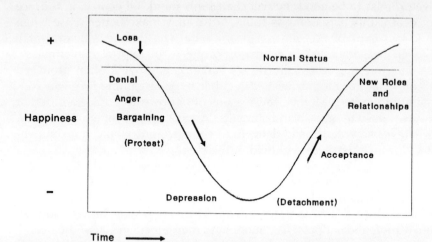

the past are loosened, a person in mourning begins to prepare for his future. He enters the stage of acceptance and becomes reconciled with his fate. He may even start forming new relationships. Still, there will probably be a period during which the baton is being handed from the old to the new. During this phase he will feel at loose ends, but before long he will emerge to take a more active part in the world. If Angela learns that her mother is incapable of love, perhaps she too will start looking for affection in more promising places. True, she will always miss her mother's love, but maybe a more satisfying alternative can be found.

The Loss Curve

The mourning process begins with a loss, proceeds to the resistance phase, moves on to acceptance of the loss, and eventuates in adopting new roles. The whole sequence can be viewed as an inverted normal curve (see Figure 3.1). It begins with ordinary living, then descends into deep sadness, at which point it reverses itself and returns to the original baseline.

On the descending slope of the curve one finds denial, anger, and bargaining. All of these are designed to prevent a slide into misery. At the bottom are located the agonies of depression. And just when all seems lost, a person starts climbing out of his unhappiness and into new life circumstances. It is on the upward slope of the curve that he enters into new relationships and negotiates new roles.

Attachment

John Bowlby (1969, 1973, 1980) has placed the mourning process in the context of attachment behavior. He has shown that loss is a corollary of attachment. Without the pre-existence of attachments, there would be no bonds that needed to be broken. Building upon the foundation established by Freud in "Mourning and Melancholia" (1959), he examined the ethological roots of attachment and argued that forming a bond with parental figures provides survival advantages. An infant who can forge firm links with significant others thereby gains refuge in a potentially hostile world.

When children are between seven months and three years of age, their need to establish solid attachments with reliable defenders is at its height. Usually this is with the child's mother, and when he is fearful, he will seek her out as a source of security. She will be used as a home base to which he can retreat in times of danger (e.g., the appearance of a stranger). From this safe place, he will also be able to emerge when he wants to explore the larger world. Without a secure attachment he would not have the confidence to master the outer world, and this lack of security would follow him into later life, where it would interfere with his ability to form solid relationships. A child who is lucky and does form good attachments is able to internalize his protective role partners, and carries comforting icons of them even in times of stress. His secure attachments form the bedrock of future satisfying relationships. They permit fair negotiations with subsequent role partners, and give him the confidence to fight for fair deals. The insecurely attached person, in contrast, begins life with a loss and faces a downhill slide the rest of the way. Unless he can establish a secure base somewhere, his lack of confidence will doom him to a lifetime of losing.

Good Attachments. Solid attachments are created within solid relationships. Ainsworth (1967) has demonstrated that secure attachments are facilitated by mutually responsive interactions. When a mother and child react to one another in a sensitive and caring manner, the bond between them is strengthened. They thereby engage in fair negotiations that give the needs of both a chance of being met. If, however, a mother exhibits blindness to her child's requirements or fails to react responsively toward him, he will become upset and will protest. If her quasi-coercive behavior continues, her baby will eventually withdraw from the interaction. Good attachments are non-coercive and safe; poor ones are insecure and injurious.

Role negotiations begin the moment a mother picks up her neonate. The gurgling and cooing between them, the faces they make, the language games they play, and their feeding behavior all form a dialogue used to construct their respective roles as mother and baby. How they interact in these situations then establishes a template for the child's future relationships.

Broken Attachments. When the initial role negotiations of babyhood are disrupted, a vital bond is broken. Necessary attachments are interrupted and the child is injured. Even when this disruption is unintentional, as when a mother is hospitalized for a long period, the child suffers from the separation. In his review of the literature on childhood separation, Bowlby has shown there is strong evidence that children who experience loss react by grieving. A child whose mother leaves him will first search for her, then failing to find her, will protest loudly. He may scream, wail, or thrash about. Some children visibly sulk in an effort to make their displeasure known. Older children may even engage in bargaining. They may promise to be good if only mother will return. Ultimately, all become sad and withdrawn if mother does not reappear. Should she be gone long enough, they will turn to other people as a source of protection and begin forming attachments with them. When mother then returns, she will be studiously ignored because her child will have started establishing loyalties in other directions.

Bowlby has summarized this data by suggesting that children go through a three-stage sequence when confronted with separation. First they protest, then they grow depressed, and finally they become detached. This, it should be noted, is very much the same sequence as observed by Kubler-Ross, though with a very different population. The mourning process seems to be a universal response to loss, one that may be expected to occur as much for adult role loss as in childhood separations.

Adult Role Loss

Good attachments depend upon good role negotiations, and hence good adult roles depend upon good childhood ones. If early role negotiations are disrupted (e.g., by separation or coercion), they set a negative pattern for subsequent negotiations. Their dire precedent sets in motion a mourning process which, unless it is successfully resolved, initiates a legacy of sadness that endures into adulthood. This grim scenario has been confirmed by Brown and Harris (1978) in their studies of depression. They have discovered that while adult depression can be precipitated by losses occurring in adulthood, the most serious distress occurs to those who have sustained a severe loss early in life.

Apparently, childhood depression can set the stage for adult sadness. Remnants of incomplete mourning remain in place to sensitize people to later trauma.

Relationship Losses. One of the most clearly recognizable of adult role losses is divorce. In it, a major relationship is obviously torn asunder. If adult role losses have the same outcome as childhood separations, this sequence should therefore be visible in divorce, as indeed it is. Weiss (1975) in his investigations of marital separation has demonstrated that marital partners go through the same pattern of mourning recognized by Bowlby in childhood separations and by Kubler-Ross in death. When the dissolution of a marriage is pending, couples often deny they are in trouble. When this maneuver no longer works, they commence fighting about who is at fault. Venomous recriminations may give expression to the anger they feel at their impending loss. At the same time, they may engage in a bargaining process—"If you do this, I'll do that"—in the hope that a reconciliation is possible. In short, a couple's first recourse is to protest. Their goal is to prevent the loss from occurring.

Should a reconciliation prove impossible, spouses in the midst of divorce usually become very unhappy, that is, they become depressed. Contrary to popular myth, divorce rarely occasions a celebration. Divorce is a failure; it is a loss people do not plan or want. Thus when they recognize it as unavoidable, they become sad.

Another myth about divorce is that people can jump successfully from one marriage into another without taking time to catch their breath. In fact, detachment does not come easily. Often years must pass before someone is ready for a new relationship. In the meantime, the connections with his former partner must be broken. Since this person is still alive, it may be psychologically painful to make a final break. The hope that past mistakes can be corrected makes it more difficult to give up the ghost. Maggie Scarf (1980) has very effectively illustrated just how devastating a relationship loss can be. In her book on women and depression *(Unfinished Business)*, she relates how unsuccessful romances can shatter a woman's existence. A need for love can be so strong that when a lover is abusive or disloyal, the depression it inaugurates is profound and protracted.

Status Changes. Adult role loss occurs in many ways besides the breakup of a love relationship. Indeed, many losses are a natural part of growing up (Viorst 1986). Leave-takings are a normal part of the transition from adolescence into adulthood, and thence into marriage and parenting. People must abandon the protection of their original home to establish residences of their own. They must also enter the job market, and perhaps move from job to job, and friend to friend. Starting as a child with few responsibilities, they progress to roles with greater and greater responsibility. If these natural moves are traumatic, they can engender significant and painful loss. A mourning process may be necessary to navigate such crucial life transitions as leaving home, work-related separations, and moving into a new cultural environment (Bloom-Feshbach and Bloom-Feshbach 1987). These changes can be more or less profound and will differ in their impact depending upon a person's vulnerability.

Clinical Loss. Adult losses can be so serious that they demand clinical intervention. When the pain of a mourning process is too severe, a person may have difficulty surviving it without help. Indeed, many clinicians believe that the focus of their work is in repairing disrupted relationships. H. S. Sullivan (1953) was explicit in arguing that relationship problems are the cause of many so-called mental illnesses. In a similar vein, Roy Grinker (1961) has written that neuroses can be attributed to "disruptions in interpersonal relations." More particularly, he has assigned an etiological role to a lack of "role complementarity." Jerome Frank (1973) similarly talks about the "maladaptive responses" people make. He explains that these have their origin in the inter- and intra-personal conflicts of childhood, and that when they erupt in adult life, can interfere with a person's ability to meet his needs. These maladaptive responses seem to be none other than dysfunctional role behaviors.

Recently, Gerald Klerman (Klerman et al. 1984) has been less ambiguous in connecting the pain of role loss with the necessity of facilitating a mourning process. His "interpersonal psychotherapy" for depression has focused attention upon role disputes and role-transition difficulties. Klerman, who extrapolates directly from Bowlby, uses techniques such as "non-judgmental exploration," the "elicitation of feelings," "reassurance," and the "reconstruction of past relationships" to speed the grieving process. His stated goal is to help clients move out of a debilitating depression into more satisfying social relationships.

ROLE CHANGE

The notion that when someone has a personal problem, something must be released before relief can be achieved, is an old one. Many in the Freudian tradition (Fenichel 1941) would endorse such an idea. Here it is suggested that what must be relinquished is social roles. Before positive change can take place, dysfunctional behavior patterns must be surrendered and new ones constructed. Our thesis is thus that failed and aborted roles must be mourned before they can be replaced with more functional relationships.

Since the process by which roles are changed is very much like the normal loss process, just as when a person dies, there are bonds that must be broken before life can proceed. For role change to occur, the following must take place:

1. A dysfunctional role must be identified and reexperienced.
2. Script elements impeding change must be unblocked and the failed or aborted role relinquished.
3. New and more satisfying roles must be negotiated to replace the failed role.

As with loss, role change follows a downward curve that ultimately reverses itself with the development of new roles. For the process to be initiated, a dysfunctional role must first be experienced. As the pain of its loss is felt, resistance is mobilized. Denial, anger, and bargaining then slow the descent into change. What is happening must next be identified before corrective action can proceed. The dysfunctional role, and the mechanisms blocking its replacement, must be recognized before it becomes possible to begin letting go of them. In particular, the cognitions, emotions, volitions, and role partner demands impeding change must be prevented from deterring progress, and normal grieving must be allowed to sever bonds with an unsatisfying past.

The sadness of relinquishing roles is also the herald of reattachment. It signals the initiation of negotiations for new and/or altered roles, and of new ways of interacting. But if these new patterns are to be valid, the renegotiation process must be non-coercive. Successful resocialization depends upon not repeating past mistakes. When all goes well, the upward slope of the role change curve will then lead to greater, not less, happiness.

Reliving the Loss

Initiating role change requires the recognition and reexperiencing of what has been lost. A person executing a dysfunctional role must understand what has gone wrong and, more than this, relive his failure to the depths of his soul. Emotionally, he has to understand that his pattern of interacting prevents him from meeting his needs. The point is that for a role to change, it must first be activated. One's loss must be brought into the present and made real. It is not enough to dispassionately recall what has gone wrong; it must be reanimated. Failed or aborted roles have to be re-enacted in the here and now. It is as if there are circuits in the brain which must be turned on before they can be rerouted (Greenberg and Safran 1987). This makes it necessary to manipulate loss directly, rather than addressing a cognitive copy of it.

Whatever the actual brain physiology of the process, there can be little doubt that experiencing the source of a problem is a prerequisite for changing it. Freudians have long recognized that an intellectual re-capitulation of the past does nothing to correct it. As Alexander (1948) has put it, there must be a "corrective emotional experience" before change can take place. Childhood traumas must not merely be remembered; they must be rekindled in all their primal terror. As Rice and Saperia (1984) observe

the essential characteristics of the [change] process seems to be reexperiencing and reprocessing, [and] bringing to bear on the re-evoked experience an exploratory stance and a processing capacity that for various reasons was not available on the original occasion.

In other words, for a role to be changed, the original role negotiation must be reactivated so that it can be renegotiated and terminated more successfully. Primordial coercion must be reversed or neutralized, and what was lost reworked, or failing that, allowed to die.

Role negotiations that result in dysfunctional roles are painful affairs. There is therefore a danger that in reliving them a person will be overwhelmed by experiences that are as unmanageable as they were when they first occurred. His original negotiations were surely frightening, enraging, shameful, and mortifying. These feelings were so intense that they interfered with the possibility of a successful role bargain. Given this fact, reactivated feelings may have a similar effect. A person who reexperiences the past thus faces the hazard of once again being stampeded into bad roles.

In order to avoid such an outcome, a role changer will have to have one foot in the present and one in the past. When he reexperiences a failed role, he must not give himself up to it entirely. Part of him must be in the present so that he can use contemporary strengths to counter past demons. In part, he must be an outside observer of his own anguish, simultaneously feeling his old feelings while calmly reexamining them from a safe distance. Only then will he have the equanimity to institute appropriate changes. Otherwise, he will be trapped in the same emotional turmoil as before, with neither the courage nor the presence of mind to correct past mistakes.

Most of the time that people try to change failed roles, they fall into this latter pitfall. The impulse to reexperience and reverse past losses is a universal one, which usually inspires people to rush blindly into repeated failures. It is this process that Freud called the repetition compulsion. It is why many people seem condemned to recycle their dysfunctional roles without ever successfully replacing them. Typically, when they reactivate painful roles, the affective and cognitive components thus aroused are so unacceptable that they are quickly repressed. This means that the feelings and thoughts that hold unsatisfying roles in place are not faced, but continue to guide behavior. Such a person's unconscious scripts remain active, and he plods through his dysfunctional roles like a sleepwalker. He is similar to the man who marries a replica of his mother, has a dreadful experience, divorces her, and then remarries a woman exactly comparable, all without knowing what he is doing. Samuel Johnson called remarriage the triumph of hope over experience, and it is the same with failed roles that are too painful to be recognized or assimilated.

A major reason for seeking professional help with role change is to avoid being overwhelmed by reactivated roles. The relationship a clinician provides her client should be a source of safety. When a client is in danger of slipping totally into the past, his helper can offer a reassuring hand from the present. The clinician's calm confidence in the face of what seems to her client to be an overpowering terror can instill the courage to persist. In many ways a resocializer acts the part of a champion, shielding her client from his fears until he has the strength to defend himself. A professional can also act the part of a safe negotiating partner. The prospect of renegotiating painful roles with people who want to maintain one's bad roles discourages many from attempting change. Since a client naturally "transfers" past role relationships into the clinical present, a resocializer will be asked to function as a trustworthy partner. If she honors this trust and plays fair, she will have disarmed many of her client's worst suspicions. By being a safe confederate, she renders less dangerous what is inherently unsafe.

Letting Go

Reactivating a role makes change possible, but does not guarantee it. A way must be found to permit mourning to proceed. The protest which forms the first part of the change process must be allowed to happen, but not enabled to become so strong that it throttles progress. Those script elements that threaten to freeze resocialization in place must be loosened. After denial, anger, and bargaining have run their course, the agony of change can then be joined in earnest. Whatever else resocialization is, it is not fun. The only reason for going through it is to get to the other side. No one would enter its trough of despond if it did not have a sunny up-slope.

Dysfunctional roles are not experienced all at once or in toto. During role change, a certain amount of denial must be overcome before a person can start to relive his painful past. As new aspects of old traumas are unearthed, role changers tend to dismiss their import. Recollected conflicts with parents are interpreted as "misunderstandings," and past fears are pictured as minor episodes in an otherwise arcadian childhood. A client may try to convince himself that if he can just forget the past, everything will be all right. His hope will rest upon the deep-seated human conviction that no problem is so big that it can't be solved by pretending it doesn't exist.

The reason that denial is so seductive is that it is a wonderful tool for keeping fears at bay. People who have faced coercive role negotiations know what it is to be frightened. They have been threatened and intimidated, abused and manipulated, and learned the terror of abandonment first-hand. No wonder then that when they start reexperiencing coercive role negotiations, they sometimes prefer to close their eyes. But if this denial doesn't work—as it won't—it will be succeeded by anger. Such anger, in turn, may be openly expressed or covertly imposed, merely obstructive or forthrightly aggressive. In any event, it is important that it not get out of hand and cause further injury.

However a role changer's anger surfaces, it may be directed at any of a multitude of targets. He may get angry at present role partners, at former partners, at himself, at the clinician, or at life in general. When it is the resocializer who becomes the object of his wrath, this may be described as "negative transference." Or if he is married, his spouse may be the victim. All of his problems may be attributed to her, and he will be certain that if only she got dinner ready on time, or managed money more carefully, his problems would be solved.

On the other hand, a client may be very aware that his present difficulties were generated in past relationships. In this case, he may rightly blame past role partners but go on to engage in an orgy of recriminations. Parents will be condemned as more than coercive; they will be characterized as virtual devils. Passionate demands will be made of them to recompense past errors and guarantee present happiness. Unfortunately, what is past is past. No matter how abject their contemporary apology, or sincere their present love, parents cannot undo the past. Current anger and current contrition do not reverse what has already happened. However necessary it may be for a person to express his rage at past injustices, by itself it will be impotent. It can no more undo old roles than it can resurrect the dead.

While the impotence of a person's anger is still sinking in, he may be tempted to engage in bargaining. Instead of negotiating new roles, he will try making deals that salvage the old ones. He will find, however, that these attempts are a waste of time. The bargains he makes will be in the present, and cannot reverse the past any better than his anger. The danger is that he will not give up, that he will stay angry and continue to bargain even though it is evident that his attempts are futile.

Fortunate role changers are the ones who discover their own limits. Despite the strength of their fear, anger, and confusion, they realize that failed roles must be allowed to die. Ultimately, they begin letting go and permit themselves to slide into the pain of sadness. Depression envelops them and attachments begin breaking. But this depression does not happen all at once. There is too much to be relinquished for that to be so. Rather, the bottom of the role-change curve is stitched together from many episodes of sorrow. First one bond is broken, then another, and then another. Such an unhappy withdrawal from human interaction is the sine qua non of role change. Sadness is the mechanism of role release. Whenever a person wants to let go of an important relationship, he must experience it. There is no alternative.

Yet this simple fact is often vigorously resisted. When a role changer expresses regret for what he has lost, there is usually someone who will urge him to cheer up. Many people seem to believe that by acting happy, they can bring happiness. Unfortunately, this is not true. Attempts to deny a loss by prohibiting sadness only prolong the losing. Sorrow which is squelched becomes sorrow that endures. For pain to end, it must be tolerated. Only then can what is lost be relinquished.

Renegotiation

The last part of the role-change process is the renegotiation of new roles. Once letting go proceeds in earnest and bonds of old role scripts begin dissolving, it is time to develop new roles that are capable of replacing them. Resocialization is not complete until viable new patterns of living emerge. As a person's dysfunctional roles are set aside, a chasm opens up that demands filling. If it is not bridged with more functional behavior patterns, the resocialization process will have been wasted. Despite the travail of change, the person will be no better off than when he started.

That new roles may be no better than the old is not merely a hypothetical possibility. The construction of satisfying social roles takes skill and courage. Unfortunately, a person who is emerging from role trouble has gaps in his negotiation skills. The coercive negotiations that led to his dysfunctional roles were not conducive to learning how to negotiate, and living within them will have blinded him to alternative ways of living and coping. For a person to renegotiate good roles, he must know how to demand what he wants and needs. If his ability to stand up for himself, or if his vision of his options is impaired, he will be laboring under a terrible handicap. The mere fact that he knows something is wrong won't be enough.

A role changer will be further handicapped if, when he begins renegotiations, it is with the same partners with whom he negotiated earlier. They, or their surrogates, may encourage him to use the same bargaining techniques that miscarried in the past. They are also unlikely to have his interests at heart. Successful negotiations depend not only upon viable bargaining skills, but upon partners who are committed to finding an agreement that is mutually advantageous.

An important service a professional change agent can provide is helping his client identify his needs and develop the skills to negotiate for them. If a person is to judge the fairness of the negotiations in which he participates, he must have valid standards of comparison. He must know when something vital to him has been denied, or when he has gone too far in asserting his own inclinations. The difference between these two extremes can be learned in interaction with a clinician. By acting as a mirror for his client, and as a representative of societal standards, he can assist the person in discovering where he stands.

Someone who is struggling with dysfunctional roles has probably been taught to discount his own needs and judgments. He will have to learn that his feelings and perceptions have value. Indeed, he may not even be directly aware of them. They may have been such a source of trouble in his earlier relationships that he learned to anesthetize them. But since emotions are an indispensable guide in determining needs, getting back "in touch" is a priority concern.

One of the more important functions of a professional resocializer is to act as a negotiating foil with whom new role structures can be constructed. If he is a fair person, this renegotiation process can be used to teach bargaining skills. The resocialization relationship can be adapted as a vehicle for explicating the nature of negotiations and for encouraging the assertion of a client's rights. It can empower a person so that he is in a stronger bargaining position vis-à-vis his other role partners. Finally, if a clinician is a fair person, he can act as a model of what a role partner should be. He can provide a standard against which other partners are judged. Through his example and his sustained good will, he can prepare his client to cope with role partners who are not always fair.

The fortunate few who have grown up sheltered by protective relationships learn the lessons of non-coercive negotiations from their families. Their parents treat them with justice and love, and validate their rights to self-assertion. This fair treatment, instead of softening them, provides a cushion that protects from the blows of later life. Thus they acquire a confidence that makes it easier to endure life's rigors. The person trapped in dysfunctional roles, however, is rarely as blessed. She has usually been denied the gift of unchallengeable self-confidence. Luckily, a fair role-change agent can correct this deficiency. His fairness too confers self-worth. A client who trusts her helper can incorporate his nurturance and carry it wherever she goes. It can then serve as a refuge when other role negotiations get rough.

4

Impediments to Role Change: The Emotions

DYSFUNCTIONALLY MAINTAINED ROLES

Role change is not automatic. The process can be blocked in many ways. Fear, anger, confusion, and pain all interfere with the replacement of dysfunctional roles. They can dysfunctionally maintain both failed and aborted roles. Impediments to change can occur at any point during resocialization. They make it difficult to identify and reexperience an unsatisfactory role, to mourn and let it go, or to renegotiate new ones. The origin of these impediments is to be found in role scripts. Though their purpose is to stabilize behavior, sometimes they freeze unsatisfying patterns in place. In consequence, if role alterations are to occur, it may be necessary to modify those parts of a person's scripts that prevent change.

All aspects of role scripts (both internal and external) are capable of interfering with change. There are cognitive, emotional, volitional, and social impediments to resocialization. Misunderstandings about the world can make it difficult to identify dysfunctional roles; fear can prevent mourning from occurring, confused values can make it difficult to seek alternative solutions, and unsympathetic role partners can demand a misplaced constancy. All these possibilities must be taken into account when assessing why a desired alteration has not materialized.

The Role-Change Curve. The manner in which scripts obstruct resocialization can be visualized by considering the role-change curve. Ordinarily it proceeds from the reexperienced role, through protest and letting go, and toward the renegotiation of viable new roles. When an impediment intervenes, however, reexperience can be thwarted; pro-

Figure 4.1
The Role-Change Curve

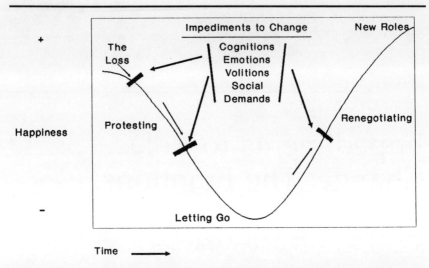

test and depression will miscarry, and renegotiations lead nowhere (see Figure 4.1).

If a person makes a cognitive mistake, such as judging himself to be weaker than he in fact is, he may not allow himself to reexperience his dysfunctional role for fear of being overwhelmed. In this case, the change process will be blocked before it begins. Or if his role is reexperienced, an erroneous perception of weakness can convince him that letting go and sliding down into sadness will have fatal consequences. He may then decide that a perpetual state of semi-misery is preferable to death. If this depression is successfully navigated, a similar perception of weakness can persuade him not to assert his rights during new negotiations. He may settle instead for an unsatisfactory bargain that obstructs suitable new roles.

An erroneous emotional reaction can have comparable effects. Extreme fear or intense anger can dissuade a person from reliving a role, or motivate him not to give up a losing proposition. Rather than admitting defeat and accepting its concomitant sadness, his emotions stimulate him to fight on forever. He remains engaged in a debilitating battle which cannot be won, instead of cutting his losses and proceeding to a better deal. Or if renegotiations do occur, fear and anger can thoroughly disrupt his bargaining techniques. Thus, he may make inappropriate demands, in an inappropriate manner, with unhappy results.

Malfunctioning volitions and excessive social demands can also block progress. Allegiance to an ill-considered value, such as a misplaced obedience to authority, can prompt someone to accede to commands that he not engage in resocialization, or if he does, to accept another's idea of what his new role should be. A person with such a value would be especially susceptible to social influence from role partners who do not have his interests at heart. Such partners may be all too willing to disrupt role change by ordering him to "shape up" and quit trying to be different. They may firmly suggest that he stop feeling sorry for himself, and get on with being who he always has been.

The Mechanisms of Blockage. Faulty cognitions, emotions, volitions, and social demands block role change because they are either wrongly directed or too intensely held. As has been indicated, internal script elements become misdirected or overly intense when they are generated in coercive negotiations. There is a tendency to respond to excessive external force with a matching internal force. Often, a person's malfunctioning beliefs, feelings, and plans are really an attempt to counter harmful beliefs, feelings, and plans imposed by unfair role partners. They are inappropriate because they are primarily designed to deflect even more inappropriate script elements initiated by others.

A cognition is wrongly directed when it misunderstands the world; it is too intensely held when a person finds it difficult to relinquish, even in the face of contrary evidence. An emotion is wrongly directed when its "goals" are misplaced (see below for the nature of emotional goals), and it is too intense when the emotion is so potent that it becomes overwhelming. A misdirected volition aims at a plan of action that is incapable of coming to fruition, and as with cognitions, it is too intensely held when it is not relinquished despite evidence that it is failing. Overly intense and misdirected social demands are, by definition, coercive in nature and incompatible with a person's real interests.

However, this is the barest outline of how script elements go wrong. Since their malfunctioning is the primary reason that bad roles persist, these mechanisms must be examined in substantially greater detail. We will begin this process with the emotions because they are the most formidable impediment to role change. More than any other factor, they make resocialization the uncomfortable enterprise that it is.

HOW EMOTIONS WORK

To understand how intense emotions interrupt role change, it is necessary to contemplate their nature. They may be thought of as having two aspects, each of which points in two separate directions (see Figure 4.2). The first of these aspects is the communication function; the second the motivation function. The first focuses attention; the second moves people to act in a particular manner. Each of these aspects can

Figure 4.2
The Structure of Emotions (e.g. Fear)

	Self	Other
Signals (Communication)	Danger Signal	Danger Signal
Motivation	Goal of Safety	Goal of Safety

then be directed at either the person experiencing the emotion or at someone with whom he is in contact.

Emotions inform people about things that are of vital import to them. They are signals that alert them to attend facts of which they must be aware. Thus, fear is a signal of danger. It tells a person there is something about which he must be careful. Fear gives him a jolt that makes it virtually impossible to ignore whatever it is that threatens. Similarly, anger signals frustration. It lets a person know when his needs have been thwarted.

Emotions also direct their messages at persons other than the one who is experiencing them. They are a social phenomenon, not merely an individual one. When someone is afraid, he not only feels something; he exhibits it. Feelings communicate with those who are interacting with the person experiencing them. These others receive signals too. The person's face, body, and voice all reveal that he is afraid, and others are thereby alerted. They too receive a jolt and become aware of the impending danger.

A second aspect of the emotions is their motivational function. It too affects both the person and those in contact with him. In the case of fear, not only is a danger signal given, but a person is pushed to do something about it. This is the famous "fight or flight" reaction (Cannon 1929). It mobilizes a person's energies to protect himself. Either he tries to overcome the danger by confronting it or he flees toward a safe haven. The adrenaline pumping in his body gives him a means to resist or run. Others who become aware of his fear have a similar reaction. In addition to being alerted to impending danger, they too are motivated to counteract it. Their fear starts their juices flowing and they too seek a way to avoid the danger or neutralize it.

This pattern of communication and motivation is repeated for all the emotions. Anger, as has been noted, signals frustration to self and others; it also energizes efforts to terminate the frustration. Sadness signals loss and helps people let go of what is defunct. Guilt, which is really an internalized form of external anger, is designed to placate the demands of others. Shame warns of socially unacceptable behavior, and helps a person desist from it. Love signals something positive about another person, and impels its subject to seek a loving relationship. Taken together, these emotions shape much of our behavior. They are far more than an ornament appended to human nature, and are at the very center of role structures. Emotions are the most compelling part of role scripts, and consequently have the most potential for blocking change.

The Goals of Emotions

As has been described, the facts highlighted by emotions and the reactions they motivate point toward particular objectives. These may be considered the goals of the emotions (Frijda 1987). They are the functions that feelings aim to implement. And as long as they are not realized, the emotions engendering them continue to push for satisfaction. An unfulfilled emotion demands completion. It does not rest until its goal has been achieved or relinquished. Unfortunately, in seeking particular goals, it can prevent the fulfillment of others. This is the genesis of many impediments to role change.

To understand how overly demanding emotions can be made quiescent, their goals must be analyzed in greater detail. For openers, it must be recognized that emotions can be reactive or teleological—or a combination of both. The goals of reactive emotions are initiated by something outside of the person; the goals of teleological emotions are chosen by the person herself. This means that reactive emotions can only be deactivated by changing their environment (or one's perceptions of this environment), while teleological ones require a person to achieve goals she has set for herself or, failing this, to abandon them and choose others.

Fear. The goal of fear is safety. It is a reactive emotion. The danger against which it guards is of external origin. For fear to achieve its objective, it must help a person become safe. Either an actual danger must be removed, or what has previously been perceived as dangerous must be reinterpreted as benign.

Anger. Anger, in contrast, is essentially teleological. The frustration it signals exists because a person first wants something. If she had no aims independent of her environment, there would be nothing to disappoint her. When someone is angry, she can assuage her frustration either by finding a way to achieve what she wants, or by changing her desires. When its internal goals are not consummated, anger escalates in intensity.

Sadness. Sadness has as its goal the relinquishment of a lost object. It is reactive in the sense that the loss is not voluntarily initiated. Loss and losing are something the world imposes. However, what is lost depends upon a person's prior attachments. This teleological aspect requires her to give up bonds that cannot be sustained. Only when she decides to renounce what she has previously chosen to embrace, will sadness have accomplished its task. Until then, it persists.

Guilt. Guilt is a complex emotion. It is primarily composed of internalized anger, but it begins with fear of another's anger. When someone else is extremely incensed at a person, fear is the typical response. To avoid the danger of the other's wrath, one tries to assuage him. This may be accomplished by becoming preemptively angry at oneself. It is this self-anger that is the essence of guilt. Its purpose is to enforce compliance with the other's wishes, so that he will be less angry.

To the extent that guilt is reactive, its goal is expiation. It aims at disarming another's rage and obtaining his forgiveness. But this other's anger is itself teleological. His indignation aspires to reduce his frustrations by achieving goals he has chosen. Insofar as a person has accepted this other's goals, they become her teleology too, and thus by helping the other obtain his desires become a path towards reducing ego's guilt. But this guilt can also be diminished by rejecting the other's goals. Instead of trying to placate him, the person can change her own teleology and stop trying to enforce alien wishes. Such a course also reduces self-anger, and hence remorse.

Shame. Shame signals that a person is the subject of negative attention. It arises when she is being ridiculed for who she is or what she has done. The message of shame is that she is not providing a suitable role model for others. Her behavior (or person) is held up as an object lesson in what not to emulate. Shame then motivates either withdrawal from negative attention or behavior that attracts positive notice. The goal of shame is to make unacceptable behavior less visible, and it encourages a person to exhibit more acceptable conduct. Someone who wishes to reduce her embarrassment wants to change the way others perceive her. Her first reaction is to shrink from sight and thus remove the offense she is causing. She may also choose to conform to their judgment and alter her behavior so that it coincides with this standard.

However, shame is more than reactive; it too has a teleological component. An act is shameful only as long as it is rejected as a model. If a person vigorously asserts the appropriateness of the behavior she is enacting, it too can set the standard. Her own teleological decision about the acceptability of behavior may ultimately induce others to change the way they perceive her actions. By firmly insisting on her own example, she can convert negative attention into positive. In this case, shame will also have achieved its goal, although through another route.

Love. Love signals the desire for an attachment to another human being. A person who experiences it wants to be close to a specific other; she also wants this other to reciprocate her feelings. A desire to achieve this bond motivates her to do what she can to make it a reality. One way she can try to get close is by making herself as lovable as possible. But love cannot be satisfied if it is unrequited, or if it demands too much sacrifice. A person may make prodigious efforts to elicit it, but if a potential partner requires her to give up too many of her own needs, the desired connection will fail. The objective of love is achieved only in a mutually satisfying relationship. Love is thus teleological in settling on its object, but reactive in its response to the way in which a commitment is reciprocated.

How Emotions Impede Role Change

When emotions are working properly, they are a powerful tool in helping people achieve their needs. The goals built into them provide vital signals about needs fulfillment, and equally vital motivation for actualizing them. When the direction and intensity of an emotion are appropriate, they foster satisfaction; when not, they prevent it.

Set Solutions. The various elements of role scripts provide people with "set solutions" for their personal aspirations. Cognitions, volitions, or emotions contain within them a method for obtaining satisfaction. The intensity and direction of these elements incorporate instructions for needs achievement. They provide ready-made answers to the problem of what will fulfill a need and how it can be procured. When an emotion is appropriate, its intensity and direction are such that the goal it signals and motivates has a good chance of being achieved. In the case of fear, it can accurately inform a person of the presence of a danger, alert him to its seriousness, suggest how to respond (e.g., by fight or flight), and provide sufficient energy to carry out this response (see Figure 4.3).

Set solutions make it possible to react to environmental challenges expeditiously. Life is too fast-paced and complex to allow for recalculating one's options every time there is an opportunity to act. A person who tried to do so would find himself frozen into inaction. As wonderful a computer as the human brain is, there are limits to what it can do. Still, when set solutions are good ones, there is no need for apprehension. The behavior patterns they set in motion are usually suitable to the situation, and adequately fulfill one's needs.

Normal socialization depends upon the establishment of effective set solutions. It is contingent upon instilling role elements that reliably guide

Figure 4.3
Set Solutions (Fear)

	Intensity	Direction
Signals	How Strong the Fear?	What Danger? (Accuracy?)
Motivation	How Strong an Impulse to Act?	What Action is Motivated (How Suitable?)

the enactment of behaviors that work. Emotions such as fear can and do provide the requisite sort of solution. They implement patterns that make social life possible. Consider how children learn to avoid running into busy streets. When a child makes the mistake of dashing into traffic, he can count on his parents becoming upset. Mother or dad will be both frightened and angry. A raised voice, a threatening fist, or a promised spanking will inform him of his error. The intensity of the reaction will undoubtedly arouse fear and discourage the child from ever again unheedingly running into the street. The scare will stay with him to provide protective habits for a lifetime. In short, his learned fear will assist him in achieving vital needs.

Wrong Solutions. However, set solutions need not be good ones. The intensity and direction of an emotion's message and motivation may be such that they preclude needs satisfaction. Wrong set solutions do not facilitate the achievement of goals and may even impede their attainment. Angela, it will be recalled, was a rejected daughter. As a child, when she asked for love, she was forcibly ejected from her family constellation. Her expressed desire elicited the very reaction she dreaded. Just as with the child who blunders into a busy street, she had the wits scared out of her. But her fear did not provide a viable set solution. It insistently signaled her that love was being denied, and strongly motivated her to cling to the source of her rejection. Although it rightly warned of the danger of repudiation, it impelled her to seek acceptance in ways that precluded success. By forever soliciting love from her mother, or mother substitutes, she virtually guaranteed not obtaining it. The solution dictated by her fears insured that her needs were not met, and prevented her from adopting more productive ones. Because her fear kept her clinging to mother, she could not shift her allegiance to more suitable attachment figures. The emotion made it difficult to recognize the source of her frustration, to let go of it, or to adopt a more satisfying attachment.

Overly intense and/or misdirected emotions impede change in several ways. First, their signals can be so intense that they cloud perceptions instead of enhancing them. The attention they command can be so fixed that important facts are missed and/or distorted. Second, the direction in which the emotions point may be in error. In the case of fear, it may not illuminate the source of danger at all. Third, emotions can motivate actions that do not reduce danger and may even enhance it. Fear may impel a person to flee into the arms of even greater danger. Fourth, the intensity of an emotion may be such that it too insistently motivates bad solutions. A person may be so frightened that he won't give up even the most disastrous of expedients.

In Angela's case, fear focused her attention too exclusively on instances of rejection and made her insensitive to other sources of satisfaction. A loss of love filled her senses with terror and assumed an importance greater than it deserved. Thus she became more frightened and more desirous of her mother's love than was sensible. Second, while Angela's dread rightly assessed her mother's rejection as dangerous, she wrongly projected it on non-dangerous sources. Lovers, employers, and welfare employees all assumed the mantle of maternal rejection. When they spurned her, she perceived their disdain as injurious as her mother's. In this she was mistaken. Third, the solution that Angela's fear endorsed was to cling to the very instigator of her jeopardy. She wanted to elicit an acceptance from this person that would wipe out the danger of rejection. But her mother was not willing to provide this sort of love. Finally, Angela's fear-motivated clinging made it difficult for her to renounce seeking love in the wrong places. The intensity of her emotion insisted that she must have the love she was denied. She must extract it from her mother no matter what the cost to herself.

Fear. Wrong set solutions make it difficult to reexperience dysfunctional roles, to let them go, or to renegotiate new ones. Intense fear, for example, can make it virtually impossible to relive an aborted role. Its danger signal may be so strong that denial, repression, or diversion blot out any hint of the cause of danger. Instead of focusing attention on what needs to be seen, the opposite occurs. Terror guarantees that awareness is aimed everywhere but where it needs to be. Indeed, a misdirected signal may persuade someone that danger is emanating from places where it is absent. Therefore the cause of a role's failure will not be apprehended, reexperienced, or changed.

Assuming that coercive role negotiations have been reactivated, intense or misdirected fears can mandate that ancient battles be refought in the same old ways. Instead of permitting a letting go which prepares the way for something new, they motivate a protest that is too long and too strong; that is, they energize a fight that never ends. Terror can suggest that a solution is possible when it is not, or that one is intolerable when it isn't.

Letting go of a role and slipping into deep sorrow can be a profoundly frightening experience in the best of circumstances. When a person is already intensely and/or mistakenly fearful, it can be a nightmare. His dread makes the slide toward depression seem unendurable. It will appear to him that he is accelerating into death itself. In consequence, he desperately clings to what little security he already has. Before giving up and having nothing, he would rather suffer the pangs of an insidious and enduring sadness. Instead of choosing a course which allows him to emerge out the other side, he prefers the apparently safer twilight zone of a more modest, but nagging melancholy.

Should the role change process enter the renegotiation phase, intense and/or misdirected fears can interfere with the correct apprehension of potential solutions, and encourage long-discredited behavior patterns. Successful renegotiation depends upon altering set solutions, and hence fears that keep them in place interfere with good bargains. They can also distort perceptions of current role partners and motivate unnecessary battles.

All in all, if a very strong and misdirected fear does not achieve its goal (namely, safety), it remains intense and misdirected and is unable to consummate itself. Fear that does not beget safety breeds more fear, and the greater the terror, the more it solidifies its grip on set solutions that don't work. When fear expands, it becomes "panic" (Barlow 1988). Among other effects, it can incite a shortness of breath, heart palpitations, profuse sweating, dizziness, numbness, a fear of going crazy, a fear of dying, hot flashes, or faintness. In combination, these reactions cause the kind of "neurotic stupidity" that Sullivan implicated in personal problems. When panic appears, a person's ability to engage in rational planning flies out the window. He still wants to be safe, but the ferocity of his emotion is just as likely to place him in harm's way.

It should be noted that among the emotions, fear has an unenviable pride of place. When other emotions are intense or misdirected, they too become dangerous. In addition to whatever individual feeling tone they may carry, they too generate fear. Thus very intense anger is frightening; very deep sadness is frightening; very insistent guilt is frightening; and so forth. This secondary fear, if it is forceful, can itself interfere with role change processes.

Anger. Anger works hand-in-glove with fear. It is often used to induce fear or to fight against its induction. Specifically, when intimidation is invoked to enforce behavior, it may be angrily resisted. If this hostility does not succeed in removing the source of intimidation (and hence frustration), it escalates to ever greater levels and becomes a problem in itself. Very intense anger is as unbearable as terror and requires containment every bit as much as does fear.

For intense anger to achieve its aim, it must reduce frustration. It must either attain its underlying goal or find a new one. If it does not, rage is expressed in set solutions that prevent success. The message and the motivation inherent in it then inhibit the very changes that would end a person's frustration.

Rage perverts the ordinary intra-personal communications of anger by blocking the perceptions and thoughts that allow one to understand why a frustration has arisen. Intense emotions of any sort interfere with one's ability to think. H. S. Sullivan compared anxiety with a blow to the head which drives out all thoughts and leaves a person feeling dizzy. Intense anger, guilt, sadness, shame, and love all do the same. They completely disrupt a person's cognitive and volitional facilities, and turn his brain into silly putty. But without cognitive and volitional competence, the attention generated by an emotion's signal is worthless. Consciousness that is not supported by productive thought does not generate enhanced understanding or planning.

The communication function of the emotions, it must be remembered, also signals role partners. In the case of anger, this assumes a special significance. One of the main mechanisms it utilizes to achieve its aim is that of persuading role partners to act in desired directions. If, however, it is too strong, the message it is designed to relay gets lost in the static. Instead of it informing others of the seriousness of one's frustration, it becomes the object of attention. Rather than providing a role partner with the information he needs in order to cooperate in frustration reduction, he is encouraged to ignore one's needs.

Misdirected anger is also a problem. If someone has mistaken the cause of his frustration, he may become furious at the wrong role partner. Should this happen, the target of his rage will resent the error. Instead of listening or wanting to cooperate, he may rejoice at his attacker's predicament. In addition, misdirected anger may try to force a change that has nothing to do with the person's real needs. In this case, even if a change is implemented, the frustration endures.

Moving on to the motivational aspects of anger, we find a similar potential for problems. Very intense anger can energize a quixotic effort to prevent a particular frustration at all costs. Indeed, the fight to resist a loss may become so furious that a person feels he is ready to explode. His passions are inflamed to the point that he is barely capable of action; all he can do is sit and sputter. Moreover, instead of impelling role partners to the desired action, intense anger motivates the opposite. It provokes counter-anger. A role partner may know what is wanted, but his own reaction will be so violent that he launches a counter-attack to enforce his will.

Worst of all, when the motivation of anger is misdirected, the outcome can be disastrous. It is not merely that misguided energy leads to failure (which of course it does), but it can cause positive, even fatal, injuries. Anger is a very dangerous emotion. It is capable of motivating physical damage, even murder. When it loses its way, it forces things to happen that don't eliminate frustration, but do leave a trail of pain. In the end, fury can induce someone to do things he will later bitterly regret. A person may even find that his rage arouses an equally violent response in his role partners. In this instance it is they who may precipitate the injury. Much against the person's wishes, he finds that he is the one who is hurt. Misdirected rage simply invites retaliation. Given this proclivity of anger toward injury, it is not surprising that it generates tremendous fear. Serious anger deserves to be feared.

As with fear, anger can activate set solutions that do not succeed. Rather than achieving its goal and being terminated, it becomes more intense and more misdirected. Like fear, anger can interfere with the very modifications that would facilitate the fulfillment of its goal. Intense and/or misguided anger reinforces tendencies not to permit change. It stiffens a person's resolve not to reexperience a loss or accept its consequences. By keeping necessary information out of awareness, rage also prevents the identification of what has really gone wrong. After all, it is the extremely angry person who mutters through clenched teeth, "I am not angry," and refuses to realize what sort of battle he is in.

Anger is especially obstructive during the protest stage of resocialization. When it is added to the ordinary passions that punctuate the change process, the combination can be staggering. Instead of merely slowing the downward slide into depression, this combined emotion stops it dead in its tracks. Rage becomes so strong and so intent upon a particular solution that it vetos any suggestion that an irreversible loss has occurred, and does not allow mourning to undo self-defeating patterns.

When role change enters the renegotiation phase, overwhelming anger makes a shambles of fairness. It is enormously coercive and fights for its prescriptions at all costs. Intense anger tries to overwhelm. It does not calmly and reasonably consider what is optimal; neither does it offer cooperation in finding a mutually suitable agreement. Ruthless anger wants to prevail so badly that it sabotages its own chances of success. By coming on too strong, it sows the seeds of an opposition that will ultimately stalemate it.

Sadness. Infants who are fed and clothed but not given loving care sometimes die. They fail to thrive because they apparently lose their will to live (Lidz 1968). Without viable attachments to other human beings, life becomes a shell that is not worth preserving. If the losses sustained in early childhood are too severe, they can literally become life-threatening. The child who is to survive will have to fight them with all his might. Thus sadness that is allowed to become too intense may break the bonds not only of particular relationships, but to life itself.

Children who have experienced intense sadness early in life carry it with them forever. They bear a constant reminder of the fragility of existence. As adults, depression stalks them with all the foreboding of death. It is not something they willingly accept or cheerfully abide. To a vulnerable person, intense sadness signals not loss but total emptiness. It makes the prospect of losing appear utterly terrifying. The message it delivers is that there is no hope, and that the slide into the nothingness of extermination is too powerful to be resisted. Total destruction is the direction in which intense sadness points. Although a person in the throes of profound sadness may be mistaken in this conclusion, he won't be capable of correcting his assessment. Phenomenologically, his sadness will seem like a black, bottomless pit from which there is no emergence.

When sadness is tolerable, it can effectuate the letting go of what is lost; when it is unendurable, it does not. The letting go which sadness mediates is something that must be allowed to happen. Depression does not work like anger; it does not try to bludgeon the world into submission. It is a more subtle emotion that makes things happen by gently permitting them to unfold. When, however, sorrow is too intense, it does not facilitate the loosening of attachments. It turns in the opposite direction and activates a fear that won't let it take place. Sadness that is too potent tries to go in reverse and hold on to what is lost.

During the early phases of role change, a person who has intimations of unbearable sadness will resist the whole process. Rather than stare into the jaws of death, a profound denial obtains. This is especially true for those who have survived a brush with life-threatening grief as young children. Instead of reexperiencing the blackness of intense depression, they feel something else. Often it will be either anger or fear. These are good masks for sadness because they are themselves so riveting. Anger, for instance, mobilizes energy, monopolizes attention, and is virtually impossible to ignore. It puts on such a good show that it diverts a person from miseries that seem worse. When this sort of defense occurs, he will remain transfixed at the reexperiencing or protest stage of resocialization.

Ordinarily, change is like a roller coaster ride on an inverse normal curve. When sadness is allowed to occur, one goes down the slope from protest into deep depression, then as forces at the bottom of the curve reverse themselves, one is hurled back up out of the pit. This trip is usually slower than one might like and there are many dips and reversals along the way, but the end result is assured. It is as if the momentum built up on the downward slope provides the energy for the upward journey. To a person burdened with intense sadness, however, this may not seem so. For him, the downward ride may feel as if it must terminate in tragedy. Because there seems to be no bottom, he will experience an irresistible impulse to jam on the brakes. This will leave him hung up somewhere on the downslope. Rather than becoming deeply sad and relinquishing his dysfunctional roles, he feels moderately sad and remains attached to behaviors that don't satisfy.

Often, people said to be clinically depressed are caught on this downslope. A major symptom of this sort of depression is a dejection that never seems to end. Such people seem to be moping about all the time, and hence it appears they have entered the sadness phase of role change. But appearances are deceptive. These individuals do not truly allow themselves to mourn what is lost. Their persistent sorrow is not a sign of letting go, but of a resistance to intense sadness. As with other emotions, when sadness is too robust, it impedes rather than facilitates its goal. The paradox is that some instances of grief actually prevent real mourning.

When true mourning does occur, it must be thoroughly worked through before productive role negotiations can take place. Sometimes people allow themselves to experience only some of their sadness. In such a case, unresolved sadness accompanies them in their renegotiations. Instead of bargaining with energy and insight, they feel a hopelessness that counteracts their efforts. Good negotiations require a sensitivity to self, to others, and to the possibilities of new role structures which an ongoing depression can vitiate. A person who is still depressed will be looking away from life and hence will not discern his options. Neither will he be able to pursue his goals with genuine conviction. Part of him still won't believe success is possible, and so he will be insufficiently motivated to seek it.

Guilt. Because guilt is a kind of internalized anger induced by external demands, it operates as an analog to anger. An intensely guilty person may misperceive his world just as does the intensely angry one. Very intense self-recriminations make it difficult to correctly evaluate the demands of others. A guilty person may even be inclined to accept external demands that he might otherwise consider invalid. Instead of calculating whether the blame being hurled at him is justified, his impaired judgment signals him to feel automatic remorse. But as with anger, guilt can be mistaken. Rage can misjudge the cause of frustration, and guilt can misjudge the basis of culpability. In short, a repentant person easily blames himself for things that are not his fault. He is then inclined to punish himself for crimes he did not perpetrate, or for frustrations it is not in his power to prevent. His self-anger expands to unmanageable proportions and he castigates himself for imaginary transgressions.

Should overly intense or mistaken guilt lurch into action, that is, should the motivation aspect of the emotion be activated, it too can refuse to give up. The overly penitent person insists upon punishing himself no matter what. Instead of reevaluating his situation, he demands instant self-compliance. Rather than crediting his impulse to resist, he ruthlessly overrides his own judgments. Moreover, intense self-blame impels him to inflict cruel punishments upon himself. The direction of his inner anger prompts enforcement strategies that actually cause injury. He may thus deny himself any source of pleasure or impose hideous pain, all in the name of forcing himself to do what he believes he must. Such internalized coercion can be far more extreme than any role partner would think of implementing.

Given the ways in which intense guilt can be corrupted, it is easy to understand how it interferes with resocialization. Such remorse generates excessive protests that simply do not allow role change to occur. The self is perceived to be at fault and is battered into submission. The fact that role negotiations have miscarried is not attributed to the malevolence of role partners, but to one's own foolish intransigence. If only one would do the right thing, past conflicts could be resolved, and apparent losses retrieved.

Intense guilt also convinces a person that he is unhappy because of something he has done, and therefore that he must change if things are to get better. Sometimes this attitude is valid, but often it is not. No matter how sweeping a person's self-reforms, there are occasions when role negotiations cannot be salvaged. Should this be the case, intense guilt will only delay the inevitable. If the self is not the cause of role failure, or if a personal failing cannot be rectified, then no amount of self-vilification will make things turn out right. Only a reduced level of guilt, one that allows for relinquishing failed roles, will serve.

Shame. Shame is another emotion that can be used, and hence misused, in enforcing role behavior. When it is very intense or misdirected, it too sends faulty signals or energizes unavailing actions. Intense shame can mistakenly indicate that a behavior merits negative attention when it does not, and acute embarrassment can make it difficult to accurately assess the value of a course of action that others find objectionable. Their ridicule leaves a person flushed with confusion and unable to decide if her behavior really is unworthy of providing a model for others.

Once a profound sense of embarrassment has been set in train, most people feel impelled to comply. Shame can be an excruciatingly uncomfortable experience. Rather than feel the draughts of such negative attention, a majority of human beings strive for anonymity or approval. Either they do what others desire, or they hide from scrutiny. It is the rare person who stands her ground and defies the crowd. This is especially true when one's humiliation is very sharp. Yet defiance is often what is needed. The ridicule inflicted by others may be misplaced, and what a person wants to do may be the proper course of action. If so, it will be better for her and others if she resists the press of shame toward invisibility. Her best policy will be to stand up and invite inspection. Sadly, intense shame makes such self-assertion very difficult. Is is more likely to motivate an ill-considered withdrawal than a courageous counter-attack.

The inappropriate withdrawal so often associated with extravagant shame can be inimical to change. A desire to hide, even when hiding is not in order, induces a person to shrink from the reexperience of her aborted roles. An old role, or merely parts of it, can feel too embarrassing to acknowledge. Someone who is hiding from the view of others will avoid this kind of self-examination. Thus a very embarrassed person may not be aware of her situation, or even want to be aware of it. Her dysfunctional role behavior is a mystery that she does not wish to reopen by reliving it.

Intense shame interrupts the protest phase of resocialization by reinforcing protest. Shame says *No!* to one's own behavior, and can be every bit as stifling as guilt. An overly embarrassed person forces herself not to be what her role partner doesn't want her to be. She remonstrates against her own contribution to an aborted role negotiation and tries to force herself into compliance with the other person's idea of a successful role bargain. In so doing, she does not allow herself to let go of what cannot work.

The depression phase of role change is also replete with danger from excessive shame. Mourning, with its attendant withdrawal, is an open display of weakness. For others so inclined, it is an invitation to ridicule. Hence, those who are sensitive to shame perceive grief to hold unnecessary risks. Consequently, to avoid negative aspersions, they elect to put on a façade of strength that impedes change.

When excessive shame invades the renegotiation stage of resocialization, it puts a person at a disadvantage relative to her negotiation partners. It may be insurmountably difficult for her to construct viable new roles if she is too vulnerable to their barbed comments. If they can easily induce her to feel shame, this feeling may unfairly pressure her to back away from solutions that are in her interest.

Love. It may seem strange to include the positive emotion of love in the company of such unsavory characters as anger, guilt, and shame. Yet love can be just as damaging to the role change process. It too can be overly intense or misdirected, and can give mistaken messages and inspire unfortunate actions. Negative emotions like anger, fear, and guilt force people to do things against their will, while love entices them to do negative things of their own accord. A person experiencing love wants to please another person. Her own desires encourage her to do what the other would like. But if the other's desires override her interests, if, for instance, the other wants stasis rather than change, then role dysfunction is a likely sequel.

When the signal given by love is too vigorous, a person may fail to perceive signs of danger. Intense love prevents her from recognizing that a beloved person is being excessively selfish or outright sadistic. Her strong impulse toward love causes her to love the wrong sort of person. She will be signaled that someone is an appropriate object for attachment when he (she) is not, and if her emotion is very intense, it may continue the same message in the face of accumulating counter-evidence. Whatever its object, intemperate love impels spirited efforts at attachment. The person signaled becomes the one sought, right or wrong. Love provides the energy to hold on, despite proof that a com-mitment is causing pain. Certainly many people maintain an allegiance to unworthy partners long after it is plain that their relationship has become an abusive one.

Misplaced love is especially evident in caretaker roles. Usually these are entered into in order to gain the love of another and terrible sacri-fices are made to obtain his/her affection. Many essential needs are jettisoned in the hope that the other will recognize one's worth and reward one accordingly. Usually this sacrifice is in vain, but sometimes it does bring a measure of love. When it does, a caretaker may be so delighted that she cannot conceive of pursuing another, potentially more rewarding, love.

When entering resocialization, a person with intensely misplaced love does not want to consider alternatives to what she thinks she already has. A caretaker may be so imprisoned by the intensity of her commit-ment that she is convinced if she only takes better care of the other, she will gain all the love and satisfaction she will ever need. In reex-periencing dysfunctional roles, her old loyalties are reanimated and her decision to hold on to failed roles is strengthened. Denial, protests, and bargaining are all reinvigorated in the hope that past errors can be corrected.

During the mourning phase of role change, the afterglow of a faded love may seem a better bargain than depression. Even an attachment to a bad love object seems preferable to letting go and having nothing. A person painfully in need of love may be seduced by a loved one into trying to "feel good" precisely because sadness feels so bad. She may willingly respond to suggestions that she cheer up and stop being de-pressed.

Finally, role change can be interrupted during renegotiations if a per-son succumbs to the unscrupulous blandishments of a loved one. A misplaced love may recommend the acceptance of another bad bargain and a person willingly accede. If she is sufficiently desperate she may happily set aside her own interests, only to pay the price of her gallantry by entering further dysfunctional roles.

Primitive Emotions

There is a certain class of emotions that has a high probability of interfering with role change. These may be called "primitive" emotions and are inherited from childhood. Primitive emotions are automatic and stereotyped reaction patterns that seem to be inborn. Such an aboriginal emotion, when actuated, seems to lead inevitably to action; its signal immediately provokes motivation. Moreover, the action motivated has a definite pattern. In primitive anger, for example, a person instinctively kicks, screams, bites, and cries. These responses appear to be pre-programmed. Thus an infant does not have to consider how to respond when he is angry; he just does.

For young children, primitive anger brings results. Screams and tears inform a parent that he is seriously unhappy and motivate the parent to eliminate the cause of his distress. But should an adult resort to these methods, he will be brought up short. Other adults will probably respond with derision and counter-anger. They will not be inclined to remove the cause of his frustration, and indeed may increase it. Adults need more sophisticated emotions. Their anger, fear, and so on must be socialized (Lewis and Saarni 1985). As they grow into adulthood, they must learn to use feelings as ever more precise instruments. The signal function of their emotions must make ever more discerning discriminations, and the motivation function invoke ever more subtle plans of action. For instance, anger must become capable of delineating finer shades of frustration, and communicating them in words, not tantrums. The adult who fails to make this transition will find his emotions becoming increasingly impotent.

Ineffectual emotions, that is, emotions that don't achieve their goals, have a propensity for preventing change. They tend to be very persistent precisely because they have not attained their ends. Instead of allowing change to proceed, they flow through the same stale channels, reiterating the same tired formulae. Thus ineffective anger makes the same threadbare demands, in the same quivering voice, with the same negative results. It never seems to learn.

More lamentably, unavailing emotions breed deeper failure. When an emotion does not achieve its goal, it is often intensified; when it intensifies, it becomes more primitive. Frustrated anger becomes angrier, and hence louder and less effective. An impulse to kick and scream becomes almost irresistible, and if acted upon, virtually guarantees a lack of success. If intense emotions are not to be primitive, they must not be automatic or stereotyped. They must be controlled so that their signal does not immediately spill into action and their motivation is deployed in effective action. Emotions that work are those that are intelligently employed. They achieve what they go after; they do not merely ventilate.

The Primacy of the Emotions

Emotions, cognitions, volitions, and social demands all guide role behaviors. Each of them, when misapplied, can interfere with role change. Yet of these components of role scripts, it is the emotions that are the most disruptive. It is emotions that are the most conservative and the most difficult to alter. When people are trapped in dysfunctional roles, more than anything else, it is because fear, anger, sadness, guilt, shame, and love prevent them from relinquishing their unsatisfying behaviors. The other script elements form impediments too, but they are far easier to remove.

This noisome quality of the emotions is what has given them such a bad reputation in some quarters. Many people wish to live their lives like Mr. Spock of *Star Trek*. Their aspiration is to be so sublimely intellectual that they are not troubled by the irrational vicissitudes of their feelings. It is precisely the intractable part of the emotions, the part that makes them so hard to change or direct, that makes people want to avoid their contamination.

The Slowness of Emotions. Above all else, what makes the emotions such formidable impediments to change is that they are altered so slowly. It is comparatively easy to transform a cognitive judgment or a plan of action. All that may be required is changing one's mind. But emotions are different. A person may recognize that one of his emotions is out of place, but it will persist anyway. He may know better than anyone that his fear is irrational, but he will remain afraid. Although there are methods for changing feelings, they are painful and protracted. It takes time to change feelings, often considerable time.

This slowness of the emotions is precisely what makes them so effective in fixing role behavior in place. They have a natural conservatism that makes roles conservative. Yet it is this same quality that induces us to call them irrational. This unfortunate word only signifies that emotions are not cognitions. They do not follow the same logical rules (Zajonc 1980; Greenberg and Safran 1987), but they do follow rules. Emotions have a logic of their own which must be respected if they are to change. The particular methods by which they can be altered will be considered at a later juncture. We will be elaborate upon them whe.. we discuss how clinicians facilitate the resocialization process. In the meantime, suffice it to reiterate that change inevitably requires time. There can be no true emotional transformation without its passage.

5

Cognitive and Volitional Impediments

HOW COGNITIONS AND VOLITIONS IMPEDE CHANGE

Earlier it was emphasized that cognitions and volitions are not the same. Although they are frequently confused with one another (Ellis and Grieger 1977), cognitions provide a kind of map of the world, while volitions contribute an itinerary for moving about within it. Nevertheless, these two script elements interfere with role change in similar ways. They both send people off in false directions which then deflect them from the steps necessary to make resocialization happen.

Like the emotions, cognitions and volitions furnish people with set solutions. They too supply answers to questions about how to meet one's needs. Unlike them, however, they do not have built-in goals. Rather, they foster the implementation of fundamental personal needs, such as safety, love, and respect, by utilizing explanations that individuals invent, inherit, and/or discover. When these cognitions and volitions provide bad solutions, they make it unlikely for someone to enact satisfying behaviors. Moreover, flawed answers, once accepted, are difficult to rectify.

A person who misunderstands his world or who devises defective plans for maneuvering within it is making mistakes about cause and effect. He is, as it were, pushing the wrong buttons. While he wants certain things to happen, he does not accurately assess how they are put together or how he can manipulate them. This reduces his chances of getting what he wants or needs. Such errors in judgment also interfere with normal role change processes. They can make it difficult to reexperience dysfunctional roles, relinquish them, or renegotiate new ones. When a person misreads the nature of his problems he can be induced to implement the wrong decisions regarding their solution. He may, for instance, decide not to let change happen, or he may decide to make the wrong changes.

The person who misconstrues what has gone wrong in his life or why it has gone wrong may see no point in reexperiencing a dysfunctional role. He may not be prepared to accept the fact that a social role has caused his unhappiness, and will be unwilling to acknowledge his own participation in precipitating this travail. Either way, he will look for alternative ways of feeling better. Whether he has allowed himself to be misled, or has positively refused to see the truth of his situation, his ability to enter the reexperience phase of resocialization will be seriously compromised.

Similarly, mistaken cognitions and volitions can block the release of failed or aborted roles. A person who cannot correctly ascertain when he has lost, or is indisposed to accept the fact that a strategy has miscarried, may be reluctant to give up a fight. His mistaken judgments will trap him within the protest phase of resocialization. He will incorrectly believe that with a little more anger, or a slightly better bargain, victory is possible. Instead of getting on with the business of changing things, his misinformed determination to win prevents real success. Satisfying role change becomes possible only when he recognizes his loss and the faulty nature of his plans, and is prepared to correct both.

Mistaken cognitions and volitions also have a negative impact on the renegotiation of roles. If resocialization is to succeed, dysfunctional roles must be improved. But negotiations based upon specious intelligence or bungled strategies make this process doubtful. A person changing roles must be able to accurately assess his needs, the needs of his role partners, their respective strengths, and the options made available by the real world if a satisfactory bargain is to be struck. If he can't, he will fail again.

Types of Error

Like the emotions, cognitions and volitions can be mistaken in both their intensity and direction. A cognition or volition can be held too strongly, or it can be mistaken in the way it understands the world or plans actions.

Errors in Intensity. A cognition can be too firmly held when a person perceives no alternative to the views he presently holds. He may have limited access to other options and simply not be aware that other interpretations are possible. This can easily happen when someone comes from an impoverished or regimented environment. Most of us learn about our possibilities by observing the models available to us. If these are limited by our social class or by family rigidity, we may never realize that other assessments exist. Moreover, cognitive understandings are not merely private; they are shared experiences. In order to be certain that a particular belief is not a fantasy, we require outside corroboration. This consensual validation builds a world in which more than one can participate. It also opens individuals to the tyranny of others. Should a role partner assert that what is, isn't, or vice versa, a person may be vulnerable to gross confusion. If the other is forceful enough, he may even have the power to arbitrarily restrict our perspective of the truth. A limited, and perhaps false, conception of the universe becomes our only world, and we clutch at it with unwarranted tenacity.

A person who has a very strong need for answers may also unnecessarily foreclose his alternatives. His longing for love or safety can be so intense that he grasps at the first apparently viable option he discovers. He then holds on for dear life because he is convinced that no other understanding can help him achieve his objective. Uncertainty makes people uncomfortable, and the more pressing a person's needs, the more discomfort he will experience when he has no explanations. Thus he will be all the more inclined to leap to false conclusions. He may also be uncomfortable if his apparent alternatives are dissonant with other of his currently held beliefs (Festinger 1957). Human beings seem to have a strong need for cognitive consistency. Sometimes, however, this yearning can impel us to reject valid interpretations. As Emerson long ago warned, a false consistency is the hobgoblin of small minds.

Volitional alternatives can be limited in the same way. A person's compelling need for answers, or the parochial models available to him, can make his choices seem narrower than they really are. Volitions are especially susceptible to the influence of others. The values and norms to which we commit ourselves are largely constructed in concert with others. If these others resolutely limit the acceptable solutions, those few that remain take on added significance. A restricted set of action strategies must then be held more firmly, since all one's potential answers must derive from them.

Errors in Direction. The direction of a cognition is in error when the understandings it imparts are wrong. Unless one is a solipsist, one must believe there is a world out there to be discovered. And the closer our interpretations come to it, the better informed our actions will be. To be sure, some of the definitions that help us understand the universe are social constructions (Thomas and Thomas 1928). But much of the cosmos is impervious to human desire. Things have a way of being what they are whether we like it or not. A person who pretends otherwise and does not seek an accurate representation of his world is likely to make very painful mistakes. He will refuse to acknowledge the existence of walls and will probably walk straight into one.

Cognitive errors can be made for various reasons. Among these are the impositions of others, the limited experience of an individual, and simple mistakes. When someone tells a person something is so when it isn't (or vice versa), the false view may nonetheless persist. This is especially so when the other is a person in authority, such as a parent. An infant has little choice but to believe his parents. If they label him stupid, or claim that their actions are in his interests when they aren't, how can he dispute them? If he believes—and he probably will—then an error of fact imposed upon him by another can persuade him to cling to the very persons who are causing him injury. Another source of error is the limitations of human experience. The world is a big place and there is more to know than any one individual can grasp. Each of us explores the vastness of the universe from his own tiny perspective. No wonder then that we are sometimes wrong. It is easy to add up two and two to get five. Yet the most serious problem is not that error is so easy, but that an intensity of a commitment may prevent remedying a mistake. It is the error which is impervious to correction that is the most dangerous.

Volitions too can point in the wrong direction. The plans a person makes can simply be ill-equipped to do the job to which they are assigned. Someone can adopt a particular value because he thinks it will lead to love when in fact it won't. As long as he persists in this direction, he reduces his chance of love. If he wants to succeed, he may have to choose a different direction and embrace different values. As with cognitions, faulty volitions can be imposed by the demands of others. Thus a parent may require a child to dedicate himself to others. This sort of caretaker morality, if it does not also include care for the self, can induce the child to work against his own interests. Given his relative weakness, he may not be able to resist since the consequence of rejecting his parent's errant value may be more painful than acceding to it.

Poor volitional decisions also result from a person's limited experience. The world is just as big when one is trying to maneuver within it as when one is trying to understand it. The number of options one faces is truly staggering. Moreover, the world does not guarantee that any specific course will succeed. Every time someone decides upon a particular action, the circumstances in which he acts must of necessity be different than those at other times. The causal chains in the world are so ramified that exact predictions are impossible. Some mistakes simply cannot be avoided. And the less experience one has, the more errors are to be expected. While this is troublesome, it is not disastrous as long as volitional decisions are flexible. As long as the intensity of a volitional commitment does not interfere with correcting errors, they can even be a source of valuable learning.

Mistakes in understanding and planning that block role change usually have their origin in coercive role negotiations. It is excessive force, more than anything else, that cultivates cognitions and volitions that are faulty in their direction and intensity. Coercion blinds us to reality and motivates the adoption of erroneous solutions. It does not allow the time or freedom to discover the truth or to evolve satisfying strategies for living.

Common Cognitive Errors

Many of the misunderstandings people have about the world are unique to themselves, but some lapses are quite standard. Errors occur in patterns. The ways we react when defending ourselves against coercive manipulations follow common pathways. For instance, some errors are mistakes about what is possible. People often incorrectly identify the way the world is constructed and how it can be manipulated. When this sort of mistake is made, we believe that something can be done when it can't, or that it can't when it can. Either way, a misinterpretation provokes an errant coping strategy. Another sort of error is that of exclusion/distortion. This depends upon refusing to see what exists, or actively misperceiving it. It is the sort of mistake that occurs when the psychological defenses are misused. When it arises, a person is denied vital information. He becomes a blind man groping through a maze.

Omnipotence. There is an apparently inborn cognitive tendency (misleadingly labeled "omnipotence" (Freud 1959)) which, when present, systematically misleads us about our capabilities. It causes us to believe that we are responsible for things over which we have no control. A person (often a child) who feels omnipotent is certain that he is the cause of most things going wrong, and that he has the power to set them to rights if he so chooses. But this is a misapprehension, for he almost never has the possibility of doing what he feels he must.

Babies have sometimes been imagined to believe themselves capable of accomplishing anything they want. The image that is conjured up is of an infant whose cries bring instant gratification, and hence who thinks he has effortlessly controlled the outcome. In fact, babies are quite helpless and exquisitely aware of this. If they exclude a recognition of their true state from consciousness, it is not because they feel omnipotent, but because they don't. Nevertheless, infants do have a bias toward believing themselves responsible for much of what happens in their world; in particular, they tend to greatly overestimate their role as a causal agent. Thus a child may indeed think he is the reason mommy entered or left his room, when in fact no connection exists. It is this tendency that convinces the young (and some adults) that their mistakes are the cause of another's unhappiness.

Infants are not born understanding the complexities of social causation. These things need to be learned. Such facts may be difficult to grasp, but are essential to fair role negotiations. If an equitable bargain is to be struck, it is imperative that each party know who is responsible for what. Each must know what he has done, or can do, before committing himself to what he will do. The child who mistakenly believes he is the cause of a problem that he didn't really initiate may undertake commitments he shouldn't make, and that won't make him happy. Thus he may have to learn that it was his partner who was at fault and hence he who must change. For example, a child who mistakenly believes himself responsible for his father's rage may unnecessarily undertake to be a good boy who won't provoke daddy, when, in fact, daddy was made furious by something totally out of the child's control, and it is daddy who needs to control himself.

Should a child's sense of omnipotence survive into adulthood, he will be at a terrible disadvantage relative to his peers. When others point an accusatory finger at him, he will be only too ready to concur. If he is trapped in a dysfunctional role, he may be convinced that it is all his fault, and hence there is nothing that can be done about his plight because his evil nature simply makes failure inevitable. Or if he is renegotiating a role, his partner may easily persuade him that he must make concessions. After all, wasn't it his selfishness that spoiled previous bargains?

The tendency of children, and some adults, to hold themselves responsible for too much does have a positive side. An exaggerated sense of responsibility provides much of the motivation for self-improvement. It focuses attention on something that is in one's control, namely, the self. Certainly this tendency toward excessive responsibility simplifies the task of socializing children, since it predisposes them to comply with social demands. And if these demands are reasonable, the formation of a viable role structure is promoted. If not, a child's mistakes in causal attribution can trap him in some very bad roles. When these mistakes extend into adulthood, as they often do, they make it more difficult for a person to understand what went wrong in his earlier socialization, or to correct it.

Self-Image. Perhaps the most crucial cognitive structure for role formation is the self-image. Role behavior requires not only an understanding of the world, but of the self as well. The kind of roles one can have depends upon the kind of person one is. An assertive person will do better in one sort of relationship, an athletic one in another, and a beautiful one in a third. When people make deals about roles, they compare their relative assets to see who should do what (Festinger 1954; Whyte 1943). How each is perceived influences the role assigned. If one is judged too clumsy to drive an automobile, then the specialty of driver may be denied her. Indeed, a person may rule herself out of such a task. Yet the assessment of personal attributes is no more definitive than the assessment of any other fact of the world. All are subject to interpretation, and consequently to misinterpretation.

Since a person's own understanding of her attributes, namely, her self-image, guides her in role negotiations, it will help her decide what demands are feasible and what concessions necessary. If her self-image is badly askew, these demands and concessions will be misplaced, and her roles dysfunctional. Unfortunately, it is very easy to be mistaken about ourselves, and hence distorted self-images are a major cause of bad roles and disrupted resocialization.

Despite the fact that notions about the self are crucial to happiness, they are not solely, or even fundamentally, of our own construction. Like so many other ostensibly personal things, self-images are largely social products. Cooley (1956) spoke of the "looking glass self." His thesis was that people learn about themselves by observing how others judge them. Quite literally, people see themselves reflected in others' eyes. A glint of anger will tell someone when she is bad, or a spark of love that she is good. The parental judgment that "Joe doesn't know how to handle money" may harden into a fact that even Joe accepts. Indeed, it may become part of him, and whenever the subject of money comes up he may demur because he knows he's not skilled with it.

Role partners may be accurate in their assessments, but then again they may not. Since they are unlikely to be disinterested bystanders, there is some probability that their judgments will be biased. Whether or not the other's point of view is distorted may be difficult to determine. Yet the further wrong it is, the more important it will be for a person to know the truth. Of course, everyone's self-image is mistaken to some extent. Errors creep in from both the self and the other. Still, serious problems arise only when image distortions are large enough to warp role negotiations and role change processes.

When an erroneous self-image critically disrupts resocialization, a way must be found to correct it. If, for instance, a person's conviction that she is helpless dissuades her from letting go of a dysfunctional role, she must learn that she does have competence. She must realize that she can face the depression of role change without being destroyed. In order for this modification in self-image to occur, she will probably need role partners who take a more optimistic view of her. If some other person can reflect her more capable features, she may come to see that she has more options than she thought. She will probably also need the strength to discount the estimations of biased role partners. If these others are out of touch with reality, or unfriendly, she must be clear-sighted enough to recognize this. It takes courage to resist another's mistakes, but significant others are only human and must sometimes be resisted. The more stalwart a person is in appraising herself and others, the less need she will have to accept their judgments wholesale.

Untoward Defenses. Psychological defenses protect people from being overwhelmed by terror, but they also exclude a great deal of vital information. When an environment is too painful, too frightening, or too frustrating, it is often wise to shut one's eyes to offending stimuli. A case in point is that heart attack victims who deny the seriousness of their affliction may actually recover more quickly (Dorpat 1985). Nevertheless, if one excludes too much, or distorts too much, one is apt to suffer negative consequences.

The classical defense mechanisms brought to public awareness by Anna Freud (1966) are a normal part of daily living. Ordinary social intercourse would not be possible without the conventional use of denial, repression, or suppression. Refusing to acknowledge the worst keeps workaday terrors and frictions at a minimum. However, overuse of these mechanisms causes problems. The person who refuses to see anything painful will sooner or later trip over his own feet. More to the point, someone trapped in a dysfunctional role who never allows himself to recognize the source of his distress condemns himself to perpetuating it. The lacuna in his world view becomes a gaping maw into which he may someday disappear. When someone becomes entangled in the repetition compulsion, it is often because he does not know he is repeating the past. People who remarry replicas of the same spouse do not learn from history because they do not allow themselves to perceive it. They travel through life like sleepwalkers staggering from one catastrophe to the next. Were they slightly less defensive, they would be better defended.

Another sort of defense is that which distorts rather than denies. This kind of mechanism, which is exemplified by projection and rationalization, does not completely eliminate information; it merely misinterprets it. In the case of projection, a person misattributes an action, judgment, or thought. Instead of acknowledging what the self has done, it is presumed to be caused by others. In the case of rationalization, one invents reasons for doing things that differ from one's actual motives. These justifications usually have greater social acceptability than the real ones, and hence are more palatable to the self and others. In either event, reality is veiled and a fabrication is put in its place. But just as with denial and repression, if a person is never able to penetrate his own masks, he is condemned to attempt resocialization under a handicap.

Common Volitional Errors

The action schemas that result from volitional decisions can be roughly classified as either ends or means. The former may be labeled values, moralities, commitments, or goals; the latter may be dubbed norms, rules, strategies, or tactics. Though these categories sometimes overlap, and means do become ends in themselves, the distinction has merit. It highlights aspects of planning that are often separately developed, and that require separate attention.

An obdurate dedication to either ends or means can interfere with resocialization. The person who is too determined to do things in a particular way is likely to have difficulty in changing his role structures. Whether it is a goal he refuses to give up, or a strategy he declines to alter, his commitments prevent him from accepting change when it is necessary. They hinder him from recognizing when a role has gone wrong, letting go of it, or considering alternative options.

As has been pointed out, very intense and misdirected volitional commitments often evolve from faulty role negotiations. Values and strategies that don't work, yet remain active, have usually developed during the course of coercive negotiations. When a role partner aggressively demands a particular course of action, it is easy for a person to accept wrong choices, and then to hold on to them tenaciously. Someone who is forced to be a caretaker may have no recourse but to acquiesce in the values that go along with caretaking. He may conclude that it is good to give uncritical love. Moreover, since caretaking may seem to him the only way he can obtain love, he may come to accept this value with unfeigned intensity. He will then refuse to recognize that a caretaker role is causing his pain. Neither will he acknowledge that there exist other roles that might better meet his needs. In short, his commitments induce him to reject the possibility of role change.

Defective Values. The world presents infinite possibilities. Before a person can act, he must be able to choose between them. His options need to be narrowed down to a do-able few. Internal standards help limit his alternatives. Indeed, this is the very purpose of values. They are personal and/or cultural criteria used for decision-making. When one is in place, it is used to select between types of relationship, objects of consumption, and physical activities. If it is good value, it leads to good choices; if a poor one, to unsatisfied needs.

Of the value systems one can employ, morality is of critical import. Moral values are a particularly intense form of commitment. They do not merely say that such and such would be nice; they insist that it must be done. There is an imperative quality to morality that makes its decisions notoriously difficult to alter or examine. This is especially true when morality spills over into moralism. In such cases, a commitment

to poor values such as perfectionism, uncritical love, and non-asser-
tiveness takes on the force of law. One is forcefully enjoined never to
make mistakes, to always love everyone, and never to state one's case
too vigorously. If one does, one is wrong, bad, or evil.

The reason morality, and particularly moralism, is so difficult to challenge is that moral values are inherently linked to emotions. Anger,
guilt, and shame pervade morality. They animate its directions and
give it its imperative quality. When people say to someone, "You are
wrong" they are in effect saying: "We are very angry with you for
what you are doing, and everyone else is angry too. So Stop! Now!"
Blame is essentially the expression of a potentially universal outrage. It
contains veiled threats of sanction wrapped in a civilized exterior.

Morality is an institutionalization of anger, guilt, and shame. It co-
ordinates social wrath and gives it structure. This means that when
something is deemed bad or wrong, it is considered emotively bad or
wrong for everyone. Should this institutionalized emotion become too
potent, one enters the realm of moralism. In this situation, feelings run
so deeply that opposing them becomes problematic. The anger of moralism is both blind and implacable, and is capable of causing no end of
personal difficulties.

Normal morality also draws the magnitude of its power from the
universality of its anger. A person who is condemned as bad has the
weight of the world descend on his head. He is in effect being warned
that he has to contend with everyone's anger, not just that of the person confronting him. Similarly, when individuals are urged to judge
that an action is wrong, an appeal is being made for them to join a
universal consensus of condemnation. The object of the exercise is to
enforce compliance—now and for always—to regulations that are deemed
particularly important to a whole community. Opposing morality, or
moralism, is extremely difficult because it entails defying this community. It is not just one person who must be contradicted, but an interlocking society of potentially hostile people. If someone wants to challenge strongly held moral judgments, he has to contend not only with
the conservatism of his own guilt, but with that of group anger. When
he stands up to say "No," he invites the wrath of the humanity to
crash down on him.

The moral consensus that enforces particular moral values is achieved
in two ways. It develops out of an appeal to either tradition or consequences. Morality has a dual nature. It is both categorical and utilitarian. The first of these aspects, the categorical, is what makes morality
seem beyond challenge. It is what has persuaded many philosophers
(Kant 1949) to describe it as emanating from natural law. They take it
as a given which is found and obeyed, not as something that can be
examined or altered. The utilitarian aspect, on the other hand, is con-

cerned with satisfying human interests. It insists that things are good if they meet human needs, and bad if they don't. In its classic expression, utilitarianism calls for "the greatest happiness for the greatest number" (Lyons 1965). Its adherents believe that consequences count. Acceptance of this outlook makes moral values negotiable. If a person can be convinced that he has made a mistake in the calculation of utility, then presumably he must be prepared to change his values. Consensus is thus understood as a prediction of utility, and not a reflection of God's will.

Historically, philosophers have pitted these two outlooks against each other. It has been assumed that morality must be either categorical or utilitarian. The debate has been about which of these views is the correct one. In reality, both are correct. People of necessity use both in making moral distinctions. There is no contradiction between them because they derive from different parts of human experience. Indeed, both must be present since morality without a dash of absolutism has no force, while absolutism that is not tempered by utility has no heart.

Categorical values originate in early childhood. Young children see everything as black or white. They are very literal in their interpretation of the world, and once they believe something to be true, they conceive of it as absolute. Read a child a story once, and it must forever be read the same way. Any changes in its rendition will strike him as wrong. Piaget (1965) has shown that young children take a similar attitude toward moral values. They may not fully comprehend why something is right or wrong, but they consider such judgments chiseled in stone. What is wrong, is *wrong!* The child who spills his milk on the floor will judge himself to be bad despite mitigating circumstances.

This attitude about the inviolability of moral values is imported into adulthood, and as such takes on the mantle of principled action. In large part, it is principles that provide the stability for morality. "Stealing is wrong!" "Murder is bad!" These are enduring values that derive from childhood and form the core of adult morality. To be sure, they must be reinterpreted to meet the complexities of adult life; there will, for instance, be questions about whether self-defense is really murder, or whether killing in war is allowable. Nevertheless, such values possess an appearance of immutability, and hence retain an authority that brings order out of chaos. They are the eternal verities to which an appeal can always be made, and which are always capable of validating specific decisions. As long as these truths are also open to revision by considerations of need, they can dictate very credible decisions.

When the anger of morality is directed at young children, it serves to rivet particular values in place. Children have a harder time coping with anger than do adults since they have fewer resources with which to resist it. In consequence, they are more apt to accept values that are imposed upon them. They may also acquire an intense guilt which makes these values persistent. Thus when a child is forced to be the "good one" or the "unselfish one," he will maintain the values attendant upon these roles as an adult. If his socialization was too coercive, they will become rigid, and can make subsequent resocialization very frightening. Changing such values will entail confronting overpowering guilt, anger, and shame. Should he try, the demands of childhood role partners will be reawakened and reexperienced as if he were still a child. He will then discover that the ancient terrors retain all their primal ferocity.

Utilitarian values, in contrast, originate much later than the categorical. They presuppose an ability to engage in cooperative endeavors with peers. Piaget (1965) describes how children gradually learn through their play that the rules of games are subject to alteration. It is only as teenagers, when they have sufficiently acquired the skills and knowledge to participate in the negotiation of rules and values, that a utilitarian perspective becomes genuinely operative. It is at this age that considerations of what works and what doesn't come into full play, when value decisions become genuinely cognizant of individual needs.

But an adult who is able to apply utilitarian considerations must have the competence to do so. He must not be so overwhelmed by a rigid moralism acquired in his childhood that he cannot contemplate the specific impact of his actions upon his needs. Neither should he be so intimidated that he cannot challenge the misjudgments of others. The child who has learned morality in an environment saturated by excessive force may as an adult find it difficult to assert himself during value negotiations. He will not have acquired the personal strength necessary for confronting his peers. Their assertions will still feel too devastating. As an adult, he may prefer to make his stand allied with traditional authorities, rather than consider what is best in the here and now. In this case, his too exclusive attachment to categorical values will deprive him of the flexibility to tailor his values to meet current circumstances. This is why the person trapped in moralism often finds himself trapped in dysfunctional roles as well.

Defective Strategies. The rules that guide behaviors come in many shapes. They can be imposed by society as social norms and laws, or can be individually designed as strategies and tactics. In either case, they are formulae that provide the way to do things. Without them, behaviors would be random and ineffectual. Most goals cannot be realized unless pursued in a rational and organized fashion. This is especially true for objectives requiring interpersonal cooperation. Rules are one of the mechanisms that coordinate behaviors. Consider how impossible it would be to assume the role of baseball pitcher unless one were playing in conjunction with others, all of whom more or less followed the same guidelines.

When personal and social rules are good ones, they facilitate the attainment of goals and, ultimately, the satisfaction of needs. When they are not, roles become dysfunctional. If rules are rigid, mistakes made are difficult to correct. Coercion is often the route through which poorly conceived, but steadfastly maintained, strategies enter a person's role repertoire. When confronted with a threatening role partner (especially in childhood), a person may rush to find some response. Even a bad plan of action will then exact allegiance because at the moment it seems the only way of coping. Once it acquires the virtue of familiarity, it also provides a comforting illusion of control.

Professional resocializers often encounter clients committed to dysfunctional rules. Albert Ellis (Ellis and Grieger 1977) has labeled many of these "irrational ideas." Certainly the "ideas" to which he alludes do not work. Although Ellis believes he is dealing with straightforward cognitions, he has correctly identified some very lame interpersonal strategies. One of these is the belief that "it is absolutely essential for an individual to be loved or approved by every significant person in his environment." Ellis then points out that "while it is desirable for individuals to be loved, the idea is irrational because it is impossible to be loved or approved by everyone and striving to attain the goal leads to behavior that is not self-directing." The idea of striving for everyone's love is a coping strategy that is indeed foolish. Anyone who attempts it will soon discover that different role partners have different requirements, not all of which can be satisfied. Also, some people are incapable of love. Trying to please them is seeking blood from the proverbial stone. It can't be done.

Another of Ellis' irrational ideas is that "it is necessary that each individual be completely competent, adequate, and achieving if the individual is to be worthwhile." He then points out that

it is impossible for any individual to be competent in every endeavor and an individual who feels he must is doomed to a sense of failure. Such an idea also leads a person to view every situation in competitive terms. Such an individual strives to beat others rather than simply enjoying the activity itself.

Again Ellis is correct in condemning perfectionism and excessive competitiveness as poor strategies. Making mistakes is part of living, and so is cooperation; people learn from mistakes and benefit from help. A person seeking to live an error-free life in total independence is courting a narrow, contradictory, and confused existence. He will be trying to win using tools more suited to defeat.

The question of why anyone would make such ill-advised strategic decisions is an important one. As may be supposed, they flow almost logically from coercive role negotiations. Thus a person whose parents deny him love may quite reasonably conclude that love is so important, and so problematic, that he must seek it everywhere. Or a person whose parents criticize him unmercifully may be convinced that his only salvation lies in never making mistakes. Finally, a coercive interpersonal environment can easily persuade someone that it is poor policy ever to be dependent on anyone. It may seem that the only way to keep others at bay is to engage in unremitting and universal competition.

Some of Anna Freud's (1966) defense mechanisms are also bad rules for living. The strategy she calls "identification with the aggressor" is one such. Sometimes, in order to protect oneself from a punitive role partner, a person may be tempted to take that partner's side. This is why some inmates of Nazi concentration camps identified with their guards and accepted jobs controlling their fellow inmates. It is also why some children identify with their punitive parents and want to be just like them. This identification can be so strong that they punish themselves just as their parents might. While such a strategy may protect them from some suffering, it has the difficulty of exposing them to a more virulent torture at their own hands.

Sublimation, another of the Freudian defenses and another strategy for living, can have both positive and negative consequences. It is a technique for turning antisocial instincts into prosocial actions. As an example, the anger one feels toward society can instead be used to protect it. Some sublimations do, in fact, function quite well. They indeed facilitate the satisfaction of needs. Some, however, are accomplished at too great a sacrifice to the self. Thus some people sublimate their hostilities by trying to take care of everyone. They become universal caretakers dedicated to serving everyone's needs—everyone, that is, except themselves.

Reaction formation too can be a strategy that misfires. In an attempt to be the opposite of a coercive role partner, many people go too far. Instead of being like a selfish parent, a child may try to be so unselfish that in the end he is the one who is hurt. Or he can hate parental violence so passionately that he adopts a passive strategy that invites attack by every unscrupulous person he meets. If reaction formation is to suffice, it must not be blind or total.

To reiterate, then, dysfunctional action schemas can block resocialization in several ways. (1) They may make it difficult to recognize or reexperience dysfunctional roles. A failed role may seem to be the only way to do things. An exaggerated commitment to a particular style of problem solving may make alternatives inconceivable and hence discourage the reexperiencing of failed roles. (2) They confuse a person's notions of what is possible. During the protest phase of role change they may give him a mistaken idea of what can be salvaged from the past. Such a person may be encouraged to fight too hard for bargains that are only chimeras. (3) They direct renegotiations along unprofitable paths. Perfectionism, unrestricted love, super-competitiveness, reaction formations, and identification with an aggressor may propel a person to make a deal that is not in his interest.

When mistaken cognitions or bad volitional commitments interfere with role change, it may be necessary to turn back the clock. The effects of the coercive relationships that encouraged ineffectual set solutions must be reversed. A person needs to be allowed the space to correct the intensity and direction of his detrimental understandings and plans. He may even benefit from the help of someone who can point him along more productive avenues. A resocializer is in a position to do this for his client by providing him with the safety from which he can challenge unfortunate ideas and commitments. He may even help his client develop the courage to stand up to the coercive demands of others. Equally important, a resocializer can provide fair validation. He can honestly let a person know when he has correctly perceived his world and when he has not, or when he is subscribing to a viable action schema and when not. This validation process can extend to the person himself. The clinician can help his client to understand that he has rights too, that he has the prerogative of pursuing his interests as much as do his role partners. This includes his right to see things as they are and to pursue goals in an efficacious manner.

6

Social Aspects of Role Change

ONGOING COERCION

Social coercion is not something that happens at one point in time, and then ends. Unlike Freud's early idea of trauma, the coercive relationships that launch dysfunctional roles do not disappear once roles have been set in place. Almost always, they survive to maintain them and to interfere with attempts at change. Coercive role partners, or their surrogates, tend to continue their use of excessive force, and their demands require a defensive reaction on the part of the subject.

Human society forms an enduring web of demands and counter-demands. The opportunity for ongoing coercion is ubiquitous. There are always some partners who insist that a person do something that is contrary to his interests. They expect him to enact behaviors that do not meet his needs, and will not abide his efforts to achieve alternative solutions. The person will then have to find at least one way to counteract these pressures. If he does not, he will have to accede to their requirements. Unfortunately, this is often the case. Indeed, it is often a person's struggle to resist these impositions that prevents productive change.

Intensity and Direction

The coercive demands imposed by role partners may be wrong in both their intensity and direction. Like other script elements, social expectations can be too strong or weak, or misguided in their goals. Coercion has been defined as excessive force and its equivalents; this means it involves an exorbitant use of power, the recipient of which is permitted no choice. Either its intensity is so extreme that it terrifies a person into compliance, or it constitutes an implacable withdrawal so complete that no plea for reengagement is possible. Whichever the case, whether there is an imposition of pain or arrant neglect, coercion denies a person the possibility of winning. Its intensity simply brooks no effective counter-measures.

When irresistible demands impose behaviors that do not meet needs, that is, when the direction of coercion is mistaken, the roles maintained will be dysfunctional. A role partner may, for instance, require that a person be a caretaker. Instead of allowing him to consider his own needs, coercion will be used to enforce actions that meet only the needs of the other. If the direction of a demand is self-contradictory as in a double bind, or cruel as when a person is required to be a scapegoat, or merely foolish as when it requests perfection, someone who attempts to comply will surely lose. He will be forced to do things that do not meet his needs. And if he does not find a different direction to pursue, he is bound to remain unsatisfied. Acceding to such a misdirected demand can not bring him fulfillment, but only grief.

Reactions to Coercion

Coercion imposes script elements that do not meet needs and/or interfere with change. The reaction to excessive or misdirected force is the creation of emotions, cognitions, and volitions that are both defective and difficult to modify. Whether these internalized elements were elicited during original role negotiations, ongoing role enactments, or attempts at resocialization, is of less importance than their continued presence. However they have been aroused, they make it difficult to reexperience, relinquish, or renegotiate dysfunctional roles. They prevent a person from correcting what has gone wrong in his role repertoire.

As has been previously indicated, coercive demands elicit, and are often intended to elicit, fear. If this emotion is intense or misdirected, it can impede change just as surely as can any intense fear. Similarly, coercion can provoke extreme anger. It can motivate a person to fight back so vigorously that he defeats his own purposes. If this anger is turned inward, it can become compulsive guilt with all the negative effects such self-blame entails. Should coercion take the form of ridicule, it will be shame that is provoked. A person may therefore be induced to withdraw from interaction when there is no reason to conceal himself. An excess of force can even instigate misguided love. Thus severe neglect or abandonment can induce a person to embark on the passionate pursuit of an unworthy role partner; that is, his intense needs can encourage him to yearn for nonviable attachments. All of these emotional reactions may be intended as protective, but actually militate against a person's interests.

Coercion also triggers cognitive and volitional mistakes. A person can be forced into misapprehending his world. At the insistence of another, he can make errors about the nature of his environment or the consequences of his actions. When a role partner, for instance, asserts that a person is weak or stupid, it may be difficult for him to disagree, especially if he is vulnerable and the other seems certain. Or if a role partner stipulates that universal unselfishness is the only way to act, enlightened self-interest may seem an unconscionable form of personal indulgence. Instead of contemplating courses of action that are both feasible and satisfying, he will be intimidated into renouncing his best choices.

An especially pernicious form of volitional error occurs in what have been labeled "personality disorders." These are aberrant role negotiation strategies that develop in reaction to persistently coercive socialization. They are ways of interacting with other people which are so inimical to a person's self-interests that they have been mistaken for diseases. In reality, they are spectacularly unsuccessful attempts to counter coercion. Rather than facilitating the construction of satisfying roles, as intended, they antagonize role partners and cripple role change processes. It is because they lead to misery, not happiness, that they can be confused with illness.

Coercion and Change

Persons attempting resocialization do not live in isolation. Coercion can intrude directly into role change processes. Those who are trapped in dysfunctional roles have families, friends, and colleagues who are interested in their behavior patterns. They are also surrounded by strangers, enemies, and such anonymous role partners as the news and entertainment media. Many of these associates are supportive or indifferent, but others are passionately concerned with imposing their own aspirations. If they perceive that a person's projected changes are against their interests, they may ardently oppose them. To work their will, they can use persuasion, intimidation, manipulations, bribes, flattery, or whatever tools are at hand. It may be their goal to mandate that a person not change, or if he does, that it be in direction they have stipulated.

Reexperience. Conflicts with role partners can intrude during any stage of the resocialization cycle. During the reexperiencing phase, coercion can make it impossible for a person to allow a dysfunctional role to invade consciousness. A role partner can positively forbid her to recognize her role performance or its consequences. If, let us say, she is a caretaker and is in a relationship with a martyr, the latter may not allow her to recognize how much she is giving or how little she is receiving in return. A martyr will insist that he is doing all the giving and that the caretaker is merely being selfish. He will say, "See how much I sacrifice. It is my needs that are not being met, not yours." And the caretaker, who has heard this refrain many times before, will be cowed into agreement. Her partner's coercive manipulation will blind her to the true situation, and she will not be able to experience its reality.

An unscrupulous other can accomplish the same end by utilizing intimidation. A person who is very frightened will be so busy protecting herself that she will have no inclination or energy to reexperience a dysfunctional role. Fear will so fill her senses that she will not be able to distinguish what is causing her pain; neither will she want to. Her sole concern will be neutralizing the current danger, not reversing the effects of historic dangers.

Letting Go. When a person enters the grieving process, a coercive role partner can turn normal protest into unending warfare. If a current partner engages the anger trapped in a person's dysfunctional role scripts within a contemporary dispute, he makes it more difficult for the person to extricate herself from old battles. Ordinarily, protests aimed at past injustices are discovered for what they are and are eventually doomed because their objective will be found to be beyond reach. When, however, one's arguments offer the illusion of being with current antagonists, there seems to be more hope of success, and a person won't give up her fight because it won't seem useless. The provocation that is directly before her eyes deflects her attention and impairs her ability to detect the futility of her quest. The very real anger emanating from the other fans her emotions and she has no time to cool down and consider her situation.

If another person offers the prospect of correcting old role bargains, letting go can also become problematic. The current partner makes it seem possible to undo the damage done by previous role partners, but the person will not realize that even if a deal is reached, the past remains untouched. An even worse outcome may transpire when a present partner remains intractable. If instead of negotiating a workable settlement, he insists that the person "do this" and "don't do that," bargaining may become interminable. Rather than moving on to relinquish a bad deal, the role changer puts all her energies into persuading the other to reconsider his position and will not herself recognize what she has lost.

Letting go can also be interrupted by the fears induced by a coercive other. The sadness inherent in role change is intrinsically dangerous since its intensity can feel like death. Consequently, a person won't let it happen when she is already extremely frightened. This is why external threats can tip the balance: if they are terrifying enough, they exacerbate an already difficult situation. The fears aroused make sadness seem too perilous, and hence intolerable. But in not tolerating sorrow, a person may unintentionally interdict change. Her disinclination to be depressed can impede her ability to relinquish failed roles. If a role partner further instructs her that it is her duty to cheer up, she may be given a rationalization for not accepting her pain. When the other says, "Forget the past, you don't need to dig it up," she may gratefully agree.

Renegotiating. Antagonistic role partners can disrupt the renegotiation stage of role change as well. They may insist that a person return to a dysfunctional role and give up this nonsense about trying to do things differently. Like the spouse of the alcoholic who urges sobriety when he is drunk but has a bottle on the table when he comes home from the detoxification center, others may be more comfortable with the old ways. Be it by bluster or deception, they will attempt to maneuver new role negotiations into producing familiar results.

Sometimes a coercive role partner may offer to act as an honest broker. He presents himself as someone who is willing to be part of new role arrangements, and then breaks faith. It is not unknown for protestations of friendship to mask treachery. Successful role negotiations depend upon true cooperation, and it is precisely this cooperation that coercive partners withhold. Coercion forces a decision rather than allowing solutions to evolve through a reciprocal exchange of proposals and adjustments. A problem-solving attitude that favors the construction of truly satisfying roles is conspicuously absent from these relationships.

NEGOTIATIONS: FAIR AND UNFAIR

One way to elucidate the pitfalls of coercive role negotiations is to contrast them with fair ones. When the power distribution between two people is relatively equal, there is a good chance that the input of both will affect the final outcome. If, however, power is unequal, there is an ever-present temptation for one to overawe the other. Given the inequality that exists in society and is an ineradicable part of family life, such snares are unavoidable. It is therefore necessary to understand how to arrange fairness despite inherent inequalities.

Pruitt's Dual-Concern Model

In the case of relatively equal contestants, Dean Pruitt's dual-concern negotiating model (1981) has many advantages for role bargainers. His two-party model is based upon the assumption that the best solution to a negotiation is the one that maximizes the interests of both parties while simultaneously minimizing their respective costs. He postulates that both parties have interests to be upheld and that how these are asserted affects the outcome. Pruitt suggests four possible permutations on how a person can approach negotiations. He can be concerned with:

1. Only his interests. In this case his most rational strategy is to contend as vigorously as he can. By pushing as hard as possible for all the concessions he can get, he may be able to maximize his outcomes.

2. Primarily the interests of his partner. If this is his goal, his best strategy is to yield. By allowing the partner to have whatever he wants, the partner's aims can be maximized.

3. The interests of both himself and his partner. In this insistence, his most sensible option is to engage in problem solving. If he and his partner can work together, they may be able to maximize the interests of both. A joint effort to seek creative solutions can result in the optimum outcome.

4. Neither his interests nor those of the other. This goal suggests a do-nothing strategy. A person who doesn't care what happens can sensibly resort to inaction. He can simply allow events to follow their natural course.

Of these four strategies, only the third is non-coercive. Each of the others relies upon some form of coercion.

Coercive Strategies. Contending which is not informed by a consideration of the interests of the other slides easily into barbarism. If an anything-goes philosophy prevails in the quest of one's own interests, then it does not matter whether the other is injured. His pain does not enter one's calculations, and so it is likely to be quite substantial. Pure contending judges the advantage of using force solely upon the consequences for ego, and the other be damned.

Yielding may not seem to have such dire repercussions, but this view is misleading. Allowing the other to have whatever he wants licenses his use of unlimited coercion. If he can contend as he sees fit, then he does not need to calculate the pain of his role partners. The result is liable to be excessive force in the opposite direction. As a practical matter, inaction is equivalent to yielding. A person who remains passive, like the one who yields, allows the other whatever he wants, except cooperation. The other is permitted to be coercive, but not to have a partner who is actively helpful. He is effectively abandoned and must shift for himself. His attempts to elicit teamwork will come to nothing and, despite what he can extort from the subject, he will lose.

Problem Solving. The appropriate strategy for fair negotiations is obviously problem solving. It is the only one that takes fair account of the interests of both parties. Since the most painful of dysfunctional roles are both basic and personal, simultaneous consideration of the self and other is paramount. The roles that form the central part of a person's identity, and upon which so many other roles depend, are fashioned in intensely intimate relationships. These relationships are inherently close and long term. This means that if the other's interests are not also considered, he will probably discover this and be in a position to take revenge. Intimate role partners who are aggrieved invariably want to renegotiate deals. They understandably demand a recision of bargains to which they have not contributed and from which they derive no benefit.

When problem solving is chosen as the suitable negotiating strategy, each side must be prepared to stand up for his own interests, but also be willing to make requisite adjustments. Pruitt calls this posture "firm flexibility." The firmness to which he alludes implies that each party must be prepared to contend for his own interests. Only then can his role partner be satisfactorily informed of the importance he attaches to particular issues. It is the firm, clear assertion of someone's needs that places them on the bargaining table; it is this that makes them visible and urgent. Yet it must be noted that to be assertive is not to be blindly aggressive. The goal is to influence, not injure.

As important as it is for each negotiator to be serious about achieving his interests, it is equally important for him to be flexible about the means he uses to achieve them. Neither party to a bargain should be so attached to a particular plan that he cannot consider alternatives that are superior. The purpose of role negotiations is to meet needs, not to win debating points. Mechanisms for implementing goals should not depend upon who proposes what, but upon what works for whom.

Since role negotiations concern the needs of both parties, it is incumbent upon both to know and appreciate their separate and joint interests. First and foremost, each must know his own needs so that he can intelligently pursue them. But when a person is trapped in dysfunctional roles, these needs may not be obvious to him. Coercive role negotiations may have forced him to suppress an awareness of his own interests. He may have rightly feared that a consciousness of them would invite punishment. Thus, before he can know what he wants, he will have to lose his fear of his own desires.

In addition to his needs, each party must understand the needs of his partner. If the two are to engage in problem solving, it is greatly to their advantage to know how their respective interests can be made to mesh. Yet a person may be as unaware of his partner's needs as of his own. Often people are so bound up with themselves, or so frightened of the other, that an accurate assessment of his situation is impossible. A person who has survived coercive socialization is typically closed off and defensive. The pain he has sustained discourages him from getting too close to others, and the frustration he has endured concentrates his attention on his personal deficits. He is likely to be overinvolved with his own suffering, at the expense of a sympathetic understanding of the other.

Moreover, a person who has difficulty understanding himself will probably have difficulty in role taking. His lack of self-insight grievously damages his ability to see into another's soul. To a large extent, people comprehend others' interests only by analogy with their own. When this tool is unavailable, their insight is fatally disadvantaged. They simply do not perceive what the other wants or why. Yet the difficulty in understanding the interests of another individual may be even deeper than this. It is not sufficient to extrapolate from one's own position to appreciate that of a role partner. The other must also contribute to this process by communicating his needs. If he too is unaware of his purposes or is reluctant to share them, it may be impossible to discover them. This ignorance then acts as the equivalent of coercion and impedes successful problem solving. It forces people to act blindly and ineffectively.

Further complicating matters are secrecy and deceit. Ordinarily, negotiators do not share all of their cards with each other. There is so great a possibility that a partner will take an unfair advantage that negotiators put a premium on privacy. Unless people have a deep trust in one another, they have reason to be guarded. They know that others often engage in cheating in order to gain a competitive edge. How then can one be sure what another has up his sleeve? It may take considerable doing before a pair is certain that they are working together, and not at cross-purposes. This trust will be hard won, but without it, inadvertent coercion is inevitable.

When role partners have sufficient confidence in one another to engage in cooperative problem solving, they will have to choose between different problem-solving techniques. If they adopt integrative solutions that enhance their interests, both may prosper. Yet the best-known bargaining technique, namely, compromise, may not actually be their best option. It merely splits their differences and may not maximize interests. Among the other alternatives they should consider are (1) expanding the pie that they are dividing; (2) cutting each other's costs; (3) compensating one another for their losses; (4) bridging their differences; and (5) logrolling.

This last may be used as an example of how alternative solutions can maximize interests. Logrolling depends upon the fact that parties to a negotiation may not have the same values. Simple compromise may not give each the best mix of available goods. Thus if one partner likes eggs while the other prefers hot cereal, compromise dictates that each gets half the eggs and half the cereal. Logrolling, on the other hand, suggests that the one who prefers the eggs get all the eggs, while the other gets all the cereal. Good negotiating requires the same sort of mutuality and responsiveness as good parenting. It is not a zero-sum game in which if one wins, the other must lose. Coercion operates upon this premise; problem solving does not.

Unequal Negotiations

Unequal negotiations, in which one partner has substantially more power than the other, have more prospect of being coercive than problem solving. A parent or employer who knows he can work his will through threats or violence may be tempted to do so. In the best of all possible worlds this might not be so, but in ours it is. People are not always fair or cooperative. Often they exploit any advantage nature or chance has thrown their way. It is then incumbent upon the weaker party to find a method of protecting himself from negotiations that are stacked against him.

In unequal negotiations, the stronger partner has the option of not using firm flexibility. He can elect to be too firm or too flexible. If he wishes, he can force the other to behave in a particular way, or can show total indifference to what the other does or wants. He can decide that only his interests count. Finally, a more powerful person need not make any adjustments, let alone creative ones. For him, there is no necessity of using problem-solving techniques, and hence there is a smaller chance of solutions that maximize mutual interests. These circumstances militate against the weaker partner constructing satisfying roles, or changing dysfunctional patterns into more viable ones. The stronger can effectively forbid or sabotage his efforts. Therefore in order to develop more valid roles, he will have to find a way of neutralizing the other's power advantage.

Parent/Child Inequality. Parents have an overwhelming advantage vis-à-vis their children, especially very young children. If they so choose, they can ruthlessly exploit this disparity. It might seem that no parent would be so callous as to misuse his position, but many do. They all too eagerly invoke their greater physical strength, knowledge, and material resources to impose their desires.

The parent who is most likely to misuse his advantage is the one who is least aware that inequalities exist. Some parents conceive of themselves as superannuated children. In their mind's eye, they are small, weak victims who are being tyrannized by their offspring. When their child fights back, they fear that they will be the one overwhelmed. Rather than sustain this intolerable loss of dignity, they elect to crush their small opponent. Because they misjudge their own strength, they do more than win: they vanquish. Their child is swept away in an irresistible rush of power, and the parent prevails. But it is the child who pays. Indeed, it is from such hellishly unequal negotiations that most dysfunctional roles evolve.

Parents who recognize their relative strength can decide to be non-coercive. They can establish a kind of artificial equality between themselves and their children. They will allow themselves to perceive their child's weaknesses, and constrain themselves from utilizing all of their advantages. As their children grow and increase in power, they use more of their strengths in order to maintain equality. There develops a kind of "moving equilibrium," which permits both to have an input into their negotiations. In such an arrangement, parents deliberately listen to their children. In essence, they allow a problem-solving atmosphere to materialize, one that permits their children to participate as active partners.

Counteracting Coercion. Adult role changers whose early negotiations were particularly difficult are especially vulnerable to coercive role partners. When a powerful person in their present life makes forceful demands, they do not know how to fight back. Either they concede at the first sign of a vigorous assertion, or they bring excessive firepower to bear in even trivial disputes. In short, they are inclined to use either too little or too much force to resist all role partners. It is difficult for them to adjust their efforts, because in their anxiety to avoid defeat they misjudge their situation and resources. If a person is not to be panicked at the prospect of unequal power, it is crucial that he know how to defend himself. He must know how to endure the onslaughts of others, how to utilize his current powers most effectively, and how to increase his resources so that he may ultimately achieve equality. Coercion is not an unavoidable destiny; it can be counteracted and overcome.

Enduring. A role changer who encounters oppressive role partners can learn to endure. Instead of allowing a powerful other to prevail, he can find ways to reduce the injuries he sustains and to persevere. His situation may be unpleasant, even perilous, but in most cases he need not give up. If he does not lose sight of who he is or what his interests are, he can hang on, and one day it may be his turn to prevail. An old saw correctly reminds us that the race is not necessarily won by the strong or the swift, but the persistent. Endurance counts.

Perhaps the surest way to deflect an abusive role partner is to leave the relationship. A person who removes himself from the line of fire reduces his chances of being hit. Coercion is most easily borne when it is totally evaded. There is no special virtue in remaining in a relationship which results in injury; better to find a safer role partner. But removal from the scene may not always be realistic. Some relationships are not easily terminated. Thus child/parent bonds can not lightly be abrogated. There may, therefore, be cases in which it is necessary to give surface compliance to an overly powerful role partner. In these situations, overt resistance reaps only pain, and discretion becomes the better part of valor.

Apparent agreement today may prepare the way for effective disagreement tomorrow. The person who overtly says "yes" does not have to believe his words. He can remain loyal to his own interests while ostensibly acceding to the demands of the other. Neither need he attempt to achieve all his satisfactions by following the other's rules. If he can find alternate satisfactions, these may take the sting out of his forced compliance. The existence of pleasures that are independent of the coercive relationship may make coercion easier to bear. They will give him a source of needs fulfillment which partially alleviates the pain of acting against his interests elsewhere.

In any event, a person can take care not to identify himself with what he is forced to do. He may not be able to avoid engaging in particular role behaviors, but he does not have to make them part of his self-image. As long as he keeps a separate sense of self, coercive others can never win an absolute victory. There is no rule that requires that he always be honest with an oppressor. After all, it is the unfair role partner who benefits from his excessive openness. What is the point in making a bully's job easier than it needs to be? If the bully cannot verify compliance on his own, why should his victim simplify the task? Thus secrecy and deception which confuse an unfair partner are themselves valid. Playing fair with someone who does not, makes little sense.

Good Tactics. Enduring a bad situation is a relatively passive way of coping with unequal power. There are other more active stances a person can take. One of these is to make more effective use of the power she already possesses. Someone who uses her strengths intelligently can thereby reduce the power disparity between herself and her opponent. The amount of force at a person's disposal is not just a function of her resources, but also of how she uses them. It is not merely a matter of the number of battalions one has, but the tactics with which they are deployed. Military men know that it is not always the larger army that wins the battle. A general who is able to concentrate his troops at the right place, at the right moment, will usually prevail. He makes the most effective use of his power and multiplies its impact. For an individual, this means that she must at least choose a battlefield that is hospitable to her. Her resources will do her no good if she cannot bring them to bear.

Many people, when confronted with an overpowering role partner, make the mistake of challenging him on his own turf. If the partner threatens physical force, they feel duty bound to defend themselves physically; no matter that the other person is a foot taller and an iron man champion, while their advantage is a superior IQ and rapier wit. Because the other person has invited them out into the alley, they go. Of course, they also lose; but that is the price one pays for ignoring one's own talents.

Secrecy and deception have already been mentioned as techniques for evading a role partner's demands; they can also be used to produce a tactical advantage. Just as armies try to maintain a veil of secrecy over their movements to achieve battlefield surprise, so can an individual. If a role partner is abusing his power, subterfuge can restore a semblance of equality. It can keep the potential bully uncertain about his superiority, and hence stay his hand. His inability to see how he can apply his power effectively nullifies it. Indeed, he may fear that the person he is threatening has powers which he does not have.

Increased Power. Another way a person can even her odds is to increase her personal power. The amount of force one has available is not an invariant quantity. It is possible to become stronger. A person can empower herself. Her personal resources can be augmented so that she can more successfully counter coercion emanating from the other. An individual's resources can be increased in a number of ways. Power can be based upon economic assets, physical strength, beauty, intelligence, competence, and so on (Bendix and Lipset 1953). While some of these may not be subject to amplification, others are. It is usually possible to become richer or to develop new competences. Even something as seemingly invariant as beauty can be enhanced by the judicious use of cosmetics.

Competence, in particular, can be increased. When a person has a substantial skill at something, she thereby becomes more powerful. She becomes an expert. The display of her skills can then be used to intimidate rivals. It will also have a halo effect that will gain her respect in areas outside her specific competence. Vocational counselors often advise their disabled clients to develop skills for precisely this reason. They argue that an expertise will provide mechanisms for self-assertion which can compensate for other liabilities.

People are forever comparing their powers with one another (Festinger 1954). They test their relative strengths to see who is best (Whyte, 1943). This process helps identify and validate their relative social positions. Once comparative strengths have been established, contests can be avoided. The parties to potential disputes will have discovered who they can dominate and to whom they must defer. This knowledge will help them circumvent interactions involving disparate power. Everyone's safety is thereby increased and unnecessary battles are evaded.

Because comparison processes are used to establish relative power, a person who increases her personal resources has to re-enter the lists in order to validate her new position. Power is of little import if it is not recognized as such. Since tests of strength are uncomfortable, a person may understandably want to avoid them. Yet they must be endured. Power is not increased unless it is asserted. Others must be made to notice that one can now defend oneself more effectively.

Symbolic Power. Power, it must be understood, is not merely a potential for doing something; it is a potential which is perceived. This means that symbols of power can be as significant as power itself. It is well known that children use physical size as an index of fighting ability though in fact these two are not always correlated. A rival's size will often mistakenly be taken as a valid indication of his potential for causing harm, and be acted upon accordingly. It will be the other's apparent power, not his real strength, that matters.

Adults are even more addicted to symbols. "Dress for success" is not merely a slogan; it is a viable strategy. The person who dresses like a banker will usually be accorded the respect typically reserved for bankers. Others may take the way he dresses as a sign of power he may or may not possess. It therefore becomes possible for a person who wants to increase his clout to do so by manipulating its external vestments. The way he walks and talks, the way he combs his hair, and the car he drives can all be used to convince others that he has muscle worth noticing.

Social Alliances. One last strategy for enhancing power is that of developing social alliances. This is a remarkably compelling method for countering coercive role partners. Up to this point, only one-on-one negotiations have been contemplated. In reality, bargaining is often between teams. People frequently group together in an effort to overpower other individuals or groups. Anyone who has ever worked in a bureaucracy knows that politics are rampant. In organizations, it is coalitions that wield the most power, not individuals. Even a weak person can attain great power if he is in the right coalition. Family therapists have also discovered the strength of alliances. They routinely analyze the coalitions that develop between parents and children. When these are employed unfairly, they know that a family is having problems. In consequence, one of the strategies they use for improving family functioning is to rearrange these groupings in ways that make intra-family negotiations more equitable.

The types of alliances a person cultivates may be either overt or covert. Both enhance power. Overt alliances are very familiar. They are affiliations contracted with specific others. In this instance, the group to which one belongs is visible to all. Covert alliances, in contrast, are established between people who may not even realize that they are working together. These are usually based upon the mutual acceptance of shared norms and values. When people are pursuing the same goals or utilizing the same rules, their actions are coordinated and their respective powers enhanced. Thus a shared legal system increases the power of all attached to it. All are entitled to the same legal processes and enjoy the same rights. Persons who are party to such systems find themselves supporting one another's prerogatives, despite their mutual anonymity. They are, in effect, allies without ever having specifically contracted to be so.

A person who has learned to work well with others or who is able to commit to cultural standards thereby becomes stronger. It is not just him against the world. Often the "baddest dude" on the block, the one who can lick everyone else single-handed, winds up in jail. It is the person who is able to form coalitions with the prevailing order who flourishes. However physically weak he is, he will have the constabulary on his side.

Two last forms of alliance that must be mentioned are the "office" and "social status." Offices are defined social positions that exist within organizations. Some examples would be president, marketing manager, and supervisor. A person who is appointed to one of these posts thereby acquires many nameless supporters. The president of the United States, whatever one may think of him as a person, has as his ally the whole U.S. military. Though he may be weak and ineffectual in mind or body, his office-connected alliances make him the most powerful man in the world. Hence, when people want to increase their power, they often seek "promotions"; they court offices that have powerful built-in alliances.

Social status is probably the least visible form of coalition, yet it is surely one of the sturdiest. The hierarchical structure of mass societies endows some people with more potency than others. A person from a higher social class automatically commands the respect of complete strangers. Despite themselves, people defer to the man who steps out of a Rolls-Royce. Increasing upward mobility is therefore a wonderful strategy for increasing one's power; it is merely difficult to accomplish.

DYSFUNCTIONAL NEGOTIATION STRATEGIES

The Personality Disorders

So-called personality disorders are really highly ineffective negotiation strategies. They are, at base, an ineffectual way of countering coercive social demands. The person with a "personality disorder" is either coercively counter-attacking a perceived threat or vainly defending against such an attack. He is usually someone who has been grievously injured during childhood role negotiations and hence has not learned to protect himself properly. He does not lose his desire to defend himself, but because he doesn't know how, his methods often make things worse.

The person with such a "disorder" is trying to even the odds. Like everyone else, his goal is to negotiate favorable role structures. The problem is that his methods alienate role partners without persuading them to give him what he needs. This leaves him more frustrated than ever, and more inclined to persist in his counter-productive strategies. And because he continues in pain, he is said to have a psychological problem.

Histrionic Personality. Let us start with the example of the histrionic personality. The DSM-III describes this sort of person as having:

A. Behavior that is overly dramatic, reactive, and intensely expressed, as indicated by at least three of the following:
  1. self-dramatization, e.g., exaggerated expression of emotion
  2. incessant drawing of attention to oneself
  3. craving for activity and excitement
  4. overreaction to minor events
  5. irrational, angry outbursts or tantrums
B. Characteristic disturbances in interpersonal relationships as indicated by at least two of the following:
  1. perceived by others as shallow and lacking genuineness, even if superficially warm and charming
  2. egocentric, self-indulgent, and inconsiderate of others
  3. vain and demanding
  4. dependent, helpless, constantly seeking reassurance
  5. prone to manipulative suicidal threats, gestures, or attempts

These indicators make it obvious that the histrionic person negotiates by way of drama (Szasz 1961; Veith 1965). He makes his demands known to role partners by using grand strokes. Perhaps he will intimate that he is sick, or even dying. In any event, he needs attention right away. He is also described as dependent, demanding, and shallow. In other words, he wants what he wants very much, and is unconcerned about role-partner needs. If he must engage in manipulations in order to win, so be it.

Despite the drama, however, a histrionic person confuses his case. Because his demands are made symbolically, others are likely to miss the point. They are distracted by his tantrums and tears, and do not hear his arguments. Soon they become annoyed with all the hoopla. And since the histrionic person is visibly egocentric and inconsiderate, role partners quickly learn that their needs don't count with him. Whatever incentives they may have to cooperate with him vanish, and negotiations between them fail. The histrionic strategy is essentially a coercive one. The drama employed makes its demands excessive, and its subterfuge makes problem solving virtually impossible. A devotee of this strategy is forever contending, and forever abrogating alliances. His is clearly a negotiating technique that has almost no chance of success.

Passive-Aggressive Personality. The passive-aggressive is described by the DSM-III as exhibiting:

A. Resistance to demands for adequate performance in both occupational and social functioning.
B. Resistance expressed indirectly through at least two of the following:
  1. procrastination
  2. dawdling
  3. stubbornness
  4. intentional inefficiency
  5. "forgetfulness"
C. As a consequence of (A) and (B), pervasive and long-standing social and occupational ineffectiveness (including the roles of housewife and student), e.g., intentional inefficiency that has prevented job promotion.
D. Persistence of the behavior pattern even under circumstances in which more self-assertive and effective behavior is possible.

From the above it is plain that the passive-aggressive negotiating style specializes in indirection. The passive-aggressive fears that he cannot openly challenge role partners, so he does this covertly by slowing down or quietly resisting. One of the main complaints against him is that he does not clearly state what he wants. Instead, he is "manipulative" and he secretly tries to control others. Of course, in the process he makes enemies. It is this extensive use of secrecy and deception that makes his style coercive.

People become passive-aggressive when earlier role partners have not permitted explicit opposition. If the only way someone can make his wants known is to pretend that he isn't asking for anything, then he must perforce be "passive." The fact that he persists in this ineffectual strategy even in the teeth of evident failure is eloquent testimony to the inherent conservatism of role scripts. But it does not constitute proof of a defective personality or of a medical "disorder." The person is only doing the best he can, although it is not really good enough.

Avoidant Personality. According to the DSM-III, the avoidant personality exhibits the following characteristics:

A. Hypersensitivity to rejection; e.g., apprehensively alert to signs of social derogation, or interprets innocuous events as ridicule.
B. Unwillingness to enter into relationships unless given unusually strong guarantees of uncritical acceptance.

C. Social withdrawal; e.g., distances self from close personal attachments, or engages in peripheral social and vocational roles.

D. Desire for affection and acceptance.

E. Low self-esteem; e.g., devalues self-achievements and is overly dismayed by personal shortcomings.

This is evidently the person who sits in the corner and doesn't want to be bothered. He has adopted a "yielding" approach to negotiations, and has taken it to extremes. He asks nothing of his role partners, and in return requests only that they leave him alone. An outsider observing his position is struck by the fact that his strategy allows no path toward victory, but the person himself is so determined to avoid defeats that he willingly abjures the possibility of success. Someone with an avoidant personality is obviously hypersensitive to rejection, and this is almost certainly because he was brutally rejected as a child. If he is especially alert to ridicule, it is because he has known the pain of extreme derision. Low self-esteem, a need for affection, and a tendency to withdraw are not produced by loving, supportive relationships. The sad fact is that cold, coercive parenting generates defensive strategies that can egregiously thwart the negotiation of more satisfying behaviors patterns.

Narcissistic Personality. The narcissist is said by the DSM-III to exhibit:

A. A grandiose sense of self-importance or uniqueness, e.g., an exaggeration of talents and achievements, a focus on the special nature of one's talents.

B. Preoccupation with fantasies of success, power, brilliance, beauty, or ideal love.

C. Exhibitionism; the person requires constant attention and admiration.

D. Cool indifference or marked feelings of rage, inferiority, shame, humiliation, or emptiness in response to criticism, the indifference of others, or defeat.

E. At least two of the following characteristic disturbances in interpersonal relationships:

   1. entitlement: expectation of special favors without assuming reciprocal responsibilities, e.g., surprise and anger that people will not do what is wanted
   2. interpersonal exploitativeness: taking advantage of others to indulge own desires for self-aggrandizement; disregard for the personal integrity or personal rights of others
   3. relationships that characteristically alternate between the extremes of overidealization and devaluation
   4. lack of empathy: inability to recognize how others feel, e.g., unable to appreciate the distress of someone who is seriously ill.

This description of the narcissistic personality makes him sound suspiciously like a histrionic person with a hard edge. Certainly both want to be the center of attention and both seek only their own interests.

But the DSM-III presents the narcissist as being exhibitionist, rather than dramatic. How this differs in real-life situations is an open question. Both types of person are self-involved and eager to win, although the narcissist appears to be more open and aggressive in his intentions. It is interesting that this personality disorder is said to involve a preoccupation with fantasies of success, power, brilliance and beauty. This would seem to indicate that a narcissist is especially concerned with increasing his sources of power. He is clearly someone who feels weak and wants to maximize his strength relative to others. Despite his words about being special, he is drowning in an unsuccessful attempt to assert himself.

The narcissistic personality is not likely to win any popularity contests. His feelings of entitlement and his willingness to exploit others are guaranteed to alienate them. They will surely suspect that he is coercing them into doing his bidding, as in fact he is. If the narcissist has no genuine feelings for others, he can hardly take account of their interests during problem solving. But then again, he will not wish to, for he obviously feels so deprived that he is capable of considering only his own needs.

Antisocial Personality. Last, let us contemplate the antisocial personality. Before we do, it must be noted in passing that dependent, paranoid, and compulsive personalities—and indeed all the personality disorders—also have negotiation problems. These persons either cling too much, or are too suspicious and inflexible, to engage in meaningful problem solving. They are overly contentious or not contentious enough, too self-interested or not self-interested enough. But whichever way they operate, their negotiations don't work, and stifle change.

To return to the anti-social personality, the DSM-III's explication of him is too lengthy to be quoted verbatim here. Let it suffice to indicate that this person is said to have difficulties sustaining consistent work, being a responsible parent, respecting the norms of lawful behavior, maintaining enduring sexual attachments, avoiding excessive aggressiveness, honoring financial obligations, or planning ahead. The picture painted is of someone who cannot construct viable social roles. His reckless aggressiveness and disregard for the law get in the way of his establishing cooperative relationships.

The anti-social person clearly has a negotiating style with an even harder edge than the narcissist's. He is not averse to violence, and utilizes coercion in its most naked forms. If he is a brutal parent, an unresponsive lover, and an unreliable employee, it is because he savagely pursues only his own goals. His strategy for surviving does not include pausing to construct mutually satisfying roles. Neither does it include changing dysfunctional roles into more rewarding ones.

Given all these examples, it should be abundantly plain that the personality disorders are really styles of social negotiation that sabotage the emergence of viable roles. Because they are so unfair, they invite role partners to impose coercive counter-demands, if only in self-defense. Thus they impede the development of satisfying patterns of behavior during role negotiations and during attempts at role change. When present, they are a major obstacle to the implementation of resocialization.

7

Identifying and Reexperiencing Dysfunctional Roles

FACILITATING CHANGE

Because role change is not automatic, because it can be impeded in so many different ways, often the person who is most in need of it has the greatest difficulty in achieving it. He finds himself trapped in dysfunctional roles by the very processes that established them in the first place. Though he may desperately want life to be better, the various elements of his role scripts conspire to keep him from changing. As much as he may desire more satisfying ways of living, a mysterious barrier seems to frustrate his ambition.

If resocialization is to occur, a person in pain will need help. The assistance of another human being, one who is skilled in facilitating the change process, is often essential. Frequently it is only an outsider who can cope with the intense and/or misdirected feelings, thoughts, plans, and relationships that interfere with change. The person himself will be too frightened, confused, and/or intimidated to take the necessary steps. Thus an alliance with another may prove critical in providing him with the requisite courage and skill.

Professional resocializers are role-change agents. The job of a clinician (whether she be a sociologist, psychologist, physician, social worker, or mental health counselor) is to remove impediments to resocialization. Her task is to make the inherent pain of change more tolerable. The expertise, courage, and concern that she brings to bear can make it easier for a person to endure what is by nature a difficult enterprise. By placing herself in the balance, she can tip the scales in favor of her client, thus making possible changes that would not otherwise occur.

A clinician can foster role transformations by promoting (1) the reexperiencing and identification of dysfunctional roles; (2) the unblocking of the change process; and (3) the renegotiation of new, more satisfying roles.

1. Before a failed or aborted role can be altered, it must be activated. The person enacting it must come to experience it, and ultimately to know what he is feeling. Reexperiencing a dysfunctional role is indispensable. A role which is merely reflected upon is as if captured in amber. It is a curious museum piece that can be discussed, but not modified. Only living pieces of behavior are capable of metamorphosizing into something better.

2. Once a dysfunctional role has been brought into awareness, a mourning process must be initiated to allow a person to relinquish what has been lost. Denials, anger, and bargaining must lead to a purging sorrow which severs attachments to unsatisfying behaviors and forges a pathway to new relationships. A necessary step in facilitating this mourning is the unblocking of emotions, cognitions, and volitions that are overly intense or misdirected. Terrors must be disarmed, confusions dispelled, plans revised, and forward-looking role bargains implemented.

3. After the change process has been unblocked, new roles can be constructed. But these roles should not have the limitations of the old. It is imperative that they allow for the satisfaction of a person's needs. And because they are real roles, they must be renegotiated in real relationships. Resocialization must conclude with a person entering a new style of life, not merely speculating about what such an existence might be like.

In this and the two chapters that follow, we will explore how a resocialization agent facilitates the change process. Because this subject covers so much ground, much must be left unsaid. There are many ways of helping people to change (Hersen et al. 1983), many more than can be surveyed in one brief monograph. Indeed, classical Freudian, object relations, Gestalt, Rogerian, existential, behaviorist, and even strategic therapists operate from a resocialization core. Though these clinicians use very different language systems, they employ similar techniques in practice. Role change apparently can be dressed in dramatically different raiments.

We will begin our task with an examination of the supportive relationship. It underlies the identification and reexperiencing of dysfunctional roles, the unblocking of change, and the renegotiation of new roles. Without a trusting and facilitative partnership, little positive can occur. Such a coalition supplies a person with the courage and skill to make resocialization happen.

Reversing Coercion

One way of viewing resocialization is as a method for reversing the effects of coercive role negotiations. This requires that whatever else a clinician is, she must not be a coercive role partner. Instead, she must be capable of forming a protective and facilitative relationship with her client. Rather than force her own superior judgment upon the person she is helping, together they must establish an environment in which the two can be partners in expediting the client's growth.

A non-coercive relationship is necessary to all phases of role change. It is a prerequisite for the identification and reexperiencing of failed roles, for the unblocking of dysfunctionally maintained roles, and for the renegotiation of satisfying new ones. The kind of relationship desired has often been called a "therapeutic alliance." It involves the clinician and her client being on the same side, namely, the client's (Weis 1982). A clinician cannot reanimate a dysfunctional role merely by commanding it. The client who is ordered to feel such and such surely will not. Rather, he must be allowed to bring back into consciousness what has hitherto been too frightening and unpleasant to perceive. This he will do only if he can be certain that he will not be injured, and that he will receive valid assistance when he does try to change. The essence of the supportive relationship is thus built on trust and responsiveness.

Trust is an assurance of non-coerciveness. It is a guarantee that an erstwhile helper will not precipitate injury. The Hippocratic oath requires a physician to swear that he will at least cause no harm; a resocializer must be prepared to do no less. She must not allow her own threats, sanctions, or inattention to jeopardize her client's safety. The kind of person a clinician is, and what she does as a professional, must be calculated to enhance the client's life, not to wound him.

Responsiveness goes beyond not causing injury; it promises the ability to provide a definitive good. A responsive role partner is one who is aware of, and reacts to, the interests of the other. Hers is a style of interacting which expedites problem solving and which facilitates the emergence of new roles that actually satisfy. In this, she might also be described as nurturing.

There is, of course, some overlap between trust and responsiveness. The characteristics that provide a warrant for one are often an indication of the other as well. Trustworthiness and responsiveness typically form part of the same package. They both depend upon the qualities and skills that a clinician brings to her task. Both require a helper who is gentle and concerned, and who knows what she is doing. In short, a clinician must be able and willing to protect her client, and competent enough to guide him in positive directions.

Clinician Qualities and Skills

What must a clinician be in order to be trustworthy and responsive? Certainly, she must be prepared to be both with and for her client. A person who is embarking upon resocialization feels alone and vulnerable. Historically, his role partners have not been worthy of trust. Almost surely, many of his friends and relatives have violated his confidence. They have advertised themselves as acting in his interests, but gone on to do him grievous harm. What such a person will need now is evidence that his prospective helper is not like his past partners.

Since role changers have reason to be wary, a resocializer must be the genuine article. She needs to be the kind of person who does not cause gratuitous injury. Her temperament and role structure must be such that she has little incentive for taking advantage of her client. Moreover, she should be prepared to have her mettle tested. She must allow her client the opportunity to discover whether her apparent integrity is a sham. Simply declaring herself trustworthy will not do, since the person who does so rarely is.

There are many qualities involved in making a person safe. Among these are courage, fairness, and tact. So too are a reluctance to be moralistic and an inclination to be emotionally present. Rogerian therapists, in particular, have been sensitive to what they have termed "nonspecific relationship factors." They emphasize that a competent clinician must possess "warmth," "genuiness," and "accurate empathy" (Rogers 1951; Truax and Carkhuff 1967). If these terms are translated to mean caring, honesty, and understanding, they clearly do form the nucleus of what a helper must be in order to be trusted and beneficial.

Courage. A person with courage has little need to protect herself by attacking others or by running away. Courage is an ability to handle fear. It is not a matter of being unafraid, but of not reacting excessively when afraid. The courageous person can select her responses to fit the circumstances. She does not shift into automatic fight or flight when confronted with danger.

During role change, some exposure to danger is inevitable. A client's dysfunctional roles will have been precipitated in dangerous relationships, and when reexperienced, will reactivate primordial perils. A would-be helper who is unduly afraid of her client's terrors will not be able to counteract them. If her own fears are aroused by contact with her client's, she may either flee the scene or denounce the client for what he is feeling. Either way, the client's task is made more difficult.

More than any other kind of fortitude, a clinician needs emotional courage. The dangers she will face with her client are primarily emotional dangers. The fears, anger, and pain that a client brings to their joint venture must not be such that she cannot tolerate them. If, for instance, a client's intense rage unhinges her, they will both be in trouble. Of course, intense emotions are usually unsettling; the ordinary person who encounters them has a right to be shaken. But a clinician who is readily intimidated by strong feelings will not be able to function. Only if she has special resources will she be able to persevere in adverse conditions.

Honesty. A clinician who is honest in her presentation of herself gives her client an opportunity to make a realistic assessment of her. For a person to be trusted, the other must know who she is. Deception breeds uncertainty. An individual who lies or covers up is naturally suspected of having something to hide. If this person is a resocializer, then her client will justly wonder what she is up to. Such a client will not know what to believe or how to proceed.

An honest clinician is one who says what she thinks, and who behaves the way she really is. She is the genuine article, and not a hypocrite. Moreover, if she is to succeed in this honesty, she must be a good person. The forthright scoundrel will no more be trusted than the deceitful saint. Honesty only allows another to make a valid assessment; a resocializer must also have the substance to back up what she advertises.

One more characteristic of the honest helper is that she answers questions. Psychoanalysis has left therapists with an unfortunate legacy of deflecting client inquiries. It has been assumed that a clinician should be a mystery upon which a client projects his own distortions. The analyst who replies frankly to questions has been accused of interfering with her client's attempts to solve his own problems. But nothing could be further from the truth. Routinely deflecting questions is disrespectful and infantilizing. It negates a client's right to know where he stands, and confuses him about what he is doing. The clinician who hides from questions is demanding that her client take her good intentions on faith. If a client is gullible enough to do so, he will have learned a terrible lesson, namely, that he has no right to examine the credentials of authority figures. Instead of discovering that he should test the designs of his role partners, he will be indoctrinated into believing that it is necessary to place oneself at the mercy of others, even the unscrupulous.

Fairness. Good role bargains have at last two sides, both of which must be taken into account. For the end result to be truly desirable, both parties must win. The interests of each must be considered and balanced. While this world rarely allows for absolute equality, role negotiators must nonetheless strive for it.

A clinician who advertises herself as facilitating role change must at least be fair. She is presumably more powerful than her vulnerable client, and hence will be in a position to be abusive. If she wishes, she should be able to manipulate her client for her own interests. Yet her commitment to help must preclude this. A sense of fairness should prohibit her taking advantage. Though she might with impunity ignore her client's needs, she must in fact resolve to compensate for his weaknesses. When the person she is helping is not able to defend himself, she must be prepared to bolster his cause.

Caring. Besides being fair, a resocializer must care about her client; she must want to see him succeed. Her client's interests should in a real sense be her own. When the person she is helping loses, this should represent a loss for her as well. Recently, the helping professions have been infused with a spirit of scientism (Saranson 1985). Too many clinicians have come to think of themselves as scientists first and resocializers second. For them, the disinterested objectivity of the researcher is the ideal, and they find "caring" faintly embarrassing. It smacks too much of a sentimental dilettantism. Sometimes caring is denigrated as a form of infantilization. The one-sided concern of the helper is assumed to impose helplessness upon the client. A clinician supposedly becomes the "strong one" who orchestrates her client's life for him. It is postulated that caring automatically forecloses independence and that a clinician who cares too much will be like an overprotective parent who is convinced that his child can do nothing for himself.

Yet caring need not eliminate dignity. Concern can be tempered by respect. A person who has role problems does not automatically become a helpless infant. Even if many of his dysfunctional roles are reenactments of failed childhood roles, he remains an adult. His problems do not cancel his competence; neither do his weaknesses abrogate his rights. As an adult human being, he can do much for himself, and he certainly has the right to try. A title to fail is part and parcel of self-determination.

In some ways, a clinician must assume a quasi-parental role. Her caring should be comparable to the concern of a loving parent. Thus she can, and should, want the best for her client. But even this does not imply infantilization. In the real world, good parents want their children to grow and prosper. They know that in order to learn their children must stretch themselves. The child who is to become an adult must be allowed to take chances and make mistakes. This requires restraint on the part of parents, but it is a productive restraint. A willingness to see him stumble is ultimately rewarded by a youngster who grows stronger. The clinician can do much the same. She can function as a parent who cares, and forbears interference when her client needs to make independent discoveries.

Tact. Tact may seem a trivial quality to require of a trustworthy helper, but it speaks directly to a role changer's need for safety. A tactful person is one who does not intentionally cause pain. She is aware of another's vulnerabilities and makes an effort not to abuse them. When she perceives that a role partner might be injured, she does not lunge straight ahead, but softens her approach so the pain is diminished. Her words are gentle and her manner cautious. The message she wishes to impart is that although some difficult subjects may be broached, they need not be handled callously.

A tactful clinician may sometimes appear indirect. Instead of telling her client that he is crazy, she will intimate that he seems to have made an error in judgment. Because her goal is not to force a particular point of view down her client's throat, she will give him room to maneuver. Tact is non-coerciveness incarnate; it does not demand an immediate or specific response.

Non-Moralism. Earlier we contrasted moralism with morality. The former was described as the coercive imposition of moral values. A clinician who is moralistic assumes that she knows what is right and that her client ought to accept her judgments unconditionally. This leaves no room for quibbling, and none for dissent. Such a clinician will force her client to adopt her opinions and abandon his own.

Sometimes non-moralism is confused with being non-judgmental (Rogers 1951). It is assumed that a trustworthy clinician will withhold judgments of her clients and offer unconditional acceptance instead. Yet this would be going too far. While a resocializer should totally accept her client as a person—this is no more than being on his side—there is no reason to uncritically accept all he says and does. The clinician who does so is not being fair, but foolish.

Emotional Presence. Another way for a clinician to demonstrate that she is a safe person is to be emotionally present. When two human beings communicate with one another, they can do so intellectually and/or emotionally. If only the former channel is used, much will be concealed. A resocializer who hides behind her professional credentials denies her client access to an important aspect of herself. The clinician's emotional presence vouches for her good intentions precisely because it puts her on the line. Her being there testifies to the fact that she is who she says she is. By abjuring her right to professional anonymity, she is permitting her client to discover if her words match her deeds. If they do, the client's trust will be based upon evidence he has personally gathered.

Authority. Since trust is based upon a person's ability to protect, it is essential that a clinician be perceived as having sufficient strength to ward off external dangers. This entails her having adequate power to repulse external threats, while simultaneously abstaining from the exploitation of her advantages. Authority is the recognized presence of this ability. It represents the legitimate exercise of power. When a person has it, it is a warrant that she is strong enough to protect, and dependable enough to abstain from abuse.

One basis of authority is personal competence. A person who knows her job, knows the world, and knows how to make things happen will be accorded the respect due an expert. Another basis is moral courage. A clinician who has the courage of her convictions also merits deference. Her words deserve weight. The client who is confused about where he stands, or where he wants to go, will value a role partner with solid moorings. As long as the clinician does not coercively impose her perspective, the power of her commitments will add legitimacy to her opinions.

Patience. A trustworthy and responsive resocializer is also a patient one. The answers to her client's role dilemmas are usually not immediately apparent. It will not be instantaneously clear why he is dissatisfied, what is impeding the change process, or how renegotiation can be resolved. These questions may take considerable time to settle. The uncertainties of resocialization are best decided by allowing solutions to emerge, rather than forcing them. A clinician who must make things happen right away will probably stop them from occurring altogether.

The facilitative change agent knows that time is on her side. Her motto is: Make haste slowly. She recognizes that some things change only with time, and that emotions, in particular, cannot be rushed. Undue speed makes for anxiety, mistakes, and, ultimately, regression. It leads to one quick step forward followed by three even quicker ones back. Though a clinician may understandably want to speed her client's journey through the rigors of resocialization, her anxiety for expedition will be more an indication of her own discomfort than of her client's interests.

Understanding. A resocializer will not be able to help her client if she does not know what her client's interests are. But responsiveness which is not informed by understanding is scarcely in a position to respond. An accurate assessment of another's needs is thus an essential prerequisite of successful role bargaining.

Understanding is in critically short supply in our world. Most people are too self-involved to take the time to notice others. This is especially true for a person trapped in dysfunctional roles. His bad roles will almost surely have been negotiated with role partners who did not understand him, and will be maintained by partners who continue to misunderstand. When genuine understanding is available to him, it will be deeply appreciated. The experience of being comprehended will make him feel far less alone. It will give him confidence that there is someone in his world with him.

In order for a clinician to enter her client's world, she must be able to experience it from the inside. To achieve this, she must be a skillful "role taker." Ultimately, an ability to comprehend another depends upon one's being a competent role performer. Among the tools needed are empathy, self-knowledge, and social knowledge.

Part of the ordinary equipment of role players is an ability to understand each other's part. A wife can best determine what it is to be a wife by comprehending the demands of her husband qua husband. Her ability to accurately predict what he is thinking and feeling will be vital to her decisions about how to respond. In her own mind, she will have to perform his role and learn his "lines" if she is to devise appropriate rejoinders. It is this role-taking ability that makes it possible for people to generate coordinated role performances.

Role taking is much more than an intellectual prediction of what another will do; it involves getting under his skin. At its best, one feels as the other would; one sees through his eyes, and appreciates his interests as one's own. It is the ability to do this that gives a clinician the possibility of truly understanding her client. Because she is a human being and a role player, she will be able to intuit what is going on inside the other. This empathetic understanding furnishes her with a far broader understanding than if she merely tried to interpret her client's words.

Empathy is often considered a mysterious concept. Perhaps the simplest way to think of it is as "emotional understanding." An empathetic person feels with another human being. He is tuned in to the other's emotional experience. It is not merely that he is sensitive to what the other is feeling, although this is part of it; it is that he may literally feel the same thing. Emotions are communicable and an empathetic person has opened himself to this channel. He often senses what the other is feeling by, as it were, scanning the vibrations that pass between them.

Since role taking requires a proficiency in accurately projecting the self into the other, it is dependent upon adequate self-knowledge. A person who does not understand himself is likely to make the same mistakes about someone else as he makes about himself. If he does not know what he is thinking or feeling, he will probably not be in touch with what is going on inside the other person.

Clyde Kluckhohn (Kluckhohn and Murray 1948) has observed that while there are ways in which all people are different, there are many ways in which we are all the same. Our basic hopes and fears are in fact very similar. We all need to be loved and respected, and we all feel uncomfortable when attacked. Therefore, in trying to understand what another person feels, we can not go far wrong by trying to ascertain what we would experience in equivalent circumstances. While our own reaction may not be precisely the same as the other's, it is usually a good starting point.

All of this, of course, is contingent upon self-knowledge. A clinician, like anyone else, can be misled by distorted self-understandings. She too can be victimized by mistaken cognitions, intense emotions, foolish volitional choices, and adamant role partners. Clients do not have a monopoly on self-delusions. It is the clinician's very humanity (that is, the qualities that make it possible for her to be a roletaker) that makes it vital for her to pierce the veil of her own ignorance. To the extent that she knows herself, she can utilize her reactions as a model for understanding others; to the extent that she doesn't, it is incumbent upon her to increase her self-knowledge.

But self-knowledge is not all a resocializer must master. How she and her client react is dependent upon more than what is going on inside each of them. Their role behaviors are also a consequence of the social world they inhabit. Their present social surroundings and the social contexts in which they were socialized inevitably channel their thoughts, feelings, and decisions in particular directions. In order to understand these pathways, the constraints that fashioned them must be uncovered.

To take a simple example, a clinician working with a client living in the barrio may be at a loss to understand the heterosexual reactions of her client if she does not understand "the culture of poverty" (Valentine 1968; Lewis 1966) or Latin *machismo*. Certain kinds of violence and sexual posturing may seem senseless when not viewed within the value context in which they are generated. Roles are never constructed totally *de novo*. They are always influenced by the social models available and by unavoidable social demands. Without knowing these, one does not know what a person is trying to do. Ethnocentrism is no virtue in a role-change agent; hence it is necessary for her to expand her knowledge of her (and her client's) reality.

Other Skills. An expert resocializer must be a jack-of-many-trades. In addition to her skills in understanding, she must be a clever investigator, an expert communicator, and a practiced negotiator. Her understanding of others will not emerge without an ability to delve beneath the surface of things; neither will it be of any use to her if she cannot share what she discovers with her clients. Unless she can accomplish these tasks, she will not be able to assist them in identifying or reexperiencing their dysfunctional roles. Moreover, a resocialization agent must be able to guide clients in defusing their intense emotions and renegotiating new roles. This requires that she be skilled in the management of emotions and in productive problem solving. Since these are not abilities with which we are born, they must be learned and perfected. Otherwise, impediments to change cannot be removed or satisfying new roles consolidated.

Proto-Identification

When people seek professional help, they rarely identify themselves as having "role problems." The complaints they typically make are more nebulous. If given specificity, they will usually be couched in medical or psychological terms. These categories are socially current, and hence familiar and acceptable. Thus resocialization clients may speculate about having a "mental illness" or suffering from a "neurosis." In this, they will be making a proto-identification of their problem. Theirs will be a tentative effort to label what is troubling them. The categories employed will not usually include "dysfunctional roles," because these have not yet achieved a social cachet. Though clients readily comprehend role difficulties when they are pointed out, they are unlikely to begin role change by complaining of them.

The closest people usually come to spontaneously recognizing a role problem is acknowledging that they may have difficulty being a proper husband or wife, or being a good mother or father. Sometimes a younger client will admit that he does not know who he is. He will describe himself as having an "identity" problem, although he may not associate this with a disorganized role structure. Similarly, mature adults may worry about their "mid-life crisis" without being aware that they are in a state of role collapse.

Usually, people coming for professional help have complaints about specific life problems. They may say that some aspect of their life is not working as desired. For example, they may worry about being trapped in a troublesome relationship from which they cannot seem to extricate themselves. Some beginning clients tend to blame themselves for all their problems because of what they perceive to be their own "badness" or "inadequacy." Others, however, ascribe their difficulties to external persecution and see themselves as the helpless victims of malicious spouses, parents, and bosses.

If a clinician is to help a client deal with his unhappiness, she must have a more precise understanding of what is causing her client's pain. The person's rudimentary protestations of discomfort must be related to distinct areas of role failure. The feelings of which he complains and the relationships he decries must be attached to particular aspects of role dysfunction. It is the resocializer's task to convert proto-identifications into more unambiguous identifications of role problems.

The discomfort of which a client is aware will have two primary sources: he will be ensnared by roles that do not meet his needs, and he will be experiencing the pain that is inherent in role change. Thus it is here that the clinician must search if she is to obtain a more precise idea of what has gone wrong in her client's life. She must be able to relate the specifics of her client's current situation to his dysfunctional roles and his place in the role-change process.

Some roles are simply not satisfying and, when present, are a sign of trouble. Whether they have failed in adulthood or been aborted in childhood, they are poor vehicles for satisfying personal needs; that is, they make it difficult for a person to feel safe, loved, or respected. Roles such as caretaker, rebel, and scapegoat are often inherently unsatisfying. A person who is living with them will have an aching sense that something is missing. He may even feel very real pain. The scripts followed by a caretaker, for instance, will dictate that he put the needs of others ahead of his own. He is often specifically mandated to do what will not make him happy.

Similarly, role change is itself traumatic. Central to the resocialization paradigm is the notion that change involves mourning, and that when people are trapped in dysfunctional roles this mourning is impeded. Grief is inherently painful, and impeded grief more so. Since most people don't understand how role change works, they easily blunder into change strategies that make things worse. Their attempts to exert willpower or to find painless solutions often entangle them in useless battles and unproductive detours. Instead of short-circuiting an unavoidably traumatic affair, they unintentionally prolong it, and a clinician must be aware of this.

IDENTIFYING ROLE DYSFUNCTIONS

A client's dysfunctional roles are identified by uncovering them. All clients live out their roles, and may even be able to communicate them. But often they cannot. At such times a clinician must become an active investigator. She can both observe what her client is doing and listen to what he says. When necessary she can also ask questions. In general, she can try to fathom her client's roles by imaginatively putting herself in his place. Thus, when she asks questions, it should be with an eye to learning what her client's situation is. Only then can she know what shoes she needs to walk in.

There are no hard and fast rules for discovering failed roles, but one point is paramount: it is the resocializer's goal to understand her client. The techniques she uses are secondary to the aim she is pursuing. As long as she keeps in mind that she is trying to comprehend dysfunctional roles, she will be all right. The clinician who relaxes, and unselfconsciously uses the knowledge and skills she has acquired through years of living, will probably do well. If she exploits her wisdom as a role player she should be able to understand most human predicaments.

Observing

Listening. Listening is the fundamental channel of observation available to a clinician. A client may blurt out what is troubling him, or, if one listens closely, his words may imply it. Nevertheless, careful listening is an art. In ordinary conversation, people are so intent upon preparing their own rejoinders that they gloss over what their companion is saying. Most of us like to be at center stage, and so we relegate others to the periphery. Making the shift to being a genuine listener takes more effort than we usually realize.

A clinician who is trying to understand must temporarily hold her own ego in abeyance. She must concentrate her attention on her client's words, while simultaneously attempting to decipher their meaning. The literal significance and implications of what is said must command her notice. A resocializer must forever be trying to read between the lines. Not only words, but tones of voice must be considered, as must strange circumlocutions, repetitive patterns, and unusual lacunae. Often what is not said is as informative as what is. If a client tells about a situation that would ordinarily make a person angry but makes no allusion to such a reaction, the clinician's ears should perk up. Why was anger not mentioned? Was it not experienced, was it suppressed, or merely not communicated? If the latter, was this intentional? Is the client trying to manage the impression (Goffman 1959) he is making? If so, why?

Listening can and should be an active process. It is not only a gathering in of words, but a fitting of them together. What is said should arouse associations which then guide further listening. If a client expresses anger at his wife while talking about his mother, is he equating the two? Is he responding to similar patterns in both? In short, is he enacting comparable roles with them? Once this question arises, additional listening may provide evidence one way or the other. While a clinician is listening, she is also thinking, and this thinking gives structure to her listening.

Watching. However, words are not enough. People communicate through other channels too. One must look as well as listen. There is, for example, body language. A person can proclaim in words that all is well, while his fidgeting body says otherwise. A raised eyebrow, or arms crossed in defiance, can speak volumes. Hands, face, and eyes are especially revealing. Many people communicate more fluently in gestures than language. A pointed finger, a clenched fist, or a trembling hand may say what a person is unwilling to enunciate any other way.

Since the face is the billboard of the mind, its expressions are specifically designed to be communicative. Emotions like anger create lines in the face which even the greatest dissemblers have difficulty hiding. They may be able to maintain a poker face with special effort, but over an extended course of interviews slips are inevitable. Finally, it is with good reason that the eyes have been called the window to the soul.

When they harden into a stare, or are misted over by the sentiment of the moment, they provide an unparalleled view of what is happening inside.

Many of the cues that a person gives are too subtle to be specified. Few of us can accurately expound on what facial patterns indicate what emotions. Nevertheless, we are all able to discriminate emotions with considerable precision. Similarly, there exist "vibes" which occur during social interactions and which a clinician can use as a guide to what is going on. Her own emotional reactions will give her clues to her client's emotions, and her physiological reactions may hint at her client's internal experiences. Thus, if she suddenly finds herself tense or tired, she should be alert to comparable processes in the other. Perhaps her client has become anxious or withdrawn. A careful observation of what has provoked her reaction will usually be rewarded with new data.

What is happening inside a client's body can also provide information. If he tenses up, has a pain in his chest, or suddenly becomes dizzy, these may indicate what he is thinking or feeling. A pain in one part of the body may be associated with previous beatings that are now being recalled through the resocialization process. Twitching, burning eyes can be the residue of long hours of crying. It is not only the hysterical client who relives his past through bodily reactions; virtually anyone can have these experiences.

Not all channels of information are so subtle or exotic. How a client acts can communicate his roles most clearly of all. For instance, does he pick fights with the clinician? What are they about? Is he also having fights with his wife? Or his father? Perhaps he is being overly solicitous of the clinician's welfare. Is it because he feels he must take care of everybody? And does this mean he is a caretaker?

Roletaking. Roletaking cannot be separated from listening and watching. What a person hears or witnesses is as much a product of what he projects outward as of what the others communicate to him. Active listeners make informed interpretations by extrapolating from their own experience. Thus a clinician who is a sensitive observer only makes sense of her client's emotions by first consulting her own. As George Herbert Mead (1934) discovered many years ago, in order for people to interact meaningfully, they must have some idea of what others are trying to do. Both parties to a social interaction must be able to put themselves in their role partner's place. They must be able to engage in a kind of projective identification before their interpersonal understandings can have substance. Without this ability to imaginatively walk in the other fellow's shoes, one is a cardboard cut-out, and social life becomes a charade.

Taking the role of another imbues him with emotional depth. A clinician who has the capacity for imaginative projection thereby gains access to her client's role scripts. She opens a channel into her client's thoughts, feelings, plans, and social reality. The other's internal and external circumstances become accessible to her. Instead of mechanically associating disjointed behaviors, she becomes privy to the larger patterns that integrate human behaviors and make them meaningful. In short, a client ceases to be a "case" and becomes a purposeful human being.

Exploring

Exploring is simply a more active form of observing. It follows up on initial observations and tries to clarify what was not immediately evident. When engaged in explorations, a clinician prods, pokes, and digs. She seeks to probe beneath the surface of things to obtain a fuller understanding of her client's roles. The primary tool she uses is the question. Its purpose is to elicit what is not voluntarily offered. Other techniques for discovery such as dream analysis, free association, reflection, and confrontation are supplementary to it. They come into play when the direct question fails. Their purpose is to elicit information more indirectly. Sometimes they even uncover material of which the client himself was unaware.

Questioning. Questions begin from the first interview between a resocializer and her client. They form a bridge between the two. Because they start as strangers, explicit indicators of what a clinician wants to know are required to launch their mutual enterprise. Sometimes professionals make the mistake of assuming they must be completely unintrusive. They fear that direct questions will automatically be leading ones and that it is the clinician's hidden agenda, not the client's real situation, that will emerge. But effective queries can be genuine ones also. It is perfectly allowable for a professional to make things happen, as long as she permits her clients to express genuine answers. Only when she puts words in their mouths is she overstepping her bounds.

For questions to be of value, they must be employed intelligently; that is, they must have a purpose. There has to be some information that the clinician wishes to elicit. Totally unpremeditated questions are pointless, and are an affront to a client's dignity. This does not mean that questions cannot be open-ended or vague; often it is precisely these queries that allow the latitude for unexpected responses. Idle curiosity and unfocused chitchat, however, must be rigorously excluded. A client who is paying for help deserves an honest effort at facilitating change, not merely a pleasant diversion.

A client's dysfunctional roles can be unearthed by exploring the elements of his role scripts. The cognitive, emotional, volitional, and social aspects of his behavior should be teased out of the morass of his experience and made available for examination. This can be achieved by asking him about the particulars of his situation. Thus he can be asked:

"What are you thinking?"
"What are you feeling?"
"What are you trying to do?"
"What demands are being made of you?"

Or if past circumstances are involved, he can be asked:

"What were you thinking?"
"What were you feeling?"
"What were you trying to do?"
"What demands were being made of you?"

Similar questions can be asked in terms of role partners. It may be possible to learn about their role scripts by inquiring after their thoughts, emotions, volitions, and social circumstances. Ascertaining these may add a vital dimension to understanding the demands influencing a client's behaviors. Moreover, inquiries about the physical and historical contexts of roles expose them as the integrated patterns of behavior they in fact are. Role scripts only make sense when one knows how they arose and to what they were a response.

Once a client has answered questions about his scripts or their context, there must be a follow-up. Answers beget further questions. The leads that a person furnishes must be pursued. Thoughts, feelings, plans, and demands can all be elaborated. Thus one thought or feeling can trigger another, and it a third, and so on. Ultimately, material may be unearthed that was not at first suspected. Moreover, the conclusions a clinician draws should always be tentative. Since this is so, additional information is continually needed to refine, change, and expand her understandings.

When it is a client's current role behaviors that are being examined, a variation of script questions can be asked. To find out what is specifically happening to a person, he can be asked, "What are you thinking now?" This sort of question has the advantage of requiring immediacy. It brings scripts to life and hence opens them to closer inspection. As a bonus, it also facilitates the reexperiencing of roles. Thinking about something now, and especially feeling it now, make for a vibrancy that cannot be ignored. And when one part of a role is relived, others may be as well.

REEXPERIENCING DYSFUNCTIONAL ROLES

As a clinician develops an accurate picture of what is troubling her client, she becomes better situated to initiate the change process. What she has uncovered about her client's dysfunctional roles positions her to start the client on the role-change curve. In identifying problem areas, she acquires the ability to draw her client's attention to them and to help him reexperience them. She can thus use her understanding to focus the client's awareness on what has gone wrong and what needs to be relived.

A major reason why people get stuck in roles that don't work is that they cannot allow themselves to reexperience or comprehend them. The habit of looking away from problems is so ingrained in most of us that we have no inkling of what we are really doing. A clinician can extricate someone from this predicament by actively redirecting his attention. What a person may not be able to conceive of for himself, a helper can inaugurate by implementing strategies that demand attention.

Facilitating Awareness

A resocializer can facilitate her client's awareness of role dysfunctions by bringing things out into the open. She can initiate this by the simple expedient of talking about them. Thus she can say to her client: "Such and such seems to be troubling you." Or: "Look, see what you're doing (feeling, etc.)." A clinician can insist that sources of dissatisfaction be acknowledged and that impediments to change be examined. In so doing, she brings unpleasant facts into consciousness by, as it were, holding them in front of the other's nose.

An awareness of pertinent information is not automatic. There are good reasons that role changers don't want to see what they must. Dysfunctional roles are by definition uncomfortable. They are failed efforts, and failure is never fun to contemplate. When a person sees that his roles are malfunctioning, he simultaneously witnesses needs that are unmet. And while this may alert him to what must be corrected, it also arouses a consciousness of what is missing. A knowledge of what he does not have will summon unwelcome emotions such as unrequited love or anger. Moreover, he may be gripped with a sense of hopelessness when he contemplates the enormity of what he lacks.

Directing Attention. There are many ways in which a client's attention can be focused. Foremost among these is the direct request to pay attention. A clinician can say, "Look, see what you are doing; see what you are feeling." If this does not work, she can describe what she expects her client to notice. She can say, "See how you are always taking care of your mother, your wife, and even me." This allusion to concrete instances may make the client's behaviors more tangible to him. If he still denies what is in plain sight, the clinician can pile detail upon detail until their sheer weight makes a difference. It may also be useful to label the other's behaviors as those of a caretaker role, if that's what they are. Sometimes, having a hook upon which to place things makes them easier to acknowledge.

Because diversions are so central to the way in which people protect themselves from pain, a resocializer must be prepared to counter them. Her client's attempts at denial or obfuscation must be recognized for what they are. When attention wanders or is deliberately shifted, it needs to be brought back. A clinician can insist that they talk about a particular subject or return to one that has been dropped. If a client persists in changing the focus, he can be asked why he wants to change it. The clinician can then indicate that she thinks it is crucial to return to the old subject, or that the shift of attention itself merits notice.

Dramatizing. Because a resocializer will want to be certain that her client sees and feels what is being pointed out, she will want mechanisms to sharpen the focus of her messages. She will need to dramatize her communications so that her client can more readily identify and experience the hidden elements of his roles. The goal will be to intensify her client's perceptions so they become easier for him to delimit. Drama is, after all, the art of heightening experience to make it more visible.

If focusing attention increases immediacy, drama redoubles it. It does not merely say, "Look at that"; it comes to life and engulfs a person. Drama is like theater; it seduces a person into imaginatively becoming part of the action. He is encouraged to experience and not merely witness events. Perhaps he may even be reduced to tears or provoked to fury. In any event, his consciousness will be captured by the vividness of perceptions that he will find difficult to deny.

One way of dramatizing a role is by using examples. Citing a concrete instance from another situation may provide a clue about what a client should look for in himself. The clinician can ask her client to compare his case with another with which they are both familiar. If the client is a "caretaker," the clinician can illustrate her points by noting other illustrations from the client's life, and/or by tapping their common culture. Newspaper stories, television shows, proverbs, or movies all can supply materials for comparison. They can act as unambiguous models of what is intended, especially when the client's own feelings are too diffuse for easy recognition.

A particularly effective conduit for giving examples is storytelling. Stories have good connotations for most of us. They elicit an aura of parental concern, and hence constitute a non-threatening intervention. A resocializer can tell stories about third parties, or herself (Jourard 1964), and then draw parallels with the client's situation. As long as her tales are kept short and are calculated to make a point, they can significantly heighten awareness. It is only the confused story or the one designed to relieve the clinician's tensions that will fail to hit the mark.

Another mechanism for increasing the vivacity of a perception is "cognitive dissonance" (Festinger 1957). If a person can be made to recognize that some of his attitudes and understandings are self-contradictory, it will be difficult for him to overlook them. They will virtually force themselves into his awareness. Similarly, exaggerations, jokes, surprises, and unusual juxtapositions can focus attention. If these are sufficiently different, or uncomfortable, or pleasant, they will become quite striking. And if they are connected with role dysfunctions, these too will, by association, be more visible.

Finally, a resocializer's style of communication can be used to dramatic effect. She may, for instance, utilize her tone of voice to express interest in what her client says. Her animation can arouse the other, just as the enthusiasm of a cheerleader generates excitement in a crowd. Since it is in the nature of emotions to engage attention, when a helper incorporates them in her face or voice, they influence awareness. Her own vividly expressed interest stimulates the other's interest in precisely what he needs to discover.

Role Playing. As a general rule, saliency can be increased by making a person do something rather than simply talk about it. Mere words can easily be drained of emotion or specific reference, while actions and feelings are more difficult to disengage. To do and to feel is to be, not just to observe. It is inherently involving. This makes role playing an excellent vehicle for intensifying a person's awareness.

During resocialization, a client can be asked to do more than talk about a dysfunctional role; he can be invited to play it out. A clinician can suggest, for example, that her client pretend he is talking to his father or ministering to his wife. Any behavior that is part of an unsatisfying pattern has the potential for being acted out. Moreover, a client can start with a small part of a role and find that it brings back other parts of his repertoire. Because roles are complex patterns of interactive behavior, acting out one part tends to release others. One piece of behavior reminds a person of another, and it of still others, and so on.

The words, postures, and tones of voice associated with a past situation can often bring that situation back. Thus a clinician who encourages a faithful representation of past interactions can breathe life into a remembered role performance. If she also joins in the role play and takes the part of a past role partner, she can further enhance the drama and saliency. She can make her client feel as if he has been transported back into a world that has vanished.

Another device for reanimating roles is role reversal. Since roles are of necessity inter-personal, they always have at least two sides. This allows the clinician and her client to turn their parts around. The clinician can play the client and the client a former role partner. In this circumstance, the client is forced to take the point of view of the former role partner. He, as it were, relives the other half of his own role, and gains an opportunity to discover the meaning behind the social demands that shaped his role behavior. His perspective is broadened and he learns things about himself and his past that he may not have known before. In addition, nothing so transfixes one's attention as seeing the familiar from an unfamiliar point of view.

Many psychotherapies have rightly used role playing to influence their clients. Systems as diverse as Gestalt therapy (Perls et al. 1951), psychodrama (Moreno 1953), and transactional analysis (Berne 1961) have relied heavily upon it. Perls, in particular, was quite prolific in the variations of role-play methods that he promulgated. His "empty chair" technique, for instance, has proved very productive. It utilizes two chairs between which a client physically shuttles and on which he plays both sides of a particular role relationship. Such an arrangement often stimulates a very intense experience of repressed materials.

Berne is less obviously connected with role-play techniques, but has accomplished the same effect by emphasizing the internalized roles (called "ego states") of "adult," "child" and "parent." His therapy encourages conversations between these often conflicting aspects of a person. The client who follows this method finds himself acting out both sides of internalized role relationships. Thus his "parent" may be a representation of his actual parent, and his "child" a reenactment of a role fragment from his own past.

In recent years there has been considerable interest in imaging techniques. These have largely been the contribution of behaivorist and cognitive psychologists (Wolpe 1973; Beck et al. 1979). They have sought to use internal images to enhance particular experiences. A client is asked to imagine himself with another person, having a particular feeling, or reliving a past event. In essence, he is being asked to engage in a kind of internalized role play. Sometimes the role partner is not explicitly present in these fantasies, but there is always an *eminence gris* lurking somewhere in the background.

Images have the advantage of being vivid, yet malleable. The pictures a person constructs in his head can have very sharp outlines, yet be changed at will. This makes it possible to imagine old roles, and then very quickly imagine new ways of enacting them. Fantasy adds a dimension of flexibility to role playing. Since the stage on which it occurs is internal, it is subject to instant manipulation. The imagination is a very convenient place for both reliving the past and rehearsing the future. It allows a person to achieve victories in imagined role negotiations that might not be possible with existent role partners. Indeed, it permits what we will soon be calling "ghost victories."

Explaining

While a resocializer is focusing her client's attention on what he needs to perceive or experience, she must also place this material in context. A client must not only reexperience his dysfunctional role, he must know that it is a dysfunctional role and that supplanting it with more satisfying ones is being inhibited. In short, a clinician must explain to her client what he is experiencing and why. Particular feelings, thoughts, plans, and social demands must be put in a role or role-change framework.

Raw experience can be a "blooming, buzzing confusion" unless set in perspective. The client who does not appreciate what is happening to him will be hard pressed to effectively participate in his resocialization. Without a framework to guide him, he is poorly positioned to manage his own efforts at change. Yet initially, the typical role changer is confused about what is happening. Although a helper may have focused his attention on a dysfunctional role, he still will not have deciphered the meaning of what he sees. It will be a new experience to him, and he will not know what to make of it.

The clinician, however, will be a more experienced and objective observer who has almost surely participated in role change before. Optimally, she will have seen other clients undergo resocialization, and may even have experienced it personally. Undoubtedly she has also learned something about the theory of resocialization and is able to recognize it when she sees it. This should equip her to explain its what, how, and whys. It should also make her capable of interpreting her client's experience and of providing an idea of how it can be modified for the better.

Explanation can begin by showing a client how his current roles are dysfunctional. The patterns connecting individual feelings, thoughts, and plans can be pointed out and correlated with his unhappiness. It can be explained that much misery is not accidental, and is often a consequence of a person's own ways of behaving. The clinician can then elucidate the various aspects of role scripts to show how specific feelings, thoughts, plans, and social demands are interfering with the client's ability to meet his needs.

Once he understands that he is having role problems, a client can be introduced to the intricacies of role change. A clinician can explain how attempts at change can go awry and cause further pain. An overall picture of the change curve can be outlined and methods for removing the impediments to resocialization suggested. Resocialization is a complex process, and the more accurately a role changer comprehends it, the more competently he can navigate it. There is no point in mystifying role change, for the less completely a client understands it, the less prepared he is to cooperate in effecting it.

Providing a Rationale. Mystery is inimical to change. That which is shrouded in darkness becomes an object of fear. A role changer who does not know what is happening to him is subjected to an unnecessary source of anxiety. His ignorance will encourage misleading flights of fancy. The unaccustomed feelings and thoughts that he experiences as a result of his clinician's explorations may lead him to imagine the worst. Negative feelings and thoughts which are a normal part of dysfunctional role scripts are compounded by his uncertainties, and deleterious sentiments become specters of doom. The client then becomes discouraged about his prospects for a better life.

Studies of psychotherapy have shown that a common feature of all change systems is a rationale (Frank 1973). All therapies have some theory to explain why they lead to improvement. Confidence in these theories seems to be part of the process of effecting successful change (Norcross 1986). It does not matter so much what the rationale is as long as the client believes it. Freudian, Jungian, Sullivanian, Ericksonian, Rogerian, behavioral, Gestalt, existential, and medical systems have all proved capable of inspiring enough respect to generate positive results.

Validating

When a person who is trapped in dysfunctional roles begins to examine his life, he may not be sure about what is real and what is not. So much of what he has experienced may have been repressed that what remains seems fragmentary or illusory. Moreover, previous role partners may have deceived him about the accuracy of his judgments. Thus, when he tried to be helpful, they may have accused him of being selfish; when they caused him injury, they may have claimed to be expressing love. This may have left him not knowing what to believe.

Reality is never an individual construction. The world, and especially its social structure, requires consensual validation. Because social roles are joint exercises, they can only be made real through the confirmation of role partners. This gives role partners great power and means that role scripts, including one's thoughts, feelings, and plans, are subject to manipulation by others. If these partners are on one's side, all is well; if they are not, the world can be a terrifying jumble of contradictions and confabulations.

Confused communications are part and parcel of dysfunctional roles. One source of this confusion is what Bateson called the "double bind" (Berger 1978). He demonstrated that some parents demand a particular behavior from their children, and when it is forthcoming, disqualify it. They may, for instance, ask for love, but when it is proffered, reject it. This kind of "poisoning the well" serves to confuse children. They do not know what they are supposed to do, and this induces them to question the accuracy of their perceptions. Children, because they have a tendency to assume everything is their responsibility, are especially vulnerable to concluding that somehow they are at fault. A child may not know what he has done wrong, but when he is on the receiving end of a double bind, his inclination to feel guilty will cause him to disconfirm his own feelings, thoughts, and plans. It will seem obvious to him that if his roles are not working, it is because his internal scripts are in error.

If a client is to reexperience his failed or aborted roles, he must have confidence in his own senses and judgments. The roles he has learned to identify must feel real, and indeed painful; otherwise they will be like someone else's experience, and become objects of curiosity rather than resocialization. Behavior patterns that appear false and distant are not accessible to alteration. Because it is only the feelings, thoughts, plans, and relationships which come alive that can be reorganized, only they can be felt, thought, and experienced, differently.

This fact places a premium on a clinician's ability to validate her client's experience. If a dysfunctional role is to be reanimated, a helper must not only see it and make it visible, but she must also make it real. What has been brought to a client's attention must not feel like an intellectual exercise or fantasy.

When resocialization encourages a client to reactivate unsatisfying roles, the confusions surrounding them will be activated too. Why he acts the way he does will not come instantly into focus. He may begin to glimpse the outlines of his dysfunctional role scripts, but will be uncertain about exactly what happened during past role negotiations. His reexperiencing of the past will be as in a haze. Indeed, as he recounts his history to the clinician, he may express his uncertainty. Instead of telling his helper, "This is what happened" and "That is what I felt," he may ask, "Is this what happened?" or "Is that the way I felt?" Part of a resocializer's task is then to clarify and reinforce her client's perceptions. She will have to sort out what is real and what not, and certify the real. When her client's experiences are valid, she must be able to say, "Yes, things are as you think. You are not crazy."

If past role partners have distorted a person's reality, current interlocutors will have to challenge it. There will need to be at least one other human being who agrees about what is out there. No matter how intelligent or forceful a person, by himself he cannot make his world real. An isolated individual is consumed with Cartesian doubt and of necessity loses his bearings. It takes a trustworthy other to nail down one corner of his experience and provide a basis for confirming other parts of it. Without such a partner, a person is adrift in an undifferentiated reverie (Hamilton 1988).

CASE STUDY: ROBERT

To fully appreciate role change, it must be understood within the context of specific human lives. An abstract description of the process needs be translated into concrete experience before it really makes sense. Let us therefore introduce Robert. He is an older man who has had a history of alcoholism and is struggling to come to grips with the ruins of his life. First, we will explore his early life to see how his dysfunctional roles evolved. Then we will examine his experience in resocialization, including how he was helped to identify and reexperience his dysfunctional roles.

Introductions

Robert endured a very troubled early life. He was born out of wedlock, and within months was sent to live with a foster family. When asked as an adult what this was like, he described his benefactors as coming straight out of "tobacco road." Yet Robert liked them, and thought they liked him. To him, they represented a home where he felt he belonged. Unfortunately, this interlude was to be very brief. By the time he turned four, his natural father returned to reclaim him. He was then taken to live in his father's bachelor house. His mother was not present, and was only a memory of someone he once met at school, and whom his father constantly castigated as being a whore. If Robert wasn't careful, he was warned, he would turn out to be just like her.

Robert's father was a brutal man. He was physically strong and bright, but also very contentious. When angry, he was not above physically beating Robert or verbally assaulting him. Although his father was a skilled craftsman, he had a prickly disposition. On the job, he was forever in conflict with his co-workers and was often sacked because of his caustic language. Nevertheless, he was justly proud of his craftsmanship, and adamantly believed that only manual labor conferred dignity.

This work ethic was quickly transferred to Robert. From the first, the boy was expected to earn his keep. There were many chores to be done around the house, and Robert was supposed to do them immediately and well. If he did not, he was the object of physical blows. At the very least, he could expect an accusation of malicious incompetence. Occasionally he was subjected to punishments such as being locked out of the house without a coat during the New England winter. Robert learned that when his father was provoked, he was capable of towering rages. At such moments, the child trembled in fear that this uncontrolled violence might terminate in his death.

Almost as bad, he found that it was virtually impossible to please his father. Thus when he did clean the house or prepare a meal, instead of being praised, he would be asked why he hadn't done the same yesterday. When his father's rages sent him cowering in fear, he was accused of cowardice; when bitter verbal tirades left him tongue-tied, the charge was mental retardation. If Robert was not strong enough to physically resist his father, he must be physically weak; if he was not motivated to do the work demanded of him, he must be lazy. Robert was simply not allowed to win. Whichever way he turned, he was a "failure." According to father, he probably took after his "artistic" mother or his "alcoholic" grandfather. All in all, he was instructed that he was "no good."

When Robert went to school, he had an understandably difficult time concentrating. He was often too preoccupied with what was happening at home to pay much attention to his teachers. When in frustration they demanded that he do better, he resisted. But no matter how fierce they attempted to be, they were a pale imitation of his father. This made it possible to successfully defy them because they were benign compared with what he was accustomed to. When his teachers then complained to father, the latter assured them that his son was "slow" and that not much could be expected of him.

Eventually, Robert was placed in classes for the retarded. Subsequent tests as an adult would demonstrate that while he indeed suffered from a form of dyslexia, his IQ was in the neighborhood of 150. In the meantime, he was grievously misunderstood, and so lost all confidence in his teachers. He was convinced that they neither knew nor cared about his home situation or his true abilities, and so he returned their disinterest in kind.

As he approached his teen years, Robert became more difficult for his father or the school to handle. In consequence, they shipped him off to a "reform" school where his continued defiance and poor academics kept him labeled as retarded. Soon he took to running away, and although he was caught several times, he eventually made a successful escape. He thus became a street person, condemned to living as best he could.

During his early twenties, Robert drifted between odd jobs and petty crime. It was only in his late twenties that he began to drink, but soon he was drinking heavily. His crime now came to be directed toward supporting his alcoholism and, in his words, he began a slide that didn't end until he became a "low bottom drunk." He wound up a common "bum" who slept in alleyways and earned his wine through burglary. Despite his cleverness, this larceny led to arrests and, ultimately, prison. One day he found himself in a high security correctional facility surrounded by murderers, thieves, and rapists. These were men of violence who reminded him of his father, and against whom his only defense was his wits. He then became an honest broker between men more powerful than himself, and although he survived, he considered these methods those of a coward.

After prison, Robert struggled to subsist. He resumed his alcoholism, but soon began to fear for his life. Around him he could see that his drinking buddies were succumbing to cirrhosis and pneumonia, or simply falling victim to street violence. Would he be next? Robert decided not to find out and entered a series of detoxification programs instead. Initially, he experienced uniform failure in them, but eventually responded to the care given him. Since the rebelliousness of his youth had not completely disappeared, he occasionally manifested an oppositionalism which got him sent to a state psychiatric hospital. Nevertheless, his indomitable spirit attracted the ministrations of a number of helpers who were genuinely concerned about his welfare.

Along the way, he found himself hooked up with Alcoholics Anonymous and discovered that this organization was well suited to his needs. Its members were mostly supportive, not coercive. Although at first he was very negative at meetings, in time he became part of the community. Much to his surprise, he was able to maintain his sobriety day by day as was recommended.

Still, something was missing. Robert began to feel that AA was too Pollyanna-ish. Members were too fond of expounding on how wonderful their lives had become now that they were sober. He, on the other hand, although sober, did not feel wonderful; he still had problems that he wanted solved. Somewhere deep inside he felt destined for better things and was determined to fashion a way to get there.

Resocialization

When Robert entered resocialization, he was a man in his early fifties who had been in many previous "helping" relationships. His most recent association had been with a state psychiatric hospital where he had been diagnosed as suffering from alcoholism, schizophrenia, and a schizoid personality disorder. Most hospital records described him as a very dependent person who had extremely low self-esteem.

Robert indeed felt very dissatisfied with his life. He thought of himself as a coward who could not solve his own problems because he had insufficient courage. Although he very much wanted his life to be better, he didn't know how to make it so. As far as he was concerned, his situation was hopeless and far beyond the capacity of a therapist to alter. He was not shy, however, in telling his counselor how much he was hurting. It was this vague dissatisfaction that he identified as his greatest problem.

On one point Robert was very clear: he did not believe that the hospital's diagnosis of him was correct. He was willing to admit to being an alcoholic, but he did not think he was crazy. Apart from this, he was unsure of his situation. He did not know precisely what he wanted, or how a clinician might help. When asked what his goal was, he talked about getting a job. Somehow he thought this would "straighten him out."

In fact, Robert did get a job but it didn't last, and this made him feel more of a failure than ever. Repeatedly, he blamed his setbacks on cowardice. He explained that his father always predicted he would not amount to anything, and as much as he hated to admit it, the old man seemed to be right. Robert described in detail how his fears stopped him from succeeding. If the clinician suggested that fear was natural in some circumstances, he would reply, "Maybe," but "John Wayne wouldn't be afraid" in any situation. No real man should be as afraid as he was.

As the clinician attempted to decode Robert's role structure, one thing became certain: standing out above all his dysfunctional roles was that of "coward." Robert was sure that any trace of fear was unmanly, and that any competent observer would confirm this cowardice. Despite having performed many acts that others might have accepted as signs of bravery, he was convinced that because he experienced fear while executing them, he must be a coward. To prove his contention, he cited an incident that took place at his apartment. It seemed that two men were in the process of assaulting a third under his window one night. When he heard the commotion, he stuck his head out the window and ordered them to desist. The perpetrators then invited him down to try to stop them. Robert quickly agreed, and shouted that he and his shotgun would join them momentarily. He then went to the phone and called the police. As he expected, the assaulters broke and ran when he mentioned a shotgun. There was consequently no need for him to go downstairs and physically confront them. In relating this story, Robert took an evident pride in his cleverness (he had no weapon), but was also certain that his deception was a proof of cowardice. A real man would have gone into the street and had it out with them; a real man would not have lied or called the police.

In addition to believing himself to be a coward, Robert was also convinced he was an unmitigated failure. His alcoholism was one sure
indicator of this. So was his determination not to do the kind of physical work his father wanted him to do. His flat refusal to work at "the
outhouse factory" was evidence that he must be no-good and/or lazy.
Manual labor, he argued, was the only road to social acceptance, and
since he would have none of it, socially sanctioned success was out of
the question. When the clinician suggested that he did not feel that
way, that he thought other kinds of work had dignity too, Robert responded that he might agree intellectually, but deep inside he did not.
Here then was another of his dysfunctional roles. Being a failure had
become part of himself, despite his conscious desire to be different.

Another of his dysfunctional roles turned out to be that of "retard."
He was the family idiot, and always would be. The words of his father
and teachers still rang in his ears. A part of him might know that he
was intelligent, and actually be proud of it, but another part still felt
like a simpleton. He found that whenever someone contradicted an
opinion of his, he was assailed by self-doubt. How could a person with
a distorted brain such as his ever trust his own perceptions? If others
differed with him, perhaps they had insights that he lacked.

After counseling had proceeded for some time, another aborted role
emerged, namely, that of artist. Robert started to become interested in
photography, and showed considerable talent for it. He even won a
local photo contest. Nevertheless, art seemed no fit vocation for a man.
It would put him in the same "no-account" league as his mother. Neither could he be content with his talent for storytelling. While it might
be okay to regale AA meetings with tales about his past, any dreams
he had about writing a book were ruthlessly quashed. Robert's triumphs
in anything remotely connected to art became occasions for a swift reaction. Thus when his photography was going too well, he had to stop
taking photos. He could not permit himself to turn the role of artist
into a functional reality.

Because of his competence as a storyteller, Robert began resocialization by relating stories. He readily described his past and present life
in stirring detail. Since he had clearly identified his ineptitude and failure on his own, these problems did not need to be pointed out to him.
Instead, the clinician concentrated on those parts of his situation that
were not accessible to him. It then quickly became evident that although Robert talked easily about his cowardice, he had more difficulty
discussing his fears.

As the two explored Robert's history, the clinician focused more on
the dangers Robert had experienced. For example, he called attention
to the many times Robert had flirted with death during his alcoholic
and criminal periods. In large part, he did this by asking questions

about what had happened and why. The more dramatic the incident, the more the attention was lavished upon it. As Robert became more aware of this behavior pattern, the clinician compared it with the dangers he had experienced at his father's hands. He explained that Robert's experimentation with death might be a recapitulation of previous experiences. Hadn't dad physically threatened him? Hadn't he been terrified that he might be killed for being too defiant? Wasn't he afraid that his difficulty in restraining himself might mean that he would die? In a way, hadn't he been defying society, and by proxy his father, by becoming an alcoholic and a criminal?

Well, yes, maybe he had. But what was the clinician going to do about it? Couldn't the clinician see that he was still afraid and still defiant? Nothing was going to change these feelings, so what was the point of reprising them?

At first, Robert merely talked about his uncomfortable feelings; he didn't feel them. His responses were designed to parry the clinician and convince him of their mutual impotence. In effect, he said he did not want to look at his dysfunctional roles or reexperience them because nothing but frustration would come of it. All this the clinician took with good humor. His own confidence in the resocialization process allowed him to persist without trying to force issues. His hope was that Robert would eventually incorporate these convictions and acquire the courage to confront his demons.

After a time, Robert commented that the clinician was different from other helpers he had had. Now he was being given the freedom to make decisions for himself. Though the clinician might nudge him in a particular direction, he was not being coerced to think or feel a certain way. Neither did he believe that the clinician was intimidated by him or the enormity of his problems. Perhaps the two could work something out after all.

As feelings of trust developed within the relationship, more and more emotion became evident in Robert's stories. Then one day as the two were discussing a current problem Robert was having with some friends, he began to tremble. He cowered in his chair and shivered quite perceptibly. When the clinician asked what was happening, at first Robert had no answer. Gradually he became capable of describing his feelings. He indicated that he felt just as he had when his father had put him out of the house on a cold winter's night. It was as if there was some task at which he had failed, and for which he must now be punished. Until this moment, Robert had never mentioned having been locked out of his father's house without a coat. When questioned, he said he hadn't thought about it for years. But here it was, not only a memory, but in the flesh. And it was hard to tolerate because the fear was so real.

For some sessions after this, Robert avoided exploring his feelings. Only slowly could he acknowledge that this evidence of the intensity of his emotions had frightened him off. When the clinician attempted to engage him in role play about his conflicts with his father, Robert refused. He admitted that while it might help them understand why his father punished him so severely, he was too frightened to proceed. This left the clinician to merely conjecture about what their relationship might have been like. He offered speculations about what could have happened and then asked Robert to confirm or deny them. This lowered the emotional intensity and allowed more information to emerge.

During their conversations, Robert and the clinician informally fleshed out their understanding of his roles of coward, retard and alcoholic. They followed no inflexible schedule, and pursued leads wherever they led. Because of Robert's anxieties, these roles were not reexperienced as intensively as they might have been, but the two did open up territories that needed exploration. Still, it would take considerable unblocking of some of his deepest fears before they could get a really adequate fix on what was troubling him.

8

Unblocking Emotions

A MODEL FOR UNBLOCKING EMOTIONS

The identification and reexperiencing of dysfunctional roles is only a first step in the role-change process. Before unsatisfying behavior patterns can be altered, the bonds holding them in place must be loosened. The protest phase of the mourning process has to be successfully navigated, and what doesn't work must be relinquished. When letting go is impeded by script elements that interfere with the resolution of a person's protests, bad roles are frozen in place. A person becomes trapped in forms of interaction that keep him unhappy, and his unsatisfying behaviors repeat themselves in an endless loop. Only when cognitive, emotional, volitional, and social barriers to change are removed can resocialization proceed; only then are denial, anger, and bargaining worked through, and sadness performs its mission of severing ties with the past.

A clinician's task is to aid in unblocking what has been obstructed. It is his job to facilitate change by helping his client alter script elements that prevent him from becoming what he would like to be. Emotional blockages in particular must be addressed and corrected. Overly strong feelings, ones that forcefully propel a person in the wrong direction, are especially inimical to change. They are hard to deal with, and harder still to alter. When emotions such as fear and anger are too intense, or are mistaken in what they communicate and motivate, they convert the protest phase of mourning into an interminable exercise. Extreme fear, for instance, can make denial too extensive, and vehement anger can make bargaining unresolvable. Instead of permitting a person to let go, they instigate a battle against losing which is never ending and never successful.

Although cognitions, volitions, and social demands also interfere with resocialization, they will not be our focus here. Resocialization is too complex to be presented in its entirety in one volume. This constraint dictates a strategy of partial exposition, and it is the emotional impediments that will be elaborated upon because of their centrality to the change process. In no way, however, should this be taken to diminish the importance of ideas, values, or social demands. They too merit serious clinical attention and can be every bit as detrimental to resocialization.

Neither do we mean to deprecate the significance of emotions other than fear, anger, and sadness. While these three will get the lion's share of our attention, guilt, shame, and unrequited love can be quite as inimical to change. Rather, fear, anger, and sadness will serve as models of emotional blockage, and an examination of them will suggest how other feelings can be worked through. These emotions do, however, deserve a certain pride of place due to their ubiquity in disrupting resocialization.

Achieving Goals

As we have tried to show, people trapped in dysfunctional roles are suffering from the aftereffects of coercive role negotiations. They have been victimized by role partners who used excessive force in pursuing their own interests. The legacy of these unequal encounters is emotional script elements that prevent happiness. In particular, intense fear, anger, and sadness are activated when a role partner exercises unfair power. The threats, deception, and/or neglect of inequitable partners impose dangers that must be thwarted, frustrations that must be countered, and losses that must be accommodated. It is the function of a person's emotions to help him cope with these challenges.

The feelings that arise during coercive role negotiations have goals that must be achieved before they can be set to rest. Fears that warn of danger must lead to safety. Resentments that bespeak frustration must eventuate in satisfaction. Sorrow that signals a loss must result in letting go. Guilt must gain absolution, or a change in internalized demands. Shame must end in behavior that has no impulse to hide. And unrequited love must either culminate in a successful attachment or the renunciation of an unsuccessful one. When an emotion is reactive, it must correctly assess its environment and initiate an efficacious response. When it is teleological, it must correctly determine what is possible and how this can be accomplished. If these outcomes are not realized, unfulfilled goals become more insistent and the untoward reactions they instigate more difficult to remedy. Failure begets more failure and emotions escalate to unbearable dimensions. It is thus not the expression of painful emotions per se that disarms them, but the achievement of their ends. Just blowing off steam does not inaugurate set solutions that work.

Correcting Intensity and Direction. If a clinician is to help his client unblock emotional impediments to change, he must help correct their intensity and direction. When it is fear that prevents letting go, a person's level of alarm has to be reduced, and the danger of which it warns must be effectively countered. Thus a role changer's fear cannot be so terrifying that it obliterates all perceptions of reality. Intense, terrifying fear negates the possibility of correctly assessing a danger or implementing viable counter-measures. Instead of assisting a person by communicating what she needs to know or by motivating competent defenses, it leaves her helpless and prostrate.

Similarly, intense and misdirected anger does not remove frustrations. Rage is dumb and brutal. It consistently misinterprets its options, and regularly underestimates the injury it inflicts. Anger that is too strong doesn't quit. It aims to force decisions, and hence often attempts the impossible while simultaneously employing methods that are wildly imprudent. A person who is trapped in such a feeling is intimately aware of its failures, but is too caught up in its automatic reactions to extricate herself from its grasp.

Very forceful emotions set up a vicious cycle. Their intensity and misdirection make it difficult for a person to perceive their aim or effectively pursue their satisfaction. This failure then increases her sense of danger, frustration, and loss, and these intensified signals make her emotions that much stronger. Once feelings pass a certain threshold, they become very difficult for a person to disarm on her own. This makes the intervention of a disinterested role partner vital during resocialization. Only someone not trapped in this emotional cycle may be able to lower their intensity, or provide a reminder of reality.

Because a clinician's emotions will presumably must not be as intense as his client's, he is well situated to accurately appraise the latter's predicament. If he has the emotional courage that he should, he will obtain a sound fix on what threatens his client and will be able to suggest potential mechanisms for neutralizing the danger. His calm, good sense will make him a steadying influence. Because he is trusted and concerned, he will be able to share the burden of his client's emotions and help make them more manageable.

Figure 8.1
Achieving the Goals of Emotions
(By Reducing Their Intensity and Correcting Their Direction)

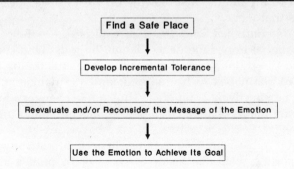

The General Model

While there are many ways in which the goals of an emotion can be achieved, there is a general model a resocializer can follow in helping his client attain them (see Figure 8.1). First, the danger inherent in coercion must be reversed. The excessive force aroused by a client's emotions must be effectively countered. Only then will he be able to relax. This requires that he have a safe place to which he can retreat in times of trouble. Reliable access to such a place affords the confidence to not be overwhelmed by arbitrary coercion.

Second, the intensity of painful emotions must be reduced. As long as fear, anger, or sadness remain so potent that they cannot be correctly appraised, their message will be blurred and the actions they inspire will be misdirected. For their intensity to be diminished, a person has to acquire an incremental tolerance of them. She must be able to experience fear, anger, and sadness in bearable doses. This can be accomplished by allowing herself to encounter them in small, digestible portions.

Third, intense or misdirected emotions must be reevaluated and reconsidered. Once it is possible for a person to examine her emotions, she needs to employ this opportunity to investigate their messages. With reactive emotions, she must decide if they are correctly assessing reality. Is fear, for instance, correctly signaling danger? With teleological emotions, she must decide if her implicit goals are realistic. Is it really possible to achieve what her anger tells her she must achieve?

Fourth, she must effectively use her emotions. The motivation inherent in powerful feelings must not be casually squandered. Fear, anger, and sadness can make things happen. If they are employed in an intelligent and controlled fashion, they can facilitate the achievement of their goals. Emotions that start out too intense or are grossly misdirected can, when astutely redirected, facilitate the implementation of objectives. It is then, and only then, that obstructive emotions can reach quiescence.

Creating a Safe Place. Intense or misdirected emotions are not safe. They are repressed with good reason. When reexperienced, clients reflexively perceive them as dangerous and routinely flee them. It takes the existence of a reliable safe place to provide a base from which they can be explored. Someone in their thrall must be convinced that she is protected from their danger before she will consent to examine them.

Coercion, it will be recalled, begins with external threats and ends with internal restraints. Physical manipulation shades into threats of violence and terminates in emotional reactions that perpetuate these threats. Thus what is initiated by the violent demands of a role partner may be consummated in the ferocious guilt of his victim. Internalized emotional coercion is often the instrument through which external coercion operates. Intense or misdirected fear, anger, guilt, sadness, and shame can be the mechanism that makes the threats of others effective.

The danger confronted by someone trapped in dysfunctional roles is thus both internal and external. Not only must she be protected from the excessive demands of role partners, past and present, but she must also guard against their internalized effigies. The intense fear, anger, and sadness aroused by such partners constitutes an internal force that must be neutralized. Otherwise, the signals of these emotions will be in constant overload and the actions they instigate will cause terrible injury. Anger is a case in point. When it is too fierce, it can literally kill or maim the self or others.

Thus a safe place must protect from both internal and external dangers. It has to prevent role partners from doing damage while simultaneously guarding against out-of-control emotional reactions. A clinician and his client must collaborate in discovering, or constructing, such places. They will need to ascertain localities or mechanisms that provide dependable protection. Indeed, it will be incumbent upon them to prepare one or more lines of defense before they can proceed to deal with the emotions themselves.

Many possibilities can be explored in the quest for safety. Some are literally "places," while others are not. They can be locations, persons, activities, objects, mental processes, or competences. In fact, a client will probably need several of each because they are adequate only when readily accessible. Such places are like portable home bases. Whenever an overwhelming danger impends, one should be handy, for without propinquity, it is not possible to have confidence in its protection. This puts a premium on having many easily reached areas of sanctuary.

1. Locations. Some places are more dangerous than others. Locations that expose a person to perilous challenges are not safe. Thus the physical presence of a threatening role partner makes his locale an unsafe one. In general, places that are saturated with external danger or provoke substantial internal danger are not secure. To move away from them to locations that are less threatening is to move toward safety. These other places allow a person to decompress and to obtain the requisite breathing room.

The office in which a clinician practices should be a reliably safe location. It must be quiet, comfortable, and secure. Its physical appointments and its separateness from more dangerous places have to provide reassurance. A client should be able to look around and say, "Ah, yes, this is nice." Indeed, he must be so comfortable that he can forget his surroundings and proceed with the business of role change.

At home or at work, he must be able to find similar places for himself. If this means retiring to bed and hiding under the covers, so be it. What is needed is a locale that works, one that actually does feel safe. Sometimes this entails entering a particular room or stepping outside of one; it may even entail taking a trip to the country. If a client does not have such places, or does not know where to find them, his clinician can instruct him on the possibilities.

2. *Persons.* Attachments are an important basis of safety. Being with a safe person makes for a sense of security. There is something reassuring about being around someone who is benign and protective. While physical locations can provide a passive defense, human beings have the advantage of supplying active protection. Bonding with a trusted other delivers a person who can be on one's side. This trusted other can actually fight in one's behalf.

Since a role changer is likely to have a restricted complement of trustworthy role partners, his clinician assumes special significance as a dependable other. The relationship between the two must be solid and reliable. When in the presence of his helper, a client should correctly perceive that he will not be attacked and that this other will make efforts to deflect impending dangers. When painful emotions arise, a client should be confident that his clinician will help keep them under control. When fear, anger, or sadness materialize, the presence of the clinician needs to make them feel less frightening, explosive, or painful.

The best way that a resocializer can provide this measure of safety is by being a safe person. He must not want to hurt the person he has promised to help. His client should sense that he is trustworthy, not because he is restraining himself, but because he genuinely cares and because he has real emotional courage. When these are present, a clinician can communicate his safety by remaining calm. His demeanor will attest to his lack of fear and to his commitment to protect. It will create a bubble of safety into which the two can retreat when emotions threaten to get out of hand.

As resocialization progresses, a client can be expected to establish other safe relationships. Current role partners, or perhaps new ones, can be enlisted to provide protection in specific contexts. In the real world, no one is completely safe, and few are predominantly dangerous. The secret of finding safe persons is in discovering who is safe, and in what ways. A client must learn to make such distinctions. He can then develop attachments with discrimination.

3. *Activities.* Doing something comforting is also a safe place. Reassuring activities have an advantage over persons in that they are under one's own control. Jogging, doing a crossword puzzle, playing a game of tennis, watching television, listening to music, or reading a good book all create areas of asylum. While doing these things, unwanted fears and rages are set aside and tranquility reigns. Of course, none of these undertakings completely solves a person's problems, but they can hold many dangers at bay. They are safe because they fill space with neutral material and provide a respite from things that are currently too difficult to handle.

A clinician can urge his client to find such activities instead of stewing about what he can't control. If necessary, relaxation techniques can be inculcated. These are activities specifically designed to keep overwhelming emotions from becoming dominant. Biofeedback or systematic muscular relaxation teach a person to manipulate his body in ways that make intense emotions more manageable.

4. *Objects.* Transitional objects are yet another way of achieving safety. Security blankets, or their equivalent, are not just the prerogative of children. Adults too have favorite chairs, lucky sweaters, cigarettes, chocolate bars, coffee, shiny automobiles, facial makeup, money, or rabbit's feet. It is easy to chalk these up to superstition, or to dismiss them as "crutches," but they are very real islands of security. There should be no shame in finding comfort in tangible things, that is, if they work. No one is so strong that "irrational" talismans are always beyond his dignity.

5. *Mental Processes.* Perhaps the least likely safe places are mental processes. These are clearly not "out there," but they offer shelter nevertheless. Distractions and fantasies clear the mind of dangers and at least temporarily make the world seem more benign. Denials, repressions, thinking about other things, and dreams all have their uses. A clinician who holds his client's feet to the fire, no matter what the pain, is doing him no service. Sometimes it is better to hide than to go crazy or commit suicide. Diversions, it must be remembered, are not final. What cannot be faced today may always be confronted tomor-

row. Better to encounter the truly frightening when one is prepared than when one isn't.

A special kind of mental safe place is the fantasy introject. Safe persons or safe locations can be called up in the imagination. Images of flowers or recollections of deceased grandparents can offer reassurance. Though ephemeral, these can sometimes seem as substantial as physical reality. Indeed, introjects of loving parents are usually a prerequisite of self-confidence. Often, resocialization permits a person without safe images to develop them by introjecting protective aspects of his helper. In times of danger, he will be able to imagine what his clinician might say or do, and this can afford solace.

6. *Competences.* Finally, a person's own ability to protect himself can be a safe place. Someone who has power, and knows he has it, can shelter behind his own competences. When one has the strength to fight back, he can be confident that although a danger impends, he will still be able to survive. Just as some feel safe when they build their muscles, others can enhance their security by augmenting their expertise. They can wield their skills like a weapon to keep others from attacking. They will know that a demonstration of superior ability can frighten coercive role partners into submission.

Incremental Tolerance. Once dependable safe places have been established, intense or misdirected emotions can safely be tackled. A client can be instructed that when dealing with powerful emotions, he should stay within his "comfort zone." If a feeling such as fear gets out of control, he must not be imprudently courageous. Instead, he should beat a judicious retreat and utilize one of his safe places. Only then will he be free to confront his offending emotions piece by piece.

Intense emotions require a person to pace himself. If they are activated too quickly, they become overwhelming. Fear can become panic and totally disrupt a person's ability to cope (Barlow 1988). Very strong feelings must be taken seriously. They have the power to inflict real damage and must not be treated cavalierly. When an emotion is too intense to be controlled, it must be divided into smaller increments and these confronted in turn. Instead of the whole fear being experienced, only one part of it should be. If this plan is followed, a tolerance of the emotion will gradually be acquired, and what was once unbearable will become familiar and controllable.

Experiencing the Emotions. The emotions that block role change are usually painful to experience. No sooner do they intrude into a person's awareness than they are expelled into the farther reaches of his unconscious. There they resist a return to consciousness, but do not on that account disappear. Despite their exclusion from experience, they continue to influence behavior. Worse still, because they are not experienced, they resist alteration. Intense or misdirected emotions that have been repressed are hard to measure or change, and hence are capable of serious mischief. If this situation is to be reversed, what is not perceived must return to experience. Feelings that have been quashed must be brought into awareness and put to productive use.

The only way to experience a feeling is to feel it. This may sound like a truism, but it is rarely obvious to a person who has suppressed his emotions. He is intent on feeling nothing. In his anxiety to avoid pain, he has probably convinced himself that there is nothing to feel. A resocializer who attempts to help him face these feelings will encounter a stone wall. His client will prefer to extend only verbal compliance. He may be perfectly amenable to talking about his feelings, but only as long as he can avoid their actuality. It is then the clinician's task to convince him that even bad emotions—especially the bad emotions—must be experienced if life is to improve.

Nevertheless, a clinician does not have to press for total, immediate experience. Intense emotions cannot be tolerated in their entirety. They must be approached one fragment at a time. Each part-emotion must be digested by itself. Familiarity will then make it less painful and will permit another part-emotion to be faced and tolerated in its turn. Ultimately, these parts will add up, and it will be possible to encompass a whole emotion without having to repress it. This process is essentially what Wolpe (1973) called "desensitization." It depends upon the possibility of learning to bear what was originally unbearable by approaching it in tolerable segments. One "gets used to" the uncomfortable feelings, and they cease being excruciatingly bothersome.

Catharsis. It has sometimes been thought that merely experiencing intense emotions holds the key to their resolution. In his early years, Freud (Breuer and Freud, 1957) advocated catharsis as a curative agent. He suggested that bringing a feeling into awareness can by itself cause it to dissipate. The implication of this view is that a violently angry person can become less angry once he expresses his rage. It is as if his pent-up rage were as ephemeral as steam, and when vented, disappears into nothingness.

Unfortunately, this simple view does not accord with reality. Merely expressing anger does not diminish it (Tavris 1983). Neither does venting rage always clear the air (Bach and Wyden 1968). If anger is expressed too forcefully, or in the wrong circumstances, it can actually make things worse. Telling one's boss to go to hell is imprudent no matter how genuinely felt. If anger is to be reduced, the frustrations causing it must be reduced. Intense emotions are made less intense by achieving their goals, not merely by displaying them. Experiencing an emotion, as in catharsis, is only a first step in accomplishing this end.

Going Slowly. Incremental tolerance is not a quick fix. It takes time to abide intense emotions. They lose their power to intimidate very slowly.

The clinician who encourages a client to integrate his passions too quickly ensures that they will remain undigested. A person's feelings become tolerable when they are in fact tolerable. There is no point in insisting on a timetable that does not coincide with one's internal schedule. A clinician must instead be responsive to what his client can accept.

The resocializer who demands too much too quickly is inadvertently fostering the development of unmanageable agglomerations of emotion. He is in effect asking his client to tackle new emotions before he is finished working through the old. Thus instead of reducing their intensity, the clinician will be making his client's task more overwhelming. One cannot facilitate desensitization if one is not patient enough to correctly assess what a client can handle. A helper who is not prepared to take progress as it comes will promote very little of it. Ultimately, going slowly is often the fastest way of getting somewhere.

A client too must learn not to push too vigorously. As much as he may want to put painful feelings behind him, desire alone will not lead to their toleration. No one can force himself to be less intimidated by his intense emotions; he must allow, not coerce, himself into being less sensitive. In this a clinician can be useful. Since he will be less pressured to pacify these uncomfortable emotions, he can counsel patience. His client can be encouraged to listen to his feelings, to acknowledge their existence, and to make haste slowly.

Reevaluation and Reconsideration. Once a person is able to examine his intense emotions without running away from them, he is ready to evaluate their message. Emotions communicate. If they are reactive, they alert a person to important circumstances in his environment. If they are teleological, they inform him of the status of his own goals. In either event, their message may be appropriate or inappropriate. A reactive emotion can accurately assess its environment, or offer a misleading account of it. A teleological one can aim at a viable goal, or encourage the impossible. When these messages and goals are out of touch with reality, they institute wrong set solutions which then need to be corrected.

If a person is to achieve the goals of his emotions, he must understand what they communicate, and react accordingly. When the messages of his emotions are appropriate, he can allow them to guide his actions; when they are not, he must revise their message and redirect his actions. There will be at least two questions he must answer: (1) Is the message of the emotion accurate? That is, is what it communicates true? (2) Is the goal of his emotion possible? Can it be achieved? Once these answers are known, he can decide what to do, what to seek, and what to avoid.

If a fear communicates danger, the person experiencing it must evaluate his actual peril. His emotion will alert him to look for some hazard; once he sees it, he must determine if his perception is valid. Does a supposed danger represent a genuine prospect of injury? Perhaps it is a false alarm. Sometimes current fears are actually imports from childhood. They may signal a danger that was once real (e.g., a spanking), but is no longer threatening to his adult self. He must be able to tell the difference if he is to respond appropriately. This reevaluation of intense emotions is necessary because the circumstances in which the feelings were originally aroused have long since disappeared. When they originated, they may have reflected dangers, frustrations, and losses that now, however, are not applicable. Still, their reemergence in the present allows one to take a fresh look. A person will be able to compare them then and now to determine what is currently true.

Similarly, the goals of emotions must be reconsidered. They too can be out of date. The frustrations that cause a person to be angry may be a response to the thwarting of goals that he may now want to renounce. He may decide, for instance, that he no longer literally craves his mother's love; thus when she withholds it, there is no longer a reason to unleash his fury.

All of this may sound easy, but emotions which endure also resist alteration. They do not crumble before one cursory reevaluation or one impulsive reconsideration. Intense emotions have been designed to conserve a person's reactions to intense learning experiences. It is their ability to stabilize important behaviors that enables us to have stable relationships and to react expeditiously in emergency situations. The conservatism of emotions serves a vital purpose, and so their alteration cannot be precipitous. Indeed, for feelings to change, they must be reevaluated and reconsidered at length. A person must be certain that his new evaluations are correct before they are implemented. Thus if something was once a danger, there must be no mistake in deciding that it no longer is. As Otto Fenichel (1941) has observed, "when a person is afraid but experiences a situation in which what was feared occurs without any harm resulting, he will not immediately trust the outcome of his new experience; however, the second time he will have a little less fear, the third time still less." This is nature's way of protecting against ill-considered mistakes.

Identifying Emotions. A clinician can encourage the reevaluation process by focusing attention on his client's emotions. A client can be asked to look at what he is feeling, and why. What specifically is he experiencing? And when does it arise? As a client becomes more comfortable with himself, his judgment in these matters becomes more accurate. To use the cliché of our day, he "gets in touch with his feelings." One way of improving a client's judgment is to help him relabel his experience. Emotions that he may once have hidden under layers of euphemism can be identified for what they are. When he is asked, "What are you feeling now?" and he replies, "I'm a little upset," he can be helped to understand that he is really afraid. Or if he answers that he is "a little annoyed," it can be suggested that he is in fact angry.

If a client resists examining his own experience, his clinician can make points by indirection. Instead of insisting that the client is angry, he may observe, "If I were in your shoes, I would feel angry." This may remove the burden from the client's shoulders and make it possible for him to avow his rage. It then becomes a feeling that can be shared with a trusted other. Sometimes a clinician will have to be more assertive. When his client adamantly refuses to acknowledge his emotions, he may have to insist. He may need to say, "You are angry." This confrontive style is sometimes indispensable. So is patience. A clinician may find it essential to restate his perception of his client's situation many times before the latter is willing to see it for what it is.

Sometimes a person has difficulty identifying his feelings because they are mixed. It is easy to become confused when contradictory emotions exist side by side. When this happens, it is the clinician's responsibility to explicate his client's multiple emotions. Together they can tease them apart. Often the realization that mixed emotions are present is enough to allay a person's fears and make it possible for him to behold them as they are.

The Context of Emotions. In their mutual effort to understand and evaluate the message of the client's emotions, resocialization partners can examine the context in which they occur. Attaching labels to feelings says something about their nature, but not enough. If a feeling is fear then it is a signal of danger, but danger from what quarter? If it is anger it warns of frustration, but what goal has been thwarted, and how? When and where an emotion occurs speaks volumes about what it communicates. Its context can help ascertain what has provoked it.

Emotions do not occur in isolation. They are reactions to situations. Moreover, the goals at which they aim are not ethereal abstractions, but palpable realities. Fear does not contemplate generalized safety, but safety from particular dangers. Anger does not seek to end frustration in general, but very particular frustrations. This means that to understand a given emotion one must understand its particular circumstances. To put the matter baldly, it is necessary to know more than that one is fearful, he has to know what he is fearful of. And if he is angry, what he is angry at.

The context, and hence the aim, of an emotion can usually be detected by questions about when it emerged. What other people were present when the feeling first appeared? And what were they doing? What was the person himself attempting? At what moment did his feeling begin? What was happening then? What was happening just before then? What thoughts was he entertaining at the time? Did he have any particular bodily sensations? Did he feel the fear in the back of his neck? His chest? Does the circumstance in which he experienced the emotion remind him of other circumstances? Now? In the past? What were these?

If a client has difficulty answering these questions, the resocialization relationship itself can be used as a tool for unearthing the background of his emotions. It too is a context of emotions. During their interchanges, the client will have emotional reactions to his clinician. Since these will be observable, they can be used to ascertain what has provoked the particular feeling in this instance. This will give the clinician an opportunity to highlight what occurred and to probe for details. What exactly was it that activated the client's reaction? Has it happened before? How would the client like the situation remedied? Has he had similar reactions with other role partners?

Making Comparisons. Reevaluating an emotion is essentially a comparative process. A person trapped in an intense or misdirected emotion must compare it with the circumstances in which it arose to see if the current feeling communicates the correct information today. Reevaluation makes comparisons between the present and the past. It attempts to determine if what appears to be true really is.

When dealing with the context of present emotions, a client must be helped to take a hard, close look at his situation. If fear says he is now in danger, what is the danger? It is not enough to assume it exists. Some independent evidence must confirm the hazard. A clinician must be prepared to ask about a specific injury. Just what is it the client believes will hurt him? And why does he think so? Is he in fact being harmed right now? Usually a mistake made in a current emotional assessment occurs because the present has been confounded with the past. The present signal has arisen because a current situation seems to be identical with a past one. If this apparent identity is mistaken, then the message will be mistaken. It then becomes necessary to disentangle now from then, and make separate judgments about both.

Let us take the example of a child who has been raised within a punitive family. He will have learned that the exercise of authority is inextricably linked with coercion. Since all of his parent's demands were preemptive orders, he assumes that all authorities issue such orders. And since his parents backed their demands with violence, he believes that violence lurks behind all authoritative demands. He will have correctly feared his parents' demands because there was a danger within them, but the question he faces as an adult is whether other authorities are also dangerous.

Emotions incorporate automatic reactions to events so that what seems similar elicits a similar response. Yet feelings are very gross instruments. Fear, anger, and sadness have difficulty making fine distinctions, especially when they originate in childhood. An authority will be deemed an authority, and all authorities will seem foreboding. Indeed, it will take a special effort to note the differences between quasi-parental figures and to react appropriately toward them.

In order to make these distinctions, a person will have to look closely at both the present and the past. If he starts with the present, he must inquire about the nature of the current authority. What kind of person is this authority? What are his motives? When he is thwarted, how does he enforce his wishes? How does he feel about the client? Does he really want to injure him? Is what the client has done so terrible that the other wants to punish him? Has the client provoked this reaction? And if the authority becomes punitive, is the client as vulnerable as he was when he was a child? Does he have ways to defend himself that he didn't have as a child?

After examining the present situation, he will have to inspect the past too. What were his father's motives? Why was he so punitive when his wishes were thwarted? Was it because of something the client did? Did he react coercively in all instances, or only some? Which were these? Why? Did he behave the same toward others? What were the father's sensitivities? His goals? How could (or couldn't) the client have protected himself from this wrath?

Going into all of these details permits a more trustworthy comparison between the past and present than was encompassed in the client's initial crude reaction. If the message encoded in his emotions is valid, it must accurately reflect the realities of both. If the situations are the same, they should feel the same; if different, they should feel different. Indeed, if he discovers that past and present authorities have similar motives and reactions, he will have reason to be fearful. Should he, however, determine that they have different attitudes and styles, he will probably not be in danger. Contrary to his original estimate, he will already be safe and will not need to protect himself further.

If a client's revised judgment is validated by future experience, his emotional structure will undergo reorganization. Gradually, the emotive meaning of "authority" and "father" will diverge, and the former will cease to hold its old terrors. This change will be slow, but when it occurs it will be stable. The client's outlook on the world will have been altered, and so will his behavior patterns.

Reconsidering Goals. When dealing with teleological emotions such as anger, it is necessary to reassess one's goals. It is essential to know if current frustrations are reversible, or whether they are inherent in one's aims. If a person is seeking the impossible, frustration is inevitable. Thus if someone is intensely angry, he must stop and ask himself if what he is after is really achievable, or whether it might be advisable to pursue more feasible alternatives. A client trapped in a rage he can't seem to reduce would do well to review the serenity prayer. He should ask himself what he must accept, and what he can hope to change. If he is conscientious, the wisdom to tell the difference between these will emerge from a careful examination of his situation. This new knowledge may then stimulate him to reorder his priorities and abandon lost causes.

Let us suppose that a person has always wanted to be loved by his parents, but was not. If he continues to seek their love, he continues to court frustration. No matter what he does, he will not get what he wants. However energetic his pleas, his efforts will fail. Most probably his parents will not cooperate, but even if they do, they cannot make up for love withheld in the past. Unless he is willing to shift his sights, he cannot win, and hence will remain angry. Only if he reconsiders his position and seeks a somewhat different goal will success be possible.

Often, clients do not wish to redirect their energies because they fear that nothing can replace their original aspirations. They believe, for instance, that no current love can supplant a past one. In this they are partly correct. It is true that nothing can exactly substitute for the all-embracing warmth of the parental love accorded infants. If this was not obtained in the past, it never will be. But what role changers fail to understand is that while the love of a spouse, child, or friend may not fully compensate for the absence of parental love, it is far better than nothing. Dreams that are not capable of fulfillment are worth no more than smoke and haze. They may be very beautiful, but they do not bring lasting satisfactions. Although the possible is not as grand as the fantasized, it has the advantage of being real. It can be touched and felt, and it meets needs.

Effective Use. When a person's emotions are no longer clouded by misleading messages, they can be used to motivate effective actions. Feelings that are too intense and/or misdirected point in the wrong directions and encourage unhelpful actions. If the communications derived from an emotion are distorted, its motivation function is distorted too. The emotion will energize behaviors that do not achieve goals or lead to personal fulfillment. It is only when freed from debilitating distortions that the emotion can achieve its ends. It then becomes an excellent indicator of what must be accomplished for a person to attain satisfaction. Such a revised emotion becomes part of a corrected set solution that is capable of meeting needs.

Once the intensity of an emotion has been reduced to manageable levels, its signal function becomes more accurate, and it can be "used" to realize its goals. Thus the actions motivated by fear can help a person achieve safety and the behaviors energized by anger can help him eliminate frustrations. Emotions that are "effectively" deployed are self-

correcting. They carry within themselves the seeds of their own fulfillment. They make a person want to do things that will make him feel
better.

Unfortunately, intense or misdirected emotions are not self-fulfilling.
They often stimulate automatic actions that are not effective. A person
in the throes of an intense emotion experiences a loss of control. His
fear or rage can induce him to do things he might not consciously desire. He may know that a particular act of violence will not accomplish
what he wants, but the impulse to commit it may be so powerful that
he cannot effectively oppose it. It will be as if he were trapped in a
rampaging river that is stronger than he is.

When a person's emotions are so potent that he is having difficulty
with impulse control, his reactions will be "primitive" ones. It will be
his under-socialized reflexes that will get the upper hand. Like an angry child, he will lash out physically; or like a frightened one, he will
cling to the very source of his danger. Either way, his action will not
be effective and will not get him what he wants. Regressive behaviors
tend to be out of place and trigger undesired consequences.

The effective use of emotions is contingent upon implementing appropriate actions. It is when feelings energize well planned and well
controlled responses that they achieve the desired effect. A certain flexibility is required to adjust an action to its circumstances. A feeling that
is too strong interferes with this malleability and instigates stereotyped
behaviors that don't succeed. Effective use of emotions, however, is
responsive and enlightened.

Fear that is properly used helps a person neutralize danger. It motivates an appropriate fight or flight which brings greater safety. Effectively used fear adjusts actions to meet particular dangers so that when
it motivates fight, it wins, and when it motivates flight, it finds refuge.
Often it walks away rather than run. Similarly, effective anger is accurately apprised of the source of one's frustrations; when it applies muscle, it does so in a way that makes things happen. It influences people
to do what is wanted, and motivates the actor to institute competent
self-help. It is not easy to use emotions effectively, but the alternative
is ineffective use. While the latter may be momentarily satisfying, in
the long run it makes things worse. Emotions that are misapplied do
not achieve their goals; they stay active and block necessary role change.

Ghost Victories. The key to neutralizing a danger is to fight it and beat
it. Usually, people trapped in dysfunctional social roles have been beaten
into submission by social dangers. The coercive relationships that shaped
their unsatisfying roles were reinforced with threats of injury. Because
they could not effectively counter these threats, they were forced to
enact unsatisfying roles. Had they been able to do battle more effectively then, they probably wouldn't need to attempt role change now.

Resocialization is to a large extent an attempt to redo the past. Past negotiations must be reworked and past coercion undone. It is only then that the fears implanted in one's soul can be truly expunged. Only when the social dangers that generated fears are successfully countered do they themselves dissipate. In short, the general goal that fear attempts to achieve is protection from the coercion of earlier role negotiations.

Yet the past is not accessible. It is gone forever. How then can coercion which occurred yesterday be countered today? How can fear which was generated by historic dangers be disarmed in present circumstances? In one sense, it cannot. What has gone wrong always stays wrong. Nevertheless, feelings initiated by past events can be altered by present events. When they are reexperienced, they can be changed. The intolerable can be made tolerable, the misinterpreted reinterpreted, and the miscarried reapplied. Emotions made to work in the present achieve a semblance of goals which really belong to the past. Thus when a facsimile of ancient coercion is successfully resisted here and now, the fear associated with it is diminished and the person can feel safe in situations that previously scared him.

One way of beating historic coercion is to do it in one's head. A person can achieve what amounts to "ghost victories." Memories of past defeats can be activated in the imagination and, in fantasy, reversed. This may make them seem to be imaginary victories, but they are real in their effects. They can, and do, have emotional consequences. Thus a person who imagines himself restraining a parent who once violently abused him can, in memory, make that parent less frightening. While the parent may be but a remembrance, the reexperienced emotional reaction to him is not. It is in the present. One's ancient terror then loses its power to be internally coercive because the parent feels less intimidating today.

Shadow Victories. Shadow victories can also counter past coercion. These are victories achieved against surrogates of past role partners. They do not occur merely in the imagination, but with real people. The possibility of shadow victories is one of the major reasons for the existence of the repetition compulsion. By reenacting past relationships in the present, old feelings are revived, along with the scenery of past events. "Repeated" roles tend to enlist role partners who reproduce the negotiating stances of past partners. This makes it easier to feel what one once felt and to plan new strategies to defeat threats that were once overwhelming. If these new negotiations go well, it will seem as if the old ones have been reversed, and the emotions connected with them will be altered.

If, for instance, a person has an employer who is similar to one of his parents, he can use the former as a substitute for the latter. If both are authoritarian, he can use the employer as a stand-in for his parent. If he can now prevent the employer from attacking him the way his parent once did, he will in one sense have gained a victory over the parent. The emotional achievement will be the same. The danger that existed in the past will not thereby be removed, but it will seem to be. Indeed, for his emotions, it will be. Manipulating a stand-in for the past role partner will have altered his feelings such that he is less fearful and much safer.

In fact, employers make terrible surrogates for parents. So do spouses. Negotiations with most current role partners are not likely to result in the desired shadow victories. These others are too powerful and too unlikely to be cooperative. Employers and spouses usually don't know that they have been chosen to be stand-ins for parents, and so they concentrate on not losing today's negotiation rather than providing an opportunity for the person to redo the past in more satisfactory ways. Indeed, they will probably not agree that what is satisfactory for the role changer is satisfactory for them. And when they vigorously resist the scripts he has devised for them, they inflict new defeats which will do nothing to alter his emotional status. This, of course, is where a clinician fits in. Presumably he does know what his client is trying to do and is prepared to be cooperative. He may not be ready to lie down and play dead, but he can negotiate in good faith and in a manner that permits his client to achieve success.

UNBLOCKING SADNESS

Unblocking sadness is a little different from unblocking other emotions. Fear, anger, and guilt require a person to actively correct their intensity and direction. For these emotions to reach their goals, a person must be prepared to fight back. Using the energy imbedded in them means trying to make things happen, but in a more satisfying way. With sadness, however, one must be more passive. For sadness to achieve its end, a person must "let go." He must be willing to allow things to happen, rather than make them happen.

Sadness, of course, is central to resocialization. Social roles cannot be changed unless role players are ready to relinquish aspects of them. This gives the process a paradoxical quality. However vital an interest a person may have in reconstructing his dysfunctional behaviors, there comes a point at which he must sit back and do nothing. For those who find safety in control, sadness is decidedly unsafe. The actual letting go of what is lost is not controllable; it is simply something that happens on its own without moment-to-moment guidance from the one to which it is happening.

Resocialization therefore requires a certain amount of vulnerability.

As the deep blackness of grief overtakes a person, he can easily feel as if he is slipping away into nothingness. A natural reaction to this is to put on the brakes and stop the process. One wants to feel better, happier, and alive. Sadness, however, will seem like a further defeat, not like a step on the path to improvement. In consequence, one actively tries to become less sad, and inadvertently blocks change.

Misusing Sadness. When someone tries to avoid the depths of his grief, he can find himself going into perpetual mourning. Instead of his sadness leading to happiness, resistance produces long-term, low-level sadness. He remains sad, but never sad enough to let go. Because the person refuses to accept the possibility of permanent loss, he condemns himself to a limbo in which there is neither loss nor success. Rather than accepting the fact that life entails a series of small deaths, each of which can initiate a rebirth, he persists in fighting, denying, and bargaining long after the hope of victory has vanished. His very terror of defeat insures that he will not win. Sometimes a person will attempt to halt the mourning process by becoming excessively detached. If he opts out of the world, perhaps there will be nothing to lose. Indeed, some withdrawal is normal to mourning; it provides an area of calm where letting go can occur. But too much withdrawal precludes the possibility of a reentry into life. It makes a person a permanent outsider in his own world.

Similarly, one can seek relief by becoming overly involved in his world. His strategy is to remain active despite his sadness. His hope will be that if he remains busy enough, the pain of loss can be cancelled out by other sensations. He may literally resort to jogging in the belief that if he runs fast enough, he can outdistance his loss. In this, he is not totally mistaken, since physical activity can postpone loss and cushion its impact. What it cannot do, however, is nullify it. Sooner or later a loss must be faced or it will fester beneath the surface.

Sadness can also be blocked by too little or too much involvement with others. Under optimal circumstances, the mourning process is a fairly private affair, but it can benefit from the unobtrusive support of concerned others. They can function as a source of courage and safety which makes it easier to cope with grief. This is one of the reasons that all cultures have ceremonies of mourning. Socially sanctioned forms of support, such as wakes and funerals, provide a transition that makes sorrow more bearable. Going it totally alone increases one's despair and makes it more difficult to move on. Still, too much interaction with others diverts the course of mourning. A certain measure of privacy is required for someone to reorganize his internal attachments. What is lost must be pondered, and what is to come considered. If a person is too social, he hasn't the time to think through issues that must be thought through.

Finally, some people avoid sadness because they simply do not believe in it. They consider it a form of weakness. Their ideal is the stiff upper lip. To them, expressing pain by crying or being downcast is unacceptably maudlin. They would rather show the world that nothing hurts them, that they are impervious to the pains that debilitate lesser souls. Unfortunately such attempts to deny sadness do not eliminate it any better than does activity. Letting go simply must be worked through in mourning. Of course, a person in the throes of grief is in a sense weaker. He is in fact more exposed to external attack because of his internal preoccupations, but he will ultimately gain strength by disengaging from areas of weakness.

Working Through the Sadness

A Safe Place. Having a safe place is crucial to achieving the goal of sadness. Because letting go of what is lost can feel like embracing death, protection is essential. A person must be certain that in allowing himself to feel sad, he will not die. His safe place must therefore be one that assures him that he is still alive. It is this affirmation of life that will give him the courage to loosen his grip, and when he does, the process of letting go will be almost automatic.

Embracing life can take many forms. In a way, it is like pinching oneself to make sure one is still alive. Primary to this approach is self-surveillance to confirm that nothing has gone wrong. One also needs some activity and some interaction to validate one's continued existence. A clinician can be very useful in this regard by confirming that sadness is not fatal. He can accomplish this by giving his client permission to be sad, support while being sad, sufficient distance to work things through, and optimism that grief does not last forever.

Giving Permission. When a client's fears incline him to resist becoming depressed, a resocializer can encourage him to experience the feeling. A client can be given permission to cry, to withdraw, and to feel sorry for himself. If he is worried about these behaviors being shameful, he can be assured that they are not. A clinician can challenge the myth of the stiff upper lip and explain the purpose and value of sadness. Although other role partners may advocate that the client tough things out, a clinician can verify the usefulness of sadness. The role changer will then not stand alone against a phalanx of opinion that denies his right to feel what he must.

Giving Support. When a client feels too frightened to be sad, when he is certain that the pain he is experiencing is dangerous, his clinician can extend an umbrella of safety. He can offer his client something to hold on to while he endures his private agony. A helping hand can assure him that he has not been abandoned by an indifferent universe.

If the two can share the client's pain, it may in fact diminish. The tears the client sheds, and the comfort he is afforded, may make the emotion more bearable.

Because sadness is a mechanism for letting go, part of what makes it so terrifying is the prospect of being trapped between two ways of life with nothing to hold on to. This transition which is a necessary part of moving from one attachment to another can seem to last forever. It may be countered by giving a person something to grasp during the process of change. By being present for his client and accessible when needed, the clinician becomes such an object. His presence fills what would otherwise be an ominous void. The client will figuratively be able to reach out and touch him when he wants to assure himself that he is not alone.

A client's terror can also be eased by teaching him how to be present for himself. A person who knows how to hold on to himself and to love himself is never completely alone. In effect, he becomes his own parent and provides himself with the protection he needs. Even simple exercises, like physically hugging oneself, can inoculate against the emptiness of sadness endured alone.

Giving Distance. While being with a person is often vital for successful letting go, it is but one half of the sadness experience. Unhappiness also requires some aloneness. Support is essential, but so is the ability to withdraw when necessary. They are opposite sides of the same phenomenon. A person in the depths of grief will sometimes want to hold on, and sometimes want space. Relinquishing what has been lost requires private mental processing which excessive stimulation can disrupt. In consequence, a clinician must be sensitive to his client's vacillating needs. When support is necessary he must be on call, but when privacy is appropriate he must be prepared to give distance. His client must not feel threatened by an "assault" just when he feels most vulnerable. Misplaced "hovering," no matter how well intentioned, can have unintended effects. It can be decidedly unsafe.

Giving Optimism. Should a client be alarmed about the prospect of relinquishing his grip on what has already been lost, his helper can inject a note of optimism. The clinician's vantage point will give him more confidence in the future than is possible for his client alone. The latter's perspective will be contaminated by his personal misery and he will be wearing the opposite of rose-colored glasses. Unless someone points out that better circumstances are possible, his pessimism may convince him that all is lost. More than one person has committed suicide because he couldn't conceive of his misery lifting. This gives the clinician an opportunity to protect his client from himself by making sure that it is understood that his current pain is temporary.

Incremental Tolerance. It is possible for sadness to be so profound that it is impossible to extricate oneself from it. When the pain of depression becomes unbearable, it inhibits all activity. The person who is too sad may not have the ability to save himself. Like the infant who wastes away from marasmus, he may lose his will to live. Instead of letting go of what is lost, he lets go of everything. The energy which one needs to fight for life will not be available to him.

It is therefore essential that total misery be avoided. Old losses must not be experienced all at once or in their entirety. For sadness to be tolerated, and ultimately used to one's advantage, it must be permitted in manageable doses. A person who obsesses about everything that has gone wrong in his life prevents himself from working through anything. Similarly, he who submerges himself in misery without coming up for breath may drown in his own juices. Letting go must occur within a person's comfort zone. Pushing too quickly to be finished with one's sorrow only extends it. Sometimes years must go by before grief is worked through.

Reevaluating and Reconsidering. When sadness is respected and dealt with in tolerable increments, its import can be appreciated. A person can recognize what he has lost and why it was lost. He can accept the necessity of letting go or rationally decide to resist it. His reevaluation of his circumstance will indicate what is feasible and what is not. The person will also be able to consider whether or not he is still alive. As he begins to loosen his grip on what is lost, he will be able to look around to see if he too is slipping away. Presumably he will discover that letting go of the lost is not equivalent to letting go of life. His observations should convince him that role change without concomitant disaster is possible.

Using Sadness. As has been stressed, the secret to using sadness is to allow it to run its course. When it does, it ends with losses being relinquished and new attachments being formed. Unhappiness can be a tool for proceeding from the bad to the good. As long as it is done gradually, it can be done well. There is no need to twist sadness so that it conforms to a preconceived notion of what change should be. A person's natural inclinations will direct him to do what needs to be done.

Paradoxical Sadness. When someone is reworking the emotions that block resocialization, he may experience a sadness that seems inexplicable. Events occur which should make him happy, but don't. Although he doesn't seem to have endured a loss, he reacts as if he did. Thus when anger or fear impel him to battle with ancient demons and he wins a ghost victory, he may not be pleased. Or, in a contest with current role partners, he may reverse the decision of a past role negotiation, yet feel no sense of victory. At such moments, one expects him to experience a rush of joy, but this rarely happens. More likely, he becomes depressed. He will, in short, be gripped by a "paradoxical sadness."

Such a person's reaction may not seem sensible, but it is. Current successes are always a reminder of past failures. The sweeter a present attainment, the more bitter becomes the past disaster, and the sharper will be the contrast between them. Therefore at the very moment of success, the past is reanimated and its pungency reinforced. A present success will vividly demonstrate that victory was always tenable, and loss not inevitable. The person will realize that the pain imposed upon him was unnecessary, and its memory will sting all the more. In short, old wounds will be reopened and their pain intensified. It is this renewed pain that forms the core of paradoxical sadness.

In addition to retrospective sadness, a person may also be seized by a prospective sadness. The memory of past failures will give him reason to distrust present successes. Instead of rejoicing at the victory of the moment, his attention may focus on a dread of the future. The present success may seem ephemeral and he will begin mourning what he is sure will be denied him at a later date. His sadness will then be for what he fears he will never have. Rather than accepting his victory and taking pleasure in it, he will treat it as a tease and prepare his defenses for the inevitable punishment to come.

CASE STUDY: ROBERT

During the letting-go phase of resocialization, Robert had to conquer many fears from his past. His role as a "coward" had virtually institutionalized his fear. Acceptance of the role made it difficult for him to change because he could not consider the possibility of relationships in which he was not afraid. As far as he was concerned, he had always been fearful and always would be. How could he let go of something that was not in his power to relinquish?

One of the tools Robert's clinician tried to employ in identifying his client's dysfunctional roles and communicating their force was the role play. But Robert had been reluctant to engage in one. He did not want to risk reexperiencing the violence-saturated relationship he had had with his father. He especially did not want to reawaken the powerlessness of his childhood or put himself in his father's pitiless shoes.

The clinician was forced to use a less evocative device. Instead of pressing Robert to experience his past in all its raw ferocity, he did something safer. He allowed Robert not to role play, but conjectured aloud about what Robert's childhood roles might have been. These verbalizations were less threatening than an emotional reenactment and permitted an incremental tolerance to develop. This strategy also established the clinician as a safe person. He visibly demonstrated that he had no desire to torture Robert as he once had been.

In time, the clinician's musings became more elaborate. As he developed a better understanding of Robert's situation, he constructed elaborate verbal fantasies of what would happen if his father joined them in the office. What would dad do? What would he say? How could Robert protect himself? Perhaps this or that might occur. What did Robert think? Might it be that way?

All of this added up to an approximation of a ghost relationship. Robert was encouraged to imagine how he might fight back. Thus he was asked if he could think of ways in which he could win. Perhaps the clinician could be used as an ally. Was this possible? "No," came the reply. Dad was so powerful that he would defeat the clinician too. But was this really so? Was the clinician so weak and dad so fearsome? Well, maybe the clinician could be of some use. Maybe dad could be beaten occasionally.

In time, as Robert felt safer, he could even imagine taking the offensive himself. His thoughts of revenge were not automatically quashed by fears of destruction at dad's hand. Still there remained a lingering suspicion that even if he could kill dad, the man would refuse to die.

As it became possible to deal more directly with Robert's relationship with his father, more and more feelings bubbled to the surface. The resocialization relationship became a sanctuary that enabled him to tolerate and reevaluate other aspects of his emotional history. More frequently he came to sessions feeling frightened or angry, but he was not panicked. When asked to explain his feelings, he could. Thus he might disclose that on the previous night he had hardly slept because he had imagined his father to be outside his bedroom. To be sure, he knew he wasn't physically present, but sometimes it felt as if he were.

As Robert's emotions became more available to him, it became possible to explore how they prevented change. Thus the better he could tolerate his fear, the more he could appreciate that it perpetuated his image of himself as a coward. He could see that if he dared to acknowledge courage in himself, he would be inviting reprisal from dad's ghost. At first, this was very intimidating. Father's remembered image seemed almost as powerful as he had been in the flesh. Robert was reluctant to challenge what he knew to be a memory because he was not sure he could defeat it.

Soon Robert saw that coming to terms with his emotions was crucial. This encouraged him to make an effort at dealing with his fear. It was not easy or simple for him, but he was determined to try. Even so, his emotions did not emerge in an orderly or predictable fashion. Instead, they came out on their own schedule. As instances of his fear and anger appeared, Robert and the clinician considered their provenance and how they might be countered. If, for example, the terror of parental punishment was aroused, they explored satisfactory ways of fighting back. What might Robert say if accused of cowardice or laziness? How could he respond if threatened with a beating? Were there safe places to go? Was there anyone he could depend upon to protect him? Could the clinician be his shield? Could he do the job himself?

When Robert's terror began to abate, he allowed himself to experience other emotions as well. First his repressed anger emerged, and eventually his sadness. The unblocking of his fear freed him to begin letting go of his dysfunctional roles. Yet Robert was surprised by this development. He had imagined that once his fear was under control, life would become a pleasant stroll in the sun. It bewildered him to become aware of how much he had missed. Despite himself, he was forced to realize how difficult and empty his life had been.

After a while, Robert became openly depressed. "I didn't know how unhappy I was; I didn't realize how much I had lost," he complained. And with this, he began to surrender his role of "coward." As he became better equipped to fight back against his father's ghost, he recognized that he had falsely been accused. He realized that fear is normal when one is being terrorized. These understandings made him less inclined to label himself a timid wretch and gave him a greater ability to accept himself as he was.

9

Renegotiating Roles

GETTING STARTED

After the major impediments to role change have been removed and a person has begun to relinquish her unsatisfying patterns of interactive behavior, she will be ready to construct new role relationships. If she is to do this successfully, she will have to negotiate more effectively than she once did. Unless she can engage in non-coercive, problem-solving negotiations, she is very unlikely to establish roles that will meet her needs. It will, therefore, be important for her to develop bargaining skills that enable her to reverse the results of coercion and to embrace structures that work.

The clinician who intends to assist in this endeavor will require a great deal of courage. If he wants to increase his client's sense of power, he cannot exert excessive power of his own. Neither can he hide behind his professional authority and enforce positive outcomes. His goal necessitates that he have the moral and emotional courage to remain vulnerable. Despite the emotional maelstroms of resocialization, he must be prepared to stand up for who he is and what he believes, and to do so in a fair way. During negotiations between himself and his client, he has to uphold his end of their differences without being overpowering. His style of contending must not prevent his client from standing up for herself.

A role-change relationship is much like a parental one in that it too should be a "moving equilibrium." There must be a real equality between the participants in spite of the inequality of their power. As long as his client is vulnerable, a clinician must be exceedingly gentle. As the former's power increases, the latter's level of assertiveness should rise to keep pace. But it will often take genuine forbearance to avoid exploitation. At any given moment, a clinician will have to exert just enough force to be heard, but not enough to be intimidating. Since the client will begin as a less skilled role negotiator, it is up to the resocializer to adjust his interventions to meet changing circumstances.

An interactive approach to role negotiations is neither directive nor non-directive. For resocialization to be fair and effective, it must be responsive. A clinician who coerces his client either by putting words in her mouth or refusing to listen to her is not allowing mutual problem solving to occur. True interaction is a dialogue. First one partner makes an assertion, which the other considers and to which he responds; then the first replies in kind, and so on. Neither side is assumed to have a monopoly on the truth or exclusive rights to have his interests met. It is understood that contributions from both parties are needed to construct a bargain that is superior to any one-sided mandate.

Firm Flexibility. A client who wishes to develop satisfying roles must be able to procure what she needs. But if her words don't have sufficient energy, they won't elicit a suitable response. There must be a firmness in her demands, along with a concomitant willingness to make concessions. The person who is obnoxiously assertive, or compliantly yielding, usually loses. It is the enlightened selfishness of someone who is secure in herself and confident in her right to pursue happiness who has the best chance of achieving success.

The resocialization process should prepare a client to act in her own interests with firmness and flexibility. If the interactions between herself and her clinician have been respectful and responsive, they should serve as a prototype for negotiating new role relationships. The practice she has had in making reasonable demands of her helper, as well as in responding to the latter's expectations, should enable her to do the same with role partners in other relationships.

Dual Concern. A non-coercive approach to negotiating should also be a dual-concern one. The interests served should be those of both parties. A person and her role partner should be aware of the interests of both so that they can develop a solution that serves mutual purposes. Non-coerciveness alone does not guarantee that their respective cases will be asserted or heard. There must also be a specific effort to understand the interests of both sides by both sides.

As it does for non-coerciveness, the resocialization process can provide a model for the dual-concern approach. If, during the first stages of role change, a client and clinician can establish a pattern of cooperation, it can carry over into the renegotiation phase of their endeavors. The client can then learn that role negotiations are not a zero-sum game, and that for a successful conclusion to emerge, both must win.

The Clinician as Negotiator

A resocializer is ipso facto a negotiator; all phases of the change process call upon him to make bargains with his client. If these are good bargains, his client will be helped to become a good bargainer herself. If not, the wrong lessons will be acquired. Before renegotiations begin, the two will have had experience in making agreements about identifying and reexperiencing dysfunctional roles, and about unblocking the impediments to change. Ultimately, skills acquired during these activities can be applied to negotiating new roles. It thus behooves a clinician to be a good negotiator who has first-rate skills to impart.

Power. The relationship between a clinician and his client is inherently unequal. The former has the power to exploit the latter's vulnerabilities. If he so chooses, he can turn a client's fears and unhappiness against her. Vanity is a near universal trait, and a resocializer who elects to enhance his self-image at the expense of the person he is pledged to help usually can do so. The fact that his own dysfunctional roles are not subjected to examination gives him a decisive advantage. Because he will be the one with the cool head and the socially sanctioned right to delve into the other's weaknesses, if he decides to use his discoveries to exacerbate his client's distress, he has the leverage to prevail.

However, power can be an instrument for enormous good. A clinician who uses it with caution can persuade a reluctant client to recognize her dysfunctional roles, to reexperience them, and to unblock the script elements that prevent change. His strength can be a guarantee of safety and a herald of what his client can become. Power commands attention and gains a respectful hearing. It can make a clinician someone who must be taken seriously when he engages in bargaining. As long as he voluntarily abstains from abusing his position, his strength will imbue him with immense influence.

There is no reason for a clinician to deny this power advantage. Power is not an evil in itself. It does not have to be used to exploit a client's secrets. Strength that expresses itself as a responsive firmness can be acknowledged with pride. Indeed, if it is not mystified or treated as inherently dangerous, it can become a tool that a client employs for her own ends too.

Fairness. The superior power of a resocializer can best be utilized when it is exercised fairly. Fairness is another way of saying that the interests of both parties are equally considered. It is the hallmark of negotiations that are oriented toward problem solving. The fair use of a clinician's power harnesses it to the needs of his client, and validates the client's right to be fair with himself. It puts the clinician's energies at the disposal of his client, and discourages arbitrary coercion.

If a clinician is to be a fair negotiator, he needs to be a fair person.

When he treats his client as an equal, his behavior should not merely imply professional duty, but reflect a personal commitment. At those moments when he must be coercive (and there are some, e.g., for the physical protection of himself or the other), it should be invoked with reluctance. It is the person who is implementing his own values, not just externally imposed standards, who is most to be trusted with the vital interests of another.

A resocializer who is fair will be pleased by his client's successes. When his client is right, he will acknowledge it; when she achieves victories, he will rejoice. Since the clinician is in a quasi-parental role, he should be capable of parental pride. His client's accomplishments should be a positive reflection upon himself, rather than a threat to his superiority.

Above all, a resocializer must avoid casual coercion. He must not force his client to do things without realizing that force has been employed. A negative outcome is possible when a clinician is so self-involved that he is insensitive to client losses. It will be difficult for him to be fair if he doesn't comprehend that he is being unfair. Similarly, he must not cavalierly dismiss his client's interests or engage in unthinking deception. He cannot be even-handed when his client's rights are unceremoniously ignored.

Counter-transference. Just as a role changer reenacts her dysfunctional roles by recruiting the clinician as a role partner, so the clinician enacts parts of his role repertoire by using his client as a foil. Both transfer roles from previous relationships into their present affiliation. Since the client's roles are dysfunctional, they will, by definition, be improperly transferred; yet the clinician's may also be out of place. When he elects to perform a role that is inappropriate to the resocialization relationship, he may be described as engaged in counter-transference.

Unsuitable counter-transference can seriously interfere with a clinician's ability to function as a cooperative negotiating partner. Instead of negotiating in his client's interests, he may be persuaded to pursue tangential interests of his own. Thus if he treats his client as if she were his irresponsible younger sister, he may be inclined to try to reform her as he once did his own sister. The client's actual strengths and interests may be ignored in favor of a fantasized representation of her. This will surely preclude the formulation of practical solutions to the current dilemma. If he is to be a proficient negotiating partner, a clinician's head must be in the here and now.

Clinician Roles. A resocializer can assume many different roles during the renegotiation phase of role change. First, he can play the part of a protagonist who negotiates real roles with his client. These roles can be on his own behalf or as a surrogate for someone else. Second, he can act as an ally during a client's negotiations with a third party. In this case, he can use his strength to augment his client's bargaining position. Third, he can assume the role of a mediator. In this case, he can make it his business to facilitate the negotiations between the client and her other role partners. This can be accomplished with them present or through a proxy.

Whichever part the clinician plays, his purpose is to facilitate a satisfactory conclusion. Whether he is a participant or an interested third party, he can use his influence to encourage a problem-solving approach. In a given situation, he will need to analyze his client's actual circumstance before deciding what role he will adopt. His choice should be based upon the opportunities that arise. Thus if his client is attempting to solve role problems in his imagination, the clinician can concretize them by assuming the negotiating stance of a surrogate. This can force his client to consider what her other role partners might be thinking. Or if a client is engaged in very salient external negotiations, the clinician can take on the role of ally and/or mediator depending upon the state of those negotiations; he will become an ally if they are unequal, and a mediator if they are symmetrical. This may weight the balances in favor of a fair conclusion.

Protagonist. There are several ways in which a clinician can function as a protagonist. First, he can negotiate on his own behalf. The relationship between him and his client can be a real one that is altered in a more favorable direction. Second, he can role-play negotiations. His client and he can consciously decide to practice negotiation skills. Third, he can act as a surrogate for another role partner. When a significant other cannot be present to negotiate for himself, the clinician can be a stand-in who helps his client achieve shadow victories.

1. The resocialization relationship involves a division of labor in which each party has definite responsibilities. These must be negotiated as must any other. Issues about money, scheduling, and topics of conversation must all be resolved. These are genuine concerns in which the clinician and his client have a real stake. The decisions they make about these matters will have consequences for both. Therefore negotiations about them involve substantial interests, and should be approached as such. And it is precisely because these negotiations are real that they can serve as a template for other negotiations. If they proceed successfully, they can facilitate the resolution of other issues in the client's life.

Suppose that a client is having difficulty in keeping appointments. Her clinician will have an interest in reducing these absences so that he can regularize their schedule. At the beginning of their relationship, he may nevertheless decide to allow his client a great deal of leeway. His reasoning may be that this client is too vulnerable to withstand pressure and that permitting flexibility will afford her some needed safety. Later, when his client is able to reexperience her dysfunctional roles and unblock impediments to change, it may be time to reopen the question of appointments. It will then be possible to be more explicit about her expected responsibilities. He and the client will be able to assertively state their cases and construct an outcome that suits both. They can then use the lessons of this negotiation as a guide for subsequent arrangements.

2. Still, not all renegotiations have to be so earnest. Some can be for practice. Role plays can enable people to act as if they were in an actual negotiation, yet with a fraction of the risk. When the interests they have at stake are only a facsimile of real ones, they needn't be so distressed if things go wrong. These role plays can have all the elements of actual situations, but be known by them to be "make-believe."

This sort of device permits a clinician and his client to pretend to negotiate with role partners whom the client is not yet ready to confront. Thus if a wife wishes to renegotiate household chores with her husband, she can practice them with her clinician first. He can then try to realistically assume the husband's strategies while she experiments with counteracting them. Once she is satisfied that she has viable alternatives, she may be prepared to face her husband directly.

3. When a clinician acts the part of a surrogate role partner, he is going a step beyond role play. His portrayal will be less explicitly make-believe, and so reality and fantasy may merge. Surrogate roles are most likely when a person is engaged in transference. The clinician may then be regarded almost as a husband, wife, father, mother, brother, sister, son, daughter, or so on. He will not literally be confused with these people, but emotionally there will be little difference.

Suppose that a client perceives her clinician to be just like her father. When she begins to negotiate for more freedom in her life, she may perceive her helper as an obstacle to her independence. There may be times when it seems to her that she is being forbidden to do something just as she once was by her deceased father. When she then resists the clinician, the latter will have an opportunity to play the part of a concerned but supportive parent. This will enable the client to assert her autonomy, and in the process achieve a shadow victory. It will feel to her as if she has renegotiated with her father, but this time the negotiation has come to a successful denouement.

Ally. When a client is engaged in renegotiations with actual others, she may need someone on her side to balance the power between herself and her role partners. Unequal negotiations are usually defective ones. If circumstances dictate that a person must negotiate with those who have substantially more power, she will probably lose unless she gets help. Without someone committed to her side—someone who will join her in asserting her interests—they may be ignored or repudiated.

A clinician can therefore function as an ally dedicated to increasing his client's power and improving her prospects of being heard.

As an ally, a clinician can also coach his client on winning tactics. He can make plain what the client's interests are, how they can be asserted, and what kind of deal may satisfy her opponents. Since presumably the clinician has a good grasp of non-coercive, dual-concern negotiations, he can share his knowledge and insights. He can, for instance, prompt his client about what level of contention is appropriate to her situation, and suggest problem-solving approaches that work.

If a client is in conflict with her employer, the clinician can almost be a cheerleader. He can urge his client on, and give her the courage to resist intimidation. Together they can assess the danger presented by the boss's maneuvers and find ways to answer them. If the client were on her own, her employer's threats might frighten her into submission, but with the resocializer at her side she may have the fortitude not to be afraid. This support can also improve her ability to be appropriately assertive. Instead of being traumatized by the prospect of losing her job, she will be able to calculate negotiating tactics that get her boss's attention and perhaps persuade him to make a deal.

Mediator. However, not all of a client's renegotiations will be with more powerful others. When she is dealing with a spouse or friends, she may not need an ally, but rather someone who can smooth negotiations and facilitate a successful outcome. In cases like these, a clinician does not want to increase his client's strength to the point that she will overawe her role partners. If a rough parity exists, he does not want to disrupt it by siding too vigorously with his client.

A mediator's job is to facilitate negotiations between others. This can be accomplished with all parties present or with the mediator acting as a consultant for one side. Thus a clinician may want to have his client and her spouse both available during a counseling session. Their joint presence gives him the opportunity to encourage fair negotiations and to make specific suggestions about resolving impasses. At the very least, he can try to persuade them to speak to each other. If, however, it is impossible to bring both partners together, he can act as if they had been. His client can be quizzed about the details of specific negotiations and suggestions offered for rectifying them. In essence, the clinician acts as a mediator whose clients refuse to sit in the same room and hence who must be dealt with separately.

There are several ways in which a mediator can facilitate successful negotiations. First, he can make them safer. By calming the passions of one, or both, parties, he can make them less inclined to be unfair, and more disposed to clear-headed problem solving. People whose anger has been assuaged are less likely to be coercive. Second, by providing information that points toward optimal solutions, he can make the task of both adversaries easier. Thus he can inform each about the other's interests and propose ways of integrating them. Third, he can facilitate communication between the parties. If they can make their goals and strategies more comprehensible to each other, it will be easier for them to discover mutually acceptable outcomes. In general, a clinician who functions as a mediator helps his client and the client's role partners by making them aware of their respective wants and by enhancing their understanding of the options they have in responding to one another.

As we will soon see for Robert, a clinician can be alternatively a protagonist, an ally, or a mediator. Thus when Robert was trying to renegotiate his roles with his father, there were times when his clinician acted as a surrogate for dad, times when he was an ally in resisting dad's coercion, and times when he mediated accommodations that were suitable for both.

Common Negotiation Mistakes

Not all responsibility for renegotiating dysfunctional roles rests upon a clinician's shoulders. It is, after all, the client whose roles are being modified and who ultimately must be responsible for herself. She will have to correct negotiating mistakes and find ways of making more satisfying deals. In particular, she will have to avoid the kinds of mistakes she made in the past, and eschew the pitfalls that are common to most role renegotiations. If, as a negotiator, a clinician must avoid coercion, so too must his client. She too must be capable of firm flexibility and dual-concern negotiations. It will be up to her to become a responsive person who is aware of her interests and those of her role partners. She too will have to be fair, informed, and innovative. And if she has not been these things in the past, she will have to become them now.

Going to Extremes. People trapped in dysfunctional roles have a tendency to go to extremes. In their anxiety to escape the misery of their failed and aborted roles, they frequently try too hard. They seem to believe that if they use enough energy, the obstacles before them will collapse and a way will be found to implement a better life. Among other things, this means that they are often too zealous in their negotiating styles.

When someone has been subjected to coercive negotiations, she tries to learn from her experience. Unfortunately, the lessons acquired may be the wrong ones. Thus someone who has been victimized by excessive force may conclude that she too should employ force, only more so. Or she could decide the opposite. She might conclude that force is evil and vow to abjure it at all costs. Either way, she will be betting that greater or less intensity is the solution to her negotiating dilemma.

The supposition of those who go to extremes is that more is better. Since the energy of a coercive role partner seemed so effective (after all, its victim could not resist it), it only stands to reason that it will take additional energy to neutralize his demands. It usually does not occur to the targets of coercion that a moderate amount of energy, appropriately directed, may be more efficacious. In fact, when power is ruthlessly exploited, negotiations suffer. The cooperation necessary for successful problem solving requires role partners who can hold up their end of the bargaining, not pawns who can be manipulated at will.

Good negotiations require a certain amount of faith. Overpowering an adversary, or running so far away that one can't be found, may seem to guarantee safety, but they cannot bring satisfaction. Since fulfillment can often be had only in relationships, it is contingent upon role partners who are willing to be cooperative. But cooperation cannot be forced; it must be enlisted. It is therefore necessary to seek out good people and to hope they can be persuaded to join in mutually beneficial activities.

Excessive Contending. A client who elects to be excessively contentious fights too hard. Instead of relaxing and allowing a solution to emerge, she tries to force the issue. She feels safe only when she has total control of the situation. Unfortunately, contending too vigorously rarely brings the kind of control desired. Because a negotiation is a two-way process, one-sided control short-circuits the exercise. It prevents the construction of what is wanted, namely, joint agreements. Indeed, overly energetic contending tends to arouse the ire of role partners and inspires them to sabotage one's goals. Sometimes it even prompts them to sacrifice their own happiness in order to insure that we will not prevail.

One type of role which usually entails excessive contending is that of "rebel." Some people feel that they must always be in the opposition. A primary purpose of their negotiations is to upset the other person's plans. Rather than seek a mutually satisfying outcome, they persist in being obstructionist. Rebels regularly find something to be unhappy about. They reject offers of friendship and fight so forcefully that their battles last forever. They simply do not allow functional roles to emerge.

Excessive Yielding. Too much yielding, however, is no better. Giving the other person what he wants, no matter what, is not likely to end in mutually satisfying solutions either. Yielding allows the other person to win, but at the expense of one's own needs. Instead of making her desires known, the yielder tries to propitiate partners by being too compliant. She hopes that this will gain their favor and bring her peace. In fact, she probably exasperates them with her obsequiousness, then whets their appetite for further concessions. By overdoing attempts at being cooperative she paves the way for unsatisfying bargains, and virtually guarantees outcomes unfavorable to herself.

"Caretakers" are the masters of yielding strategies. They are so intent upon helping others achieve their needs that they concentrate all of their attention on them. When they engage in role negotiations, they are so aware of the other's interests, and so determined to avoid their displeasure, that it is only the other's point of view that is considered. They, as it were, join the other person on his side of the encounter, and leave no one to argue their side. If a person reaches role renegotiations without having corrected this tendency, she condemns herself to repeating past mistakes. Indeed, in her anxiety to please she will probably not notice that she is falling into the same old traps.

Excessive Inaction. Inaction has consequences similar to those of yielding. A client who adopts this negotiating strategy hopes that passivity will prevent a repeat of the coercive patterns she once knew. She believes that if she is quiet and doesn't make waves, her bargaining partners will have no reason to force her to do anything. Perhaps they may not even notice her presence, and hence will not be provoked into action. Unlike the yielder, she does not actively try to give the other what he wants, but neither does she make an overt effort to meet her own needs. It is as if she wants to run so far away from trouble that it will never find her. Sadly, she will also run so far from appropriate assertiveness that if happiness befalls her, it will be by sheerest chance.

A strategy of avoiding all contention is especially attractive to those who have become "scapegoats." Clients who have been picked on all of their lives reasonably conclude that dodging every possibility of strife is the best course. Life has taught them that human interaction is replete with danger and that restricting contacts prevents abuse. For the scapegoat, inaction will seem to be the surest way of not getting involved. She will choose to avoid satisfactions in the hope that this sacrifice will forestall dissatisfactions. She would rather not negotiate at all than have a bad deal imposed upon her. But in making this decision, she precipitates a greater problem. During her renegotiation of dysfunctional roles, she abandons herself to the good will of others; if they are not what she would wish, she is in trouble.

Problem Solving. The proper alternative, of course, is problem solving. It sidesteps the extremes. Problem solving does not try too hard or too little. Neither does it seek a one-sided solution to negotiating dilemmas. Satisfactory role negotiations require a certain amount of restraint. Instead of following one's primitive reactions, they demand an ability to think things through and to make suitable calculations of advantage. The best resolutions of role difficulties are not always obvious; they take patience to discover and work out.

Going to extremes is the quick answer to negotiating enigmas. People who are trapped in dysfunctional roles want something better right away. This is why they are so inclined to jump at solutions that seem close at hand. Energetic contending, yielding, and inaction are strategies known to all children; they have the virtue of familiarity and ease of implementation. Problem solving, on the other hand, takes time to master and is infinitely complex in its application. It is therefore a negotiating pattern that must be bolstered during resocialization, that is, if the process is to end happily.

UNDERSTANDING INTERESTS

When social roles emerge from coercive negotiations, they are usually based upon a distortion of the interests of both partners. A person who has been forced to comply with another's demands rarely develops a good understanding of her own needs or those of the person with whom she has been negotiating. The very act of being compelled to accept another person's desires results in losing sight of what one really wants or what the other person is aiming at. One's contributions to the negotiating process thus take place in the dark and one's ability to correct errors is impaired.

The insistent demands of a coercive role partner tend to occupy a person's attention to the exclusion of her own desires. Instead of being able to get in touch with her personal feelings or to construct individual plans of action, she is compelled to deal with feelings and plans initiated by the other. Her own reactions, the ones derived from her needs, are obscured by external interference and she is rendered blind to her personal interests.

Neither is a person who is subject to excessive coercion likely to have a good fix on role partner interests. Though the other makes demands that require attention, their energy level is such that communication is distorted. Instead of a clear message being received and acted upon, the intensity of the transaction invites opposition. The person who is being forced to act against her will has no incentive to clarify the other's intentions; rather, she is motivated to resist whatever the other demands. She will thus probably misinterpret the other's interests because part of her wants to misunderstand.

Since the construction of viable role structures depends upon an accurate understanding of the needs of both role partners, it is imperative that during the renegotiation phase of resocialization a role changer overcome the residues of earlier coercion. Any tendencies she has to misinterpret the interests of the other, or to overlook her own, must be surmounted. She must learn to understand what it is that the other wants, and what she herself needs. If she cannot ascertain both of these, she will not be able to participate in the renegotiation of serviceable behavior patterns. All her efforts at resocialization will be in vain, for the end result of the enterprise will not be satisfying roles, but another array of dysfunctional ones.

However, if the resocialization relationship has been non-coercive, true dual-concern negotiations should be facilitated. The cooperation that evolves between a clinician and his client should open doors to a more accurate understanding of mutual interests in other negotiating situations. Since the client will presumably have discovered that within the clinical relationship she has the possibility of being herself, she will no longer be motivated to deny either her needs or those of the clinician when the two are engaged in bargaining. The experience of getting in touch with her inner self, while not needing to resist the dogmatic commands of another, will open her eyes to the things that are there to be seen, and this ability may generalize to other situations. Such a client will find that she has the capacity to transfer her new-found objectivity to relationships in which it has not existed before. She will discover how to participate in negotiations in which she has an equal chance to contribute and a reasonable chance to succeed.

Developing Values

A person's interests are usually embodied in the values to which she subscribes. Values are, as it were, vest-pocket judgments about what will meet needs. Whether developed by societies or individuals, they are generalizations about what kinds of actions lead to what consequences. When a particular objective is valued, the implication is that its attainment will result in needs fulfillment. Values then are short-hand guides to actions that should work. They save people the time of laboriously sorting through all the potential consequences of their actions, or those of their role partners, before deciding upon a strategy.

Values that work are based upon the accumulated experience of societies and individuals. Beliefs that "honesty is the best policy" or that "loving relationships are worth pursuing" have long histories. Civilizations acquire a wisdom about these things and pass them on to their children. It is then up to the children to adjust these hypotheses to their own life circumstances. In their interactions with significant others, they must decide how much honesty is a good policy and how worthwhile love actually is. The values they inherit must thus be tailored to their situation and become part of their own orientation.

When a person has grown up in coercive circumstances, the beliefs she acquires rarely stand her in good stead. Often, they are either a copy of parentally imposed standards or a reaction to coercive manip-ulations that don't generalize well to other situations. Thus authoritar-ian parents frequently demand that their children subscribe to stan-dards that are not in the children's interests. For example, they may force a child to believe that it is her responsibility to care for her parent no matter what the consequences for herself. If a child internalizes this value, as she probably will, she will have acquired an ideal that will not help her meet her own needs. As an adult, her plans of action derived from this value will not aid her in her attempts to construct viable roles.

Even when such counter-productive standards are not explicitly im-posed upon her, a child may still draw conclusions that are not in her interest. She may, for instance, decide that love is not a worthwhile goal because her experience has demonstrated that "loving" relation-ships are always stacked against her. As an adult, she will avoid inti-macy because she is certain it only leads to pain. The value she has acquired then points her away from the very role structures she will need if she is ever to be happy.

Because life is complex, it is invariably difficult to develop a value system that adequately serves one's interests. It is always hard to know what will work and what won't. For the person who has been trapped in dysfunctional roles, such decisions may have been nearly impossible while she was growing up. It will, therefore, be vital for her to develop new values as she approaches the task of renegotiating roles. She will need to construct commitments that do in fact meet her needs and free her from directions that were coercively imposed. Only then will it be possible for her to be on her own side when she makes bargains with current role partners.

Fortunately, entering adulthood requires one to reorganize one's value system. The need to reexamine commitments is imposed upon all of us by the stresses of growing up. This means that even those who get off to a bad start have an opportunity for making corrections. The sim-ple principles that are the legacy of childhood are inevitably inadequate to meet the challenges of adult life and must be reworked. Questions about issues such as lying, cheating, and stealing must be reopened in the context of the mass-market society one is about to enter. This forces would-be adults to reconsider their beliefs and alter them to suit changed circumstances. The person trapped in dysfunctional values is also given a chance to alter her values to conform to her new situation. She too gets to make improvements. And since she has more to change, she also has more to gain.

Similarly, the role-renegotiation phase of resocialization presents a clinician with a marvelous occasion to help his client develop new and more viable values. During their conversations, he can suggest that some outlooks are more in his client's interest than others. Thus enlightened selfishness, non-perfectionism, and tolerance are standards that most people would do well to adopt. Role changers usually need to learn that they too have a right to have their needs met, that in seeking these it is okay to make mistakes, and that role partners don't always have to conform to their desires. Such values foster problem solving and, ultimately, the attainment of interests. They make it possible for someone to confront her social environment with flexibility and imagination, and to construct satisfying patterns of living.

What then must a client do in order to adopt more workable values? First, she must be on her own side. A person who is not trying to meet her own needs has little chance of developing standards that further them. Second, she must be able to recognize when her previous ambitions were futile. The illusions she has carried around in her knapsack must be replaced with a better appreciation of the world's limitations and possibilities. Third, she will need the courage to be herself. It will be necessary for her to look within to see what is missing and to look without to see what is feasible. Finally, she will have to allow herself to dream. Unfulfilled needs will percolate to the surface if only she permits herself access to her own fantasies. She will then be able to explore what has the best prospect of success.

Understanding Others

A dual-concern orientation to role negotiations is predicated upon an understanding of both one's own and one's role partners' interests. A client who is trying to reconstruct her life will not only need to develop sound values, but to understand her role partner's ambitions. Unless the interests of both contribute to the final outcome, one or the other is bound to be dissatisfied. The loser will then be motivated to engage in disruptive actions. Only if both feel that their needs have been met will they accept the results of their transaction without trying to reassert individual demands.

In a world with perfect communications, understanding others might be simple. As things are, it is a challenge to determine people's interests. Both a client and her role partners will be motivated to perpetuate misunderstandings. A role changer who is still reacting to earlier coercion is geared to misperceiving current partner's objectives, while her opposite number—even if he has the best of intentions—has the normal negotiator's tendency to hide some of his cards. Since all negotiations are partly power-plays, a certain amount of caution is indicated. Indeed, some suspicion and secrecy are valuable. They allow for the slow, prudent accretion of role bargains. It is only when distrust escalates to levels which prevent accurate communication that problem solving is jeopardized.

Understanding others, and being understood, are not automatic; they have to be worked at. If a fair and non-coercive negotiating environment has been established, this should be possible. As long as a client or her role partner are not motivated to stonewall each other, they can engage in exploring their mutual and separate situations.

Role-Partner Interests. Current role-partner interests are a puzzle to be solved. It may take the combined ingenuity of a client and her helper to figure out what is going on in a role partner's head and heart. If the person with whom the client is negotiating is candid and articulate, their task will be greatly simplified. If he is not, they must be prepared to be mindreaders. Of course, no one can literally read the mind of another, but it is surprising how much can be deciphered when one is determined to do so. This, after all, is one of the bases of resocialization. If resocializers couldn't identify their client's dysfunctional roles, it would be difficult to facilitate change.

The tricks that a clinician uses in understanding his client can also be used by the latter to understand her role partners. The resocialization relationship can serve as a model from which she can crib useful techniques for other relationships. She too can be a patient observer who listens, watches, and, when necessary, does role-taking. She can also be an eager explorer who tirelessly questions, probes, and interprets her partner. As long as her goal is genuine understanding, she may find a way to achieve it.

Just as the client was asked, "What do you want?," so may the team of client and clinician ask, "What does so-and-so want?" In their mind's eye, they can put themselves in his shoes and try to figure out his goals and values. By going through a series of successively closer approximations, they may eventually come very close to the truth. Assuming that they are not seduced by their own preconceptions, they will find that their intuitions are an excellent guide in understanding a role partner's purposes. He too, of course, is a human being who has needs very similar to their own. And as long as they are prepared to use feedback from him to determine the accuracy of their judgments, they will not go too far wrong.

Past Relationships. Since many renegotiations recapitulate historic role negotiations, it is often as important to understand the motives of past role partners as those of present ones. If this is not achieved, serious mistakes can be made. A very common error is to confound a present other with someone from the past. If he seems to have the same goals as someone who once coercively imposed dysfunctional roles, it may seem vital to frustrate his purposes. Because a renegotiator will not want to lose the same battle twice, she may intensify her efforts to see to it that this time it is the other who loses.

Although successful resocialization often depends upon reversing the decisions of ancient role controversies, usually these are best abrogated by proxy rather than in the flesh. It is ghost and shadow victories that are wanted, not decisions over present-day innocents. If current role partners had nothing to do with past abuses, defeating them will be counter-productive. By forcing them to undergo the humiliations that might be appropriate to others, they are denied the possibility of participating in the construction of satisfying new relationships. If they are forced to defend themselves from unwarranted assaults, they will have neither the time nor inclination to cooperate in negotiating mutually satisfying contemporary roles.

Past relationships belong in the past. It is in memory that past injustices are best corrected. The reversal of historic coercion should not result in present coercion. This can be avoided if a role changer distinguishes the here and now from what is long gone. She can then explicitly choose to explore the motivations and interests of her past role partners. In her head, she can ascertain what was going on during past interactions, and then try to formulate winning counter-strategies. Her subsequent victories will be in her imagination and emotions, but will not for that reason be less satisfying. If anything, she will have the additional pleasure of knowing that her internal victories have not been at the expense of bystanders.

A role changer trying to determine whether her understanding of past role partners is accurate can gauge her success by monitoring her own reactions. If her speculative understanding of them leads to a resolution of internal conflicts, she is probably on the right track. Interpretations that result in emotional changes have an undeniable validity. Their efficacy in bringing change confirms the truth of the insights.

When trying to fathom the interests of past role partners, a person can attempt to uncover their personal histories. If the pressures they were under can be comprehended, it will be easier to understand what they were trying to accomplish. What makes this difficult is that the interests and goals of past role partners were usually systematically distorted when coercive negotiations are at their height. Because the person was a dependent child when they occurred, she could not afford to see things as they really were. It would be especially important for her not to perceive parental weaknesses. Consider the plight of a child whose parents are beating her to cover up their own anxieties. Can the child afford to perceive this? If she does, she may realize that her parents are not strong enough to protect her, and this too will be unacceptable. It would subject her to intolerable levels of anxiety. Instead, it may be better for her to accept personal responsibility for a beating, and fantasize her parents as stronger than they are. But if she does this, she will not be able to understand why they treated her as they did. And when these misinterpretations are carried forward into adulthood and applied to other role partners, they too will be misconstrued.

To rectify this situation, a person will need to stand back from her past and try to comprehend former partners as human beings, with human motives and human weaknesses. It will be necessary to understand their interests not merely as a function of their needs, but as a reaction to the social circumstances in which they functioned. Their expressed desires were in part a product of underlying urges, but also of what they believed their world would allow them to achieve. Thus their behaviors were shaped by internal exigencies and by parameters imposed by their role partners. If these latter can be understood, the coercive tactics employed against ego will make sense, and her alternatives will become visible. This understanding facilitates ghost victories by making it possible to imagine non-coercive solutions to which a coercive other might have subscribed had he recognized their feasibility.

Projection and Transference. If a client is to distinguish the interests of past role partners from present ones, she will need to determine her contribution to her efforts at understanding. Her perception of what another is attempting may be contaminated by her own projections and transferences. It may be her own feelings and interests that she mistakenly attributes to the other. Instead of the here and now being seen for what it is, it may be masked by preconceptions that have nothing to do with a current other's true interests.

Projection is a cognitive style that interprets personal reactions as coming from external sources. Freud identified it as a defense mechanism that a person uses to avoid seeing unpleasant truths about herself. It makes the other person responsible for things that would otherwise be condemned in the self. The antidote to such misperceptions is self-knowledge. When a person knows she is angry, she is less likely to attribute her anger to role partners. If she can accept her imperfections, she will not have to locate them where they do not exist. In this, a resocialization client can take advantage of her collaboration with a clinician she trusts. Her resocializer can then reflect a more accurate and non-judgmental appraisal than she can herself.

Transference is a byproduct of normal role reenactments. It applies role scripts from the past to current circumstances. New role partners are seen as comparable with old ones. If this assumption is in error, then current partners are grossly misperceived. More particularly, if a person believes that coercive relationships from the past are being repeated in the present, the demands of a present partner can be completely misconstrued. Thus if a man interprets his wife as a replication of his demanding mother, he may not give her an opportunity to prove her reasonableness. He will be so convinced that her current requests are as intractable as his mother's that he will combat them with excessive vigor. Instead of being open to an examination of his spouse's interests, he will conflate them with his mother's, and adamantly deny both.

A clinician can interrupt this cycle by pointing out when inappropriate identifications have been made. He can, for instance, show how a wife and mother are the same or different, and when a vigorous response is suitable, and when not. Moreover, he can demonstrate that he himself is different from the client's past role partners. Since the resocialization relationship is as open to transference as any other, the clinician too will occasionally be misrepresented. When he is, he can clearly state how his interests and demands differ from those of the person with whom he has been confused. By making it plain that a mistake has been made, he can sensitize his client to similar errors. The two will then be positioned to ferret out other transference confusions and prevent them from derailing current negotiations.

CASE STUDY: ROBERT

Robert grew up in the care of a father who was relentlessly coercive. When he tried to persuade his father to be more reasonable, he only succeeded in increasing his own discomfort. He quickly learned that he was not strong enough to counter dad's wrath and that no matter what he did, dad could not be converted into a cooperative role partner. Neither contending, nor yielding, nor inaction seemed to work. Robert tried them all and they all resulted in further losses; none effectively neutralized parental coercion. Neither was problem solving feasible, because dad simply wouldn't allow it.

Some of the roles Robert adopted incorporated negotiating strategies which, though they didn't succeed, seemed better than nothing. Thus in becoming a "coward," he institutionalized yielding and inaction. His self-image persuaded him that he could not win and that the best course was either to let people have their way or to flee. Starting as a child, he opted to run away rather than to fight battles he kept losing. Even when he was imprisoned and there was no place to run, he arranged to placate stronger opponents rather than confront them.

The role of "alcoholic" also contributed to this pattern. It allowed Robert to hide in a bottle when he was frightened. When drunk, he could sink into the total inactivity of a street bum. Instead of resisting the world, he let it do its worst without any opposition from himself. His hope was that if an alcoholic stupor prevented him from knowing what was happening, it could not hurt. He would be in a protective cocoon of his own.

Yet underneath this façade, there was another story. A part of Robert did not want to give up. If he stopped fighting his father, it was not because he wanted the old man to win but because he did not want to participate in his victories; better passive resistance than cooperation with a tyrant. His roles of "alcoholic" and "coward" served as a kind of cover. They gave him an excuse for being uncooperative and camouflaged many of his manipulative machinations. In prison, he could be an entrepreneur who made cunning deals; on the outside, he could bluff dangerous opponents into thinking he was tougher than he was. Indeed, the part of himself that wished to be contentious had never disappeared; it was only disguised.

During resocialization, Robert was at first reluctant to renegotiate his dysfunctional roles. His intense fear and anger persuaded him that open confrontations were too dangerous. Either he would be beaten badly, or he would savagely beat others. He had first to learn that fighting back was possible, and that victory was no chimera. Of course, Robert began trying to renegotiate his dysfunctional roles as soon as he started to reexperience them. His desire from the outset was to construct new and more satisfying roles. Even before he fully understood what had gone wrong, and before he could relinquish the behavior patterns that caused him such misery, he knew that he wanted something better. Nevertheless, he found himself stymied. He seemed to have a "fear of success." Every time he came close to getting what he ostensibly wanted, he hastily retreated. When asked what was happening, he described himself as a little boy whose nose was pressed up against the store window, but who couldn't allow himself to go inside and collect the goodies.

At first, Robert believed that what he feared was responsibility. He correctly assumed that any new role would be replete with new demands, and he was in no mood to comply with the expectations of others. Neither did he think himself capable of tolerating these demands. He imagined that new roles would embroil him in perpetual fights, which he had neither the energy nor the inclination to sustain. Furthermore, he was sure that no role partner would ever let him win. They would all be like his father and intensify their efforts to defeat him the closer he came to victory. Since he also believed that others were inherently stronger than he, they would always prevail; and this was unacceptable.

The more Robert explored these matters, the more he realized he was also afraid of what he might do. A part of him desperately wanted to get even with his father. If other people frustrated him in the same way, they might easily become targets. Nevertheless, he did not want to destroy them. As much as he might hate others and what they represented, he did not want to be alone in the world. He did not want his rage to condemn him to isolation.

Finally, he was reluctant to do good. Entering a successful role negotiation might reward others by meeting their needs. And as long as others were surrogates for his father, he had no wish to see them happy in any way. If this meant that he had to deprive himself of satisfaction too, he would. Moreover, the mere thought that his father might take pride in his successes made success abhorrent. Better to be a failure than to have dad think he had done a good job as a father.

Once Robert had decided to risk role change, he needed role partners. In particular, he needed non-coercive partners who would help him change. Besides the clinician, he had only his friends available. Unfortunately, they did not provide the kind of assistance he craved. When he told them about his anger or aspirations, they would reply, "Don't be that way!" They were comfortable with "Robert the Bum," and were not prepared for a more respectable version of him. Neither were they comfortable with his negative emotions. Since many of his friends were alcoholics, they found his passion for change too challenging. For some of them, the reaction was: "If I can pretend your emotions don't exist, they can't hurt me." And Robert's response to this was: "What's wrong with me? Why does everyone reject my efforts to get better? Maybe it's because I'm crazy. Maybe they know I'm no good, and I don't deserve any better."

When Robert brought this problem to his clinician, the two talked at some length about why his friends were acting as they were. The clinician functioned first as an ally and then as a mediator. Because Robert had been intimidated by his friends' reactions, he needed to know that there was someone on his side, and that his friends' judgments were not universal. When the clinician assured him that he was not crazy and that wanting something better was not wrong, he was better able to relax. Once he had settled down, he then needed a better fix on what others were doing. Perhaps they had purposes which had nothing to do with his own? The fact that they denigrated him might be serving their interests, while neglecting his. If he was going to make a deal with them, he would need to understand what they were about.

After the clinician had validated Robert's perceptions of his friends and confirmed his human worth, it became possible for him to be more assertive. He was more ready to fight back. Indeed, when one night he found himself physically assaulted by an inebriated stranger while walking near his home, instead of running for cover as he previously might, he physically pushed the man aside. The next day, he was startled by his own impulsive courage. He had protected himself without thinking about it and, what was more, no one had been hurt.

At about this time, Robert became involved with a young, and very attractive woman. He loved having a sexual relationship with her, but was pained to discover that she had severe emotional problems. For a while they lived together, and he was distressed to see her spend most of her days in bed. When he tried to stimulate her, she fought back with bitter invective. His first reaction to this was counter-anger, but he did not want to attack her; she seemed too vulnerable. His father might have been provoked to violence by her "laziness," but he would not be. He would not negotiate in the same coercive and insensitive manner. While father might have described this forbearance as a weakness, he began to think of it as compassion. He identified with his girlfriend and didn't want to hurt her. Putting himself in her shoes made him aware of her fears, and he saw no benefit in taking advantage of her frailties. He would surely not achieve the relationship he wanted by exploiting her.

Some months later, when he was back on his own, he decided to take a trip to his boyhood home. He visited the town in which he grew up and surveyed the houses in which he had lived. While he met no one he remembered or who remembered him, the place reminded him of the ambience in which he had been raised. What stood out in his imagination was the Puritan work-ethic. He wondered if this might be the origin of his father's insistence on manual labor. On the bus trip back home, he found himself wrestling with ghosts from the past. In his mind, he contrasted his artistic and entrepreneurial values with the aggressively blue-collar standards of his childhood, and decided he would stick with his own point of view. He had, in effect, explored the interests of significant role partners, and in the process reinforced his own. Looking at the past on his own terms had neutralized its coercive effect and allowed him to better understand both it and the present.

When Robert next saw the clinician, they reviewed what had happened and compared his strength with that of the ghosts. They talked about the process of negotiating new values and how he had revised his evaluation of weakness and compassion. They noted that his understanding of cowardice and laziness had shifted and that he was beginning to accord himself new value. The clinician then sought to strengthen this trend and enhance Robert's ability to negotiate on his own behalf.

One subsequent manifestation of this development was Robert's decision to change his living quarters. In the past he had asked the world for very little because he thought he would get still less. Now his appetite for material rewards was growing. Thus when he encountered problems in the apartment in which he was living, he took the opportunity to move to a better place. He was surprised to be able to give something to himself, but he was gratified also.

Now Robert felt ready to develop new relationships. His successes had emboldened him. Perhaps he was ready to venture out into the world? He developed plans for going to school and for getting a job. At first, however, everything went wrong. He panicked when he took an entrance exam for college, and a job that he got at a half-way house for alcoholics ended acrimoniously. In both cases, he had met new people and found new ways of interacting, but he had not found a style that suited him.

He also made new friends at Alcoholics Anonymous, some of whom were very successful. Much to his surprise, he found that he could hold his own without being engulfed by their values. They might have the money, but he knew what he believed. If they wanted to be friends with him, it would have to be on his terms.

The closer Robert came to full independence, the more the clinician retreated into a mediator role. Robert became more insistent on making his own decisions and only wanted advice on how to approach new relationships. Although he did not achieve the kind of worldly success others might consider the sine qua non of successful role change, he did evolve meaningful new roles. In place of his detached, yet combative, attitude toward the world, he became capable of greater intimacy. In place of perpetual failure, he obtained respect for his speaking ability at AA and for the quality of his photography. Though he remained dissatisfied with where he was, he developed a measure of self-acceptance. Robert found that progress was painfully slow, but that it was possible to negotiate new and more gratifying relationships.

10

Conclusion

AN EMERGING CONSENSUS?

The resocialization paradigm is a culmination of many professional trends and therapeutic orientations. It builds upon Freudian, Rogerian, Sullivanian, cultural, family systems, Gestalt, existential, object relations, cognitive/behavioral, conflict theory, exchange theory, structural/functional, and symbolic/interactionist traditions to develop a unified framework for helping people solve their personal problems. The paradigm synthesizes apparently disparate perspectives into a harmonious whole. In so doing, it applies the best of many outlooks to the task of assisting people to live more satisfying lives.

Sociology, psychology, social work, and the various counseling specialties seem to be converging upon the same truths. They have independently discovered that personal problems are often a product of social interactions. To be sure, the language used is often very different, but the insights are similar. Thus, frameworks as apparently dissimilar as psychoanalysis and family systems theory have moved closer together, finding common ground in their discovery that people with problems are enmeshed in dysfunctional social relationships (Nichols 1987).

One of the ironies of this process is that a perfectly good word such as "social" has been studiously avoided by practitioners in many disciplines. Apparently, its use might disadvantage them in interdisciplinary disputes. Rather than admit the social aspects of what they analyze, and perhaps inadvertently acknowledge sociological precedence, they stick to language with which they are familiar. The result is that similarities in viewpoints are obscured. People trained in a given tradition come to believe that their own perspective is unique, and that parallel outlooks are mired in ignorance.

A recent example of convergence has been the progressive transformation of psychoanalysis into object relations theory. Although psychoanalysts continue to follow Freudian tradition in labeling role partners as "objects," they have moved away from rudimentary instinct and ego perspectives toward a relationship approach. They have come to recognize that personality is constructed during socialization (despite their usual avoidance of this latter term). It is now understood that children develop through interactions with their caregivers. An earlier emphasis on the internal defects of clients has thus been replaced with an awareness of relationships gone wrong.

Similarly, family systems theory has been evolving away from its former cybernetic approach. Instead of conceptualizing families as mechanical systems, family therapists now see them as congeries of individual human beings. Originally, family theorists actively rejected sociological theories involving role systems, but they are now openly willing to discuss symbolic-interactionist and structural-functionalist contributions to their field (Wynne 1986). Still, there is a tendency among them to use awkward locutions such as "behavioral isomorphisms" (Fishman 1986) when they clearly mean to describe social roles.

It would be gratifying if the next step in this process were the straightforward recognition of social role problems. This would open the prospect of a unified psycho-social approach within the helping professions. Personal difficulties would be seen within the context of a lifetime of development and change, and it would be possible to perceive loss as applying to relationships as well as people. The internal and external conflicts that plague human life could be understood within the context of social organization, and their resolution accepted as dependent upon changed role scripts.

Advantages of a Resocialization Perspective

The resocialization paradigm has definite advantages over competing perspectives when dealing with personal problems. First, it is a more accurate and comprehensive reflection of the nature of the difficulties troubling people. Second, it is a better guide to the change processes which must be used to remedy these difficulties. Third, it is an inherently humane approach toward helping others, one that recognizes both the clinician and his client as moral agents engaged in a two-way relationship. Because it is intrinsically psycho-social, it treats people as the social animals we are, and hence can produce better results.

Reality is quite complex. Characterizing the problems for which people seek help as medical illnesses or as personality disorders does not do them justice. The concept of dysfunctional roles, dysfunctionally maintained, comes closer to the mark. It is a more accurate reflection of the fact that a clinician and his client are addressing complex patterns of inter- and intra-personal behavior. It also makes possible a fuller understanding of why it is so difficult to alter unsatisfying ways of life.

The resocialization paradigm encompasses the cognitive, emotional, volitional, and social factors underlying human behavior. It is a balanced account that does not focus on one component to the detriment of others. In particular, it recognizes the dual social and psychological nature of personal problems. Despite the fact that psychologists and other helping professionals have recently developed a greater appreciation of this truth, their institutional and intellectual allegiances bias them toward one-sided medical and psychological solutions.

A social role-change perspective, however, is by its very nature both social and psychological. It allows for a more even-handed emphasis on individuals and their interactions. The rich complexity of a person's internal life, and the cultural and institutional fabric in which he is embedded, are built into the concept of the social role. It makes it more difficult to mentally separate factors that belong together. A role viewpoint allows for an inclusive appraisal of personal problems. It does not attribute them to a specific illness or particular psychological trauma, but recognizes that their etiology is in long-term interpersonal role negotiations. This removes therapy from the realm of short-term problem solving and places it within a framework of an ongoing change process that inevitably entails social renegotiation. Such resocialization excludes instantaneous or painless "cures," and emphasizes corrective, non-coercive relationships.

It may sound self-serving to describe the resocialization paradigm as inherently humane, but this would seem to be the case. Medical and purely psychological perspectives take a more disembodied view of human beings. They are likely to treat a part of the person as "broken," rather than comprehend his dilemma in its proper social context. A role-change viewpoint, however, has a better grasp of a person's humanity. It treats him as a responsible moral agent who both acts and is acted upon.

Because a role perspective understands a person within his social environment, it can more accurately assess individual responsibilities and rights. Its recognition that social roles are negotiated products permits a balanced appraisal of the contribution of the person and his role partners to role problems. Instead of placing exclusive blame on him or his interlocutors, it becomes possible to specify more precisely who has influenced what. Each party is seen as contributing to the end result, and each must carry his share of responsibility for what happens.

This most emphatically includes both the clinician and his client; both must shoulder the burden for what occurs between them.

Resocialization does not view morality as a transcendental phenomenon, but as a product of particular social transactions. This allows the individual to have more control over his fate. Instead of values descending upon him from the heavens, it is understood that all social actors are responsible for developing their own ethical commitments. To be sure, he is not a completely free agent—society does have influence—but ultimately, it is up to him to decide what he believes and to stand by his determinations. The clinician too is seen as a moral actor, and so his value orientations become a legitimate object of scrutiny by himself and his client. He too must be responsible for what he does and what he demands.

Last, this view permits a distinction between responsibility and blame. Responsibility reflects the causal aspects of human relationships. It is the person who can change things who should be asked to do so. After all, he who has control over his destiny is best positioned to affect it. But blame goes much further; it attempts to coerce responsibility. It tries to force a person to do what is deemed essential. Although blame is a necessary mechanism of social control, it can easily be used to excess. And when it slides into moralism, it impedes rather than facilitates change. Instead of inducing people to behave in more satisfying ways, it traps them in dysfunctional patterns.

A resocialization outlook implies an awareness of these facts. It thus encourages responsibility and discourages blame. The humanity of the perspective grows out of its understanding of the exigencies of role change. Since effective role alteration depends upon knowing that change occurs within individuals who are in interaction with non-coercive others, resocializers must learn how to help them, not to force adjustments upon them. Change agents are catalysts who make movement easier and less painful, not surrogates who do the changing or enforcers who impose correct solutions.

Bibliography

Ackerman, N. W. 1958. *The Psychodynamics of Family Life.* New York: Basic Books.

Ainsworth, M. D. 1967. *Infancy in Uganda: Infant Care and the Growth of Attachment.* Baltimore: Johns Hopkins Press.

Alexander, F. 1948. *Fundamentals of Psychoanalysis.* New York: W. W. Norton.

Alexander, F. and French, T. 1946. *Psychoanalytic Therapy.* New York: Ronald Press.

Allport, G. 1985. "The Historical Background of Social Psychology." In Lindzey, G. and Aronson, E. (eds.), *Handbook of Social Psychology* (3rd ed.). New York: Random House.

American Psychiatric Association Committee on Nomenclature and Statistics. 1968. *Diagnostic and Statistical Manual of Mental Disorders* (2nd ed.). Washington, DC: APA.

American Psychiatric Association Task Force on Nomenclature and Statistics. 1980. *Diagnostic and Statistical Manual of Mental Disorders* (3rd ed.). Washington, DC: APA.

Arieti, S. and Bemporad, J. 1978. *Severe and Mild Depression.* New York: Basic Books.

Aronoff, J., Rabin, A. I., and Zucker, R. A. (eds.) 1987. *The Emergence of Personality.* New York: Springer Publishing Co.

Babad, E., Birnbaum, M., and Benne, K. (eds.) 1983. *The Social Self: Group Influence on Personal Identity.* Beverly Hills: Sage Publications.

Bach, G. R. and Wyden, P. 1968. *The Intimate Enemy.* New York: Avon.

Barlow, D. H. 1988. *Anxiety and Its Disorders: The Nature and Treatment of Anxiety and Panic.* New York: The Guilford Press.

Basch, M. 1980. *Doing Psychotherapy.* New York: Basic Books.

Bateson, G. 1972. *Steps to an Ecology of Mind.* New York: Ballantine Books.

Bavelas, J. 1978. *Personality: Current Theories and Research.* Monterey, CA: Brooks/Cole.

Beck, A. 1967. *Depression: Clinical, Experimental and Theoretical Aspects.* New York: Harper and Row.

———. 1976. *Cognitive Therapy and the Emotional Disorders.* New York: International Universities Press.

Beck, A., Rush, A., Shaw, B., and Emery, C. 1979. *Cognitive Theory of Depression.* New York: Guilford Press.

Beckham, E. E. and Leber, W. R. (eds.) 1985. *Handbook of Depression: Treatment Assessment and Research.* Homewood, IL: Dorsey Press.

Beitman, B. D. 1987. *The Structure of Individual Psychotherapy.* New York: Guilford Press.

Bendix, R. and Lipset, S. M. (eds.) 1953. *Class, Status, and Power: Social Stratification in Comparative Perspective.* New York: The Free Press.

Berger, D. 1987. *Clinical Empathy.* Northvale, NJ: Jason Aronson.

Berger, M. M. (ed.) 1978. *Beyond the Double Bind.* New York: Brunner/Mazel.

Berne, E. 1961. *Transactional Analysis in Psychotherapy.* New York: Grove Press.

Bettleheim, B. 1977. *The Uses of Enchantment.* New York: Vintage Books.

———. 1987. *A Good Enough Parent: A Book on Child-rearing.* New York: Knopf.

Biddle, B. 1979. *Role Theory: Expectations, Identities and Behaviors.* New York: Academic Press.

Bierstadt, R. 1950. "An Analysis of Social Power." *American Sociological Review* 15 (December).

Blanck, R. and Blanck, G. 1986. *Beyond Ego Psychology: Developmental Object Relations Theory.* New York: Columbia University Press.

Bloom-Feshbach, J. and Bloom-Feshbach, S. (eds.) 1987. *The Psychology of Separation and Loss.* San Francisco: Jossey-Bass Publishers.

Bowlby, J. 1969. *Attachment.* New York: Basic Books.

———. 1973. *Separation: Anxiety and Anger.* New York: Basic Books.

———. 1980. *Loss: Sadness and Depression.* New York: Basic Books.

Bratter, T. E. and Forrest, G. G. 1985. *Alcoholism and Substance Abuse: Strategies for Clinical Intervention.* New York: The Free Press.

Breuer, J. and Freud, S. 1957. *Studies on Hysteria.* New York: Basic Books.

Brim, O. and Kagan, J. (eds.) 1980. *Constancy and Change in Human Development.* Cambridge, MA: Harvard University Press.

Brim, O. and Wheeler, S. 1966. *Socialization after Childhood.* New York: John Wiley.

Brown, G. and Harris, T. 1978. *Social Origins of Depression.* New York: The French Press.

Cannon, W. B. 1929. *Bodily Changes in Pain, Hunger, Fear and Rage: An Account of Recent Research on the Function of Emotional Excitement.* New York: Appleton-Century-Crofts.

Carkhuff, R. 1969. *Helping and Human Relations.* New York: Holt Rinehart and Winston.

Chess, S. and Thomas, A. 1986. *Temperament in Clinical Practice.* New York: Guilford Press.

Chessick, R. D. 1974. *The Technique and Practice of Intensive Psychotherapy.* New York: Jason Aronson.

Choca, J. 1980. *Manual for Clinical Psychology Practicums.* New York: Brunner/Mazel.

Clausen, J. (ed.) 1968. *Socialization and Society*. Boston: Little Brown.

Clausewitz, C. 1908. *On War*. New York: Penguin Books.

Cooley, C. H. 1956. *Human Nature and the Social Order*. Glencoe, IL: The Free Press.

Corsini, R. 1966. *Roleplaying in Psychotherapy: A Manual*. Chicago: Aldine.

———. (ed.) 1981. *Handbook of Innovative Psychotherapies*. New York: John Wiley & Sons.

Cotter, S. and Guerra, J. 1976. *Assertion Training*. Chicago: Research Press.

Davis, M. 1973. *Intimate Relations*. New York: The Free Press.

Dean, A., Kraft, A., and Pepper, B. (eds.) 1976. *The Social Setting of Mental Health*. New York: Basic Books.

Deegan, M. J. 1986. "The Clinical Sociology of Jessie Taft." *Clinical Sociology Review* 4.

Dewald, P. A. 1972. *The Psychoanalytic Process*. New York: Basic Books.

Dollard, J. and Miller, N. E. 1950. *Personality and Psychotherapy: An Analysis in Terms of Learning, Thinking and Culture*. New York: McGraw-Hill.

Dorpat, T. L. 1985. *Denial and Defense in the Therapeutic Situation*. New York: Jason Aronson.

Durkheim, E. 1933. *The Division of Labor in Society*. New York: The Free Press.

Dushkin Publishing. 1973. *Encyclopedia of Sociology*. Guildford, CT.

Egeland, B. and Sroufe, L. A. 1981. "Attachment and Early Mistreatment." *Child Development* 52.

Eisdorfer, C., Cohen, D., Kleinman, A., and Maxim, P. (eds.) 1981. *Models for Clinical Psychopathology*. New York: Spectrum Publications.

Ellis, A. and Grieger, R. (eds.) 1977. *Handbook of Rational Emotive Therapy*. New York: Springer Publishing.

Erikson, E. 1950. *Childhood and Society*. New York: W. W. Norton.

———. 1968. *Identity: Youth and Crisis*. New York: W. W. Norton.

Eysenck, H. J. 1986. "A Critique of Contemporary Classification and Diagnosis." In Millon, T. and Klerman, G. L. (eds.), *Contemporary Directions in Psychopathology: Toward the DSM-IV*. New York: Guilford Press.

Fein, M. 1988. "Resocialization: A Neglected Paradigm." *Clinical Sociology Review* 6.

Fenichel, O. 1941. *Problems of Psychoanalytic Technique*. New York: Psychoanalytic Quarterly.

Festinger, L. 1954. "A Theory of Social Comparison Processes." *Human Relations* 7.

———. 1957. *A Theory of Cognitive Dissonance*. Evanston, IL: Row, Peterson.

Fishman, H. C. 1986. "The Family as a Fugue." In Fishman, H. C. and Rossman, B. L. (eds.), *Evolving Models for Family Change*. New York: Guilford Press.

Fishman, H. C. and Rossman, B. L. (eds.) 1986. *Evolving Models for Family Change*. New York: Guilford Press.

Frank, J. 1973. *Persuasion and Healing: A Comparative Study of Psychotherapy*. Baltimore: Johns Hopkins Press.

Freud, A. 1966. *The Ego and the Mechanisms of Defense*. New York: International Universities Press.

Freud, S. 1953–74. *The Standard Edition of the Complete Works of Sigmund Freud.* Edited by J. Strachey. London: Hogarth Press.

———. 1959. *Collected Papers, Volume IV.* Translated by Joan Reviere. New York: Basic Books.

———. 1961. *Civilization and Its Discontents.* New York: W. W. Norton Co.

Frijda, N. H. 1987. *The Emotions.* Cambridge: Cambridge University Press.

Fritz, J. 1985. *The Clinical Sociology Handbook.* New York: Garland.

Fromm-Reichmann, F. 1950. *Principles of Intensive Psychotherapy.* Chicago: University of Chicago Press.

Gallagher, B. 1980. *The Sociology of Mental Illness.* Englewood Cliffs: Prentice-Hall.

Gallant, D. M. 1987. *Alcoholism: A Guide to Diagnosis, Intervention, and Treatment.* New York: W. W. Norton.

Garbarino, J., Schellenbach, C. J., and Sebes, J. 1986. *Troubled Youth, Troubled Families.* New York: Aldine De Gruyter.

Garfinkel, H. 1967. *Studies in Ethnomethodology.* Englewood Cliffs: Prentice-Hall.

Gerth, H. and Mills, C. W. (eds.) 1946. *From Max Weber: Essays in Sociology.* New York: Oxford University Press.

Glass, J. 1979. "Renewing an Old Profession." *American Behavioral Scientist* 22 (4).

Glass, J. and Fritz, J. 1982. "Clinical Sociology: Origins and Development." *Clinical Sociology Review* 1.

Glassner, B. and Friedman, J. 1979. *Clinical Sociology.* New York: Longman.

Goffman, E. 1959. *The Presentation of Self in Everyday Life.* Garden City: Doubleday and Co.

———. 1963. *Stigma.* Englewood Cliffs: Prentice-Hall.

———. 1974. *Frame Analysis.* New York: Harper and Row.

Goldberg, A. (ed.) 1980. *Advances in Self Psychology.* New York: International Universities Press.

Goode, W. J. 1972. "Presidential Address: The Place of Force in Human Society." *American Sociological Review* 37.

Gordon, S. L. 1985. "Micro Sociological Theories of Emotion." In Helle, H. J. and Eisenstadt, S. N. (eds.), *Micro Sociological Theory.* Beverly Hills: Sage Publications.

Goslin, D. (ed.) 1969. *Handbook of Socialization Theory and Research.* Chicago: Rand McNally.

Gove, W. (ed.) 1982. *Deviance and Mental Illness.* Beverly Hills: Sage Publications.

Greenberg, L. and Safran, J. 1987. *Emotion in Psychotherapy.* New York: Guilford Press.

Grinker, R. 1961. "A Transactional Model for Psychotherapy." In Stein, M. (ed.), *Contemporary Psychotherapies.* New York: Free Press of Glencoe.

Gurman, A. S. and Kniskern, D. P. (eds.) 1981. *Handbook of Family Therapy.* New York: Brunner/Mazel.

Hamilton, N. G. 1988. *Self and Others: Object Relations Theory in Practice.* New York: Jason Aronson.

Helle, H. J. and Eisenstadt, S. N. (eds.) 1985. *Micro Sociological Theory.* Beverly Hills: Sage Publications.

Heller, D. 1985. *Power in Psychotherapeutic Practice*. New York: Human Services Press.

Henry, J. 1965. *Pathways to Madness*. New York: Vintage Books.

Herink, R. (ed.) 1980. *The Psychotherapy Handbook*. New York: Meridian.

Hersen, M., Kazdin, A., and Bellack, A. (eds.) 1983. *The Clinical Psychology Handbook*. New York: Pergamon Press.

Hobbes, T. 1956. *Leviathan*, Part 1. Chicago: Henry Regnery Co.

Hollingshead, A. and Redlich, F. 1958. *Social Class and Mental Health*. New York: John Wiley.

Holmes, T. H. and Rahe, R. H. 1967. "The Social Readjustment Scale." *Journal of Psychosomatic Research* 11: 213–18.

Horney, K. 1939. *New Ways in Psychoanalysis*. New York: W. W. Norton Co.

Horwitz, A. 1982. *The Social Control of Mental Illness*. New York: Academic Press.

Ingleby, D. (ed.) 1980. *Critical Psychiatry: The Politics of Mental Health*. New York: Pantheon Books.

Ivey, A. and Authier, J. 1978. *Microcounseling: Innovations in Interviewing, Counseling, Psychotherapy and Psychoeducation*. Springfield, IL: Thomas.

Izard, C. 1977. *Human Emotions*. New York: Plenum Press.

Joas, H. 1985. "Role Theories and Socialization Research." In Helle, H. J. and Eisenstadt, S. N. (eds.), *Micro Sociological Theory*. Beverly Hills: Sage Publications.

Jourard, S. M. 1964. *The Transparent Self: Self Disclosure and Well Being*. Princeton, NJ: Van Nostrand.

Kagan, J. 1984. *The Nature of the Child*. New York: Basic Books.

Kagan, J. and Lamb, S. (eds.) 1987. *The Emergence of Morality in Young Children*. Chicago: University of Chicago Press.

Kant, I. 1949. *Critique of Practical Reason*. Chicago: University of Chicago Press.

Kemper, T. D. 1968. "Reference Groups, Socialization and Achievement." *American Sociological Review* 33.

Kennedy, D. B. and Kerber, A. 1973. *Resocialization: An American Experiment*. New York: Behavioral Publications.

Klerman, G. L., Weissman, M. M., Rounsaville, B. J. and Chevron, E. 1984. *Interpersonal Psychotherapy of Depression*. New York: Basic Books.

Kluckhohn, C. and Murray, H. A. (eds.) 1948. *Personality in Nature, Society and Culture*. New York: Knopf.

Kohlberg, L. 1987. *Child Psychology and Childhood Education: A Cognitive-Developmental View*. New York: Longman Inc.

Kohn, M. 1969. *Class and Conformity: A Study in Values*. Homewood, IL: Dorsey Press.

Kottler, J. 1986. *On Being a Therapist*. San Francisco: Jossey-Bass.

Kubler-Ross, E. 1969. *On Death and Dying*. New York: MacMillan.

Kuhn, T. S. 1970. *The Structure of Scientific Revolutions* (2nd ed.). Chicago: University of Chicago Press.

Kurtines, W. M. and Gewirtz, J. L. (eds.) 1987. *Moral Development Through Social Interaction*. New York: John Wiley & Sons.

Kutash, I. and Schlesinger, L. (eds.) 1980. *Handbook on Stress and Anxiety*. San Francisco: Jossey-Bass.

Landy, D. 1960. "Rehabilitation as a Sociocultural Process." *Journal of Social Issues* 16.

Leary, M. 1983. *Understanding Social Anxiety: Social, Personality and Clinical Perspectives.* Beverly Hills: Sage Publications.

Leifer, R. 1969. *In the Name of Mental Health.* New York: Science.

Lennard, H. and Bernstein, A. 1960. *The Anatomy of Psychotherapy.* New York: Columbia University Press.

Leventhal, H. 1984. "A Perceptual-Motor Theory of Emotion." In L. Berkowitz (ed.), *Advances in Experimental Social Psychology.* New York: Academic Press.

Lewin, K. 1935. *A Dynamic Theory of Personality.* New York: McGraw-Hill.

Lewis, M. and Saarni, C. (eds.) 1985. *The Socialization of Emotions.* New York: Plenum Press.

Lewis, O. 1966. *La Vida: A Puerto Rican Family in the Culture of Poverty—San Juan and New York.* New York: Random House.

Lewontin, R., Rose, S., and Kamin, L. 1984. *Not in Our Genes: Biological Ideologies and Human Nature.* New York: Pantheon Books.

Lidz, T. 1968. *The Person: His and Her Development Through the Life Cycle.* New York: Basic Books.

Lindzey, G. and Aronson, E. (eds.) 1985. *Handbook of Social Psychology* (3rd ed.). New York: Random House.

Linton, R. 1936. *The Study of Man.* New York: Appleton-Century-Crofts.

Lippitt, R. et al. 1958. *Dynamics of Planned Change.* New York: Harcourt, Brace and World.

Lofland, J. 1971. *Analyzing Social Settings.* Belmont, CA: Wadsworth.

London, P. 1964. *The Modes and Morals of Psychotherapy.* New York: Holt, Rinehart and Winston.

Lynd, H. M. 1958. *On Shame and the Search for Identity.* New York: Harcourt, Brace and World.

Lyons, D. 1965. *Forms and Limits of Utilitarianism.* Oxford: Clarendon Press.

McClelland, D. 1975. *Power: The Inner Experience.* New York: Irvington Pub.

Maccoby, E. E. (ed.) 1966. *The Development of Sex Differences.* Stanford: Stanford University Press.

McGoldrick, M., Pearce, J. K., and Giordano, J. (eds.) 1982. *Ethnicity and Family Therapy.* New York: Guilford Press.

McKechnie, J. (ed.) 1971. *Webster's New Twentieth Century Dictionary.* Cleveland: World Publishing.

Mahler, M., Pine, F., and Bergman, A. 1975. *The Psychological Birth of the Human Infant: Symbiosis and Individuation.* New York: Basic Books.

Maslow, A. 1954. *Motivation and Personality.* New York: Harper and Row.

May, R. 1950. *The Meaning of Anxiety.* New York: W. W. Norton Co.

Mead, G. H. 1934. *Mind, Self and Society.* Chicago: University of Chicago Press.

Mechanic, D. 1969. *Mental Health and Social Policy.* Englewood Cliffs: Prentice-Hall.

Menninger, K. 1958. *The Theory of Psychoanalytic Technique.* New York: Harper and Row.

Merton, R. 1949. *Social Theory and Social Structure.* New York: The Free Press.

Miller, G. A., Galanter, E., and Pribram, K. 1960. *Plans and the Structure of Behavior.* New York: Holt, Rinehart and Winston.

Miller, J. 1978. *The Body in Question*. New York: Vintage Books.

Millon, T. and Klerman, G. L. (eds.) 1986. *Contemporary Directions in Psycho-pathology: Toward the DMS-IV*. New York: Guilford Press.

Mischel, W. 1968. *Personality and Assessment*. New York: John Wiley & Sons.

Moreno, J. 1953. *Who Shall Survive?* New York: Beacon House.

Murray, H. A. et al. 1938. *Explorations in Personality*. New York: Oxford University Press.

Nicholi, A. (ed.) 1978. *Harvard Guide to Modern Psychiatry*. Cambridge: Belknap Press.

Nichols, M. P. 1987. *The Self in the System: Expanding the Limits of Family Therapy*. New York: Brunner/Mazel.

Norcross, J. C. (ed.) 1986. *Handbook of Eclectic Psychotherapy*. New York: Brunner/Mazel.

Nye, F. I. 1976. *Role Structure and the Analysis of the Family*. Beverly Hills: Sage Publications.

Papp, P. 1983. *The Process of Change*. New York: Guilford Press.

Parsons, T. 1951. *The Social System*. New York: The Free Press.

————. 1970. *Social Structure and Personality*. New York: Macmillan.

Parsons, T. and Bales, R. F. 1955. *Family, Socialization and Interaction Process*. New York: The Free Press.

Perls, F., Hefferline, R., and Goodman, P. 1951. *Gestalt Therapy*. New York: Delta Publishing.

Pfeiffer, J. 1977. *The Emergence of Society*. New York: McGraw-Hill.

Piaget, J. 1965. *The Moral Judgment of the Child*. New York: The Free Press.

Pruitt, D. G. 1981. *Negotiation Behavior*. New York: Academic.

————. 1983. "Strategic Choice in Negotiation." *American Behavioral Scientist* 27 (22).

Rainwater, L. 1970. *Behind Ghetto Walls: Black Family Life in a Federal Slum*. Chicago: Aldine Publishing.

Redlich, F. and Freedman, D. 1966. *The Theory and Practice of Psychiatry*. New York: Basic Books.

Rice, L. and Saperia, E. P. 1984. "Task Analysis and the Resolution of Problematic Reactions." In Rice, L. and Greenberg, L. (eds.), *Patterns of Change*. New York: Guilford Press.

Rice, L. and Greenberg, L. (eds.) 1984. *Patterns of Change*. New York: Guilford Press.

Richards, M. 1974. *The Integration of a Child into a Social World*. London: Cambridge University Press.

Riley, M. W., et al. 1969. "Socialization in the Middle and Later Years." In Goslin, D. (ed.), *Handbook of Socialization Theory and Research*. Chicago: Rand McNally.

Rogers, C. 1951. *Client Centered Therapy*. Boston: Houghton-Mifflin.

————. 1961. *On Becoming a Person*. Boston: Houghton-Mifflin.

Roman, P. and Trice, H. (eds.) 1974. *The Sociology of Psychotherapy*. New York: Jason Aronson.

Rosenberg, M. 1979. *Conceiving the Self*. New York: Basic Books.

Rosenhan, M. 1973. "On Being Sane in Insane Places." *Science* 179.

Rounsaville, B. J. et al. 1985. "Short-Term Interpersonal Psychotherapy (IPT) for Depression." In Beckham, E. E. and Leber, W. R. (eds.), *Handbook of Depression: Treatment Assessment and Research*. Homewood, IL: Dorsey Press.

Sager, C. J. and Kaplan, H. S. (eds.) 1972. *Progress in Group and Family Therapy*. New York: Brunner/Mazel.

Sarason, S. 1985. *Caring and Compassion in Clinical Practice*. San Francisco: Jossey-Bass.

Sarbin, T. and Allen, V. 1968. "Role Theory." In Lindzey, G. and Aronson, E. (eds.), *Handbook of Social Psychology*. Cambridge, MA: Addison Wesley.

Sarbin, T. and Scheibe, K. (eds.) 1983. *Studies in Social Identity*. New York: Praeger.

Scarf, M. 1980. *Unfinished Business: Pressure Points in the Lives of Women*. New York: Ballantine Books.

———. 1987. *Intimate Partners: Patterns in Love and Marriage*. New York: Random House.

Schaffer, H. 1971. *The Growth of Sociability*. Baltimore: Penguin Books.

Scheff, T. 1966. *Being Mentally Ill: A Sociological Theory*. Chicago: Aldine.

———. (ed.) 1967. *Mental Illness and Social Process*. New York: Harper and Row.

Schmitt, D. 1964. "The Invocation of Moral Obligation." *Sociometry* 27.

Selye, H. 1956. *The Stress of Life*. New York: McGraw-Hill.

Sennett, R. and Cobb, J. 1972. *The Hidden Injuries of Class*. New York: Vintage Books.

Shibutani, T. 1961. *Society and Personality*. Englewood Cliffs: Prentice-Hall.

Silverman, H. 1972. *Marital Therapy: Psychological, Sociological and Moral Factors*. Springfield, IL: Charles Thomas.

Skinner, B. F. 1953. *Science and Human Behavior*. New York: Macmillan.

Spotnitz, H. 1976. *Psychotherapy of Preoedipal Conditions*. New York: Jason Aronson.

Stein, M. (ed.) 1961. *Contemporary Psychotherapies*. New York: Free Press of Glencoe.

Stone, L. J., Smith, H. T., and Murphy, L. B. (eds.) 1973. *The Competent Infant: Research and Commentary*. New York: Basic Books.

Storr, A. 1979. *The Art of Psychotherapy*. New York: Metheun.

Straus, R. (ed.) 1969. "Clinical Sociology." Special issue of *American Behavioral Scientist* 22(4).

———. (ed.) 1985. *Using Sociology: An Introduction from the Clinical Perspective*. New York: General Hall.

Strauss, A. 1959. *Mirrors and Masks: The Search for Identity*. Glencoe, IL: Free Press.

———. 1978. *Negotiations: Varieties, Contexts, Processes and Social Order*. San Francisco: Jossey-Bass.

Strean, H. 1985. *Therapeutic Principles in Practice: A Manual for Clinicians*. Beverly Hills: Sage Publications.

Stryker, S. 1968. "Identity Salience and Role Performance." *Journal of Marriage and Family* 30: 558–64.

———. 1980. *Symbolic Interactionism*. Menlo Park, CA: Benjamin/Cummings.

Stryker, S. and Statham, A. 1985. "Symbolic Interaction and Role Theory." In Lindzey, G. and Aronson, E. (eds.), *Handbook of Social Psychology* (3rd ed.). New York: Random House.

Sullivan, H. S. 1940. *Conceptions of Modern Psychiatry*. New York: W. W. Norton Co.

———. 1953. *The Interpersonal Theory of Psychiatry*. New York: W. W. Norton Co.

Susskind, L. and Rubin, L. (eds.) "Negotiations from a Behavioral Perspective." *The American Behavioral Scientist* 27(2).

Szasz, T. 1961. *The Myth of Mental Illness: Foundations of a Theory of Personal Conduct*. New York: Dell.

Tavris, C. 1983. *Anger: The Misunderstood Emotion*. New York: Simon & Schuster.

Thomas, W. I. and Thomas, D. S. 1928. *The Child in America: Behavior, Problems and Progress*. New York: Knopf.

Truax, C. B. and Carkhuff, R. R. 1967. *Toward Effective Counseling and Psychotherapy: Training and Practice*. Chicago: Aldine Publishing.

Turner, F. 1978. *Psychosocial Therapy: A Social Work Perspective*. New York: The Free Press.

Turner, R. H. 1962. "Role Taking: Process vs. Conformity?" In Rose, A. M. (ed.), *Human Behavior and Social Processes*. Boston: Houghton Mifflin.

———. 1978. "The Role and the Person." *American Journal of Sociology* 84: 1–23.

———. 1985. "Unanswered Questions in the Convergence between Structuralist and Interactionist Role Theories." In Helle, H. J. and Eisenstadt, S. N. (eds.), *Micro Sociological Theory*. Beverly Hills: Sage Publications.

Turner, S. M., Calhoun, K. S. and Adams, H. E. 1981. *Handbook of Clinical Behavior Therapy*. New York: John Wiley & Sons.

Valentine, C. A. 1968. *Culture and Poverty*. Chicago: University of Chicago Press.

Vandenbos, G. (ed.) 1980. *Psychotherapy: Practice, Research, Policy*. Beverly Hills: Sage Publications.

Veith, I. 1965. *Hysteria: The History of a Disease*. Chicago: University of Chicago Press.

Viorst, J. 1986. *Necessary Losses*. New York: Fawcett.

Walker, C. E. (ed.) 1981. *Clinical Practice of Psychology*. New York: Pergamon Press.

Weber, M. 1947. *The Theory of Social and Economic Organization*. New York: The Free Press.

Wegscheider-Cruse, S. 1980. *Another Chance: Hope and Health for Alcoholic Families*. Palo Alto, CA: Science and Behavior Books.

Weis, J. 1982. "Psychotherapy Research: Theory and Findings." *Mt. Zion Hospital and Medical Center Bulletin* 5.

Weiss, R. S. 1975. *Marital Separation*. New York: Basic Books.

Wentworth, W. 1980. *Context and Understanding: An Inquiry into Socialization Theory*. New York: Elsevier.

Westen, D. 1985. *Self and Society: Narcissism, Collectives and the Development of Morals*. Cambridge: University of Cambridge Press.

White, R. W. 1959. "Motivation Reconsidered: The Concept of Competence." *Psychological Review* 66: 297–333.

Whyte, W. F. 1943. *Street Corner Society*. Chicago: University of Chicago Press.

Windmiller, M., Lambert, N., and Turiel, E. (eds.) 1980. *Moral Development and Socialization*. Boston: Allyn and Bacon.

Wirth, L. 1931. "Clinical Sociology." *American Journal of Sociology* 37.

Wittgenstein, L. 1953. *Philosophical Investigations*. New York: Macmillan Co.

Wolberg, L. 1967. *The Technique of Psychotherapy*. New York: Grune and Stratton.

Wolman, B. (ed.) 1976. *The Therapist's Handbook: Treatment of Mental Disorders*. New York: Van Nostrand Reinhold.

Wolpe, J. 1973. *The Practice of Behavior Therapy*. New York: Pergamon Press.

Wrong, D. 1961. "The Oversocialized Conception of Man in Modern Sociology." *American Sociological Review* 26(2).

Wynne, L. C., Cromwell, R. L., and Matthysse, S. 1978. *The Nature of Schizophrenia: New Approaches to Research and Treatment*. New York: John Wiley & Sons.

―――. 1986. "Structure and Lineality in Family Therapy." In Fishman, H. C. and Rossman, B. L. (eds.), *Evolving Models of Family Change*. New York: Guilford Press.

Yalom, I. D. 1980. *Existential Psychotherapy*. New York: Basic Books.

Zajonc, R. B. 1980. "Feeling and Thinking: Preferences Need No Inferences." *American Psychologist* 35.

Zander, A., Cohen, A., and Stotland, E. 1957. *Role Relations in the Mental Health Professions*. Ann Arbor: University of Michigan Press.

Zartman, I. W. 1978. *The Negotiation Process: Theories and Applications*. Beverly Hills: Sage Publications.

Zurcher, L. 1983. *Social Roles: Conformity, Conflict and Creativity*. Beverly Hills: Sage Publications.

Index

About the Author

MELVYN L. FEIN is a certified clinical sociologist who has a private practice in resocialization in Rochester, NY. He holds a doctorate in sociology from the City University of New York, and has almost 20 years of experience helping individuals solve their personal, relationship, and vocational problems. Among his current interests are the medical model of individual problems, emotional coping strategies, and role negotiation disorders.